AF538543

ENV BOOKS SERIES

MICROBIOLOGICAL AND PHARMACOLOGICAL ASPECTS OF BIODIVERSITY

Editors

Dr. Pankaj Sharma
Department of Botany
M.L.S.M. College, Sunder Nagar
Himachal Pradesh (India)

Dr. Neha Gautam Sharma
Department of Microbiology
St. Bede's College, Navbahar
Shimla - 171 002
Himachal Pradesh (India)

Dr. Pankaj Sharma
Sr. Scientific Professional
Himachal Pradesh State Biodiversity Board
Himachal Pradesh State Council for Science
Technology & Environment (HPSCST&E)
Shimla (HP) (India)

Series Editor

Dr. Pawan Kumar 'Bharti'
Society for Environment, Health, Awareness of
Nutrition & Toxicology (SEHAT)
1775, Sohan Ganj, Near Clock Tower
Delhi - 110 007 (India)
E-mail: gurupawanbharti@rediffmail.com

DISCOVERY PUBLISHING HOUSE PVT. LTD.
INDIA

Published by:

Namit Wasan

DISCOVERY PUBLISHING HOUSE PVT. LTD.
4383/4B, Ansari Road, Darya Ganj
New Delhi-110 002 (India)
Phone : +91-11-23279245, 43596064-65
Fax : +91-11-23253475
E-mail : discoverypublishinghouse@gmail.com
namitwasan9@gmail.com
sales@discoverypublishinggroup.com
web : www.discoverypublishinggroup.com

***First Edition:* 2017**

ISBN: 978-93-5056-878-1

Microbiological and Pharmacological Aspects of Biodiversity

Printed at:
Infinity Imaging Systems
Delhi

ENV Books Series, India

Calls descriptive and error free chapters for upcoming volumes of books on various environmental issues. Send your manuscripts to envbooks@gmail.com

Founding Editor (Editor-in-Chief)

Dr. Pawan Kumar 'Bharti'

Society for Environment, Health, Awareness of Nutrition & Toxicology (SEHAT-India)

1775, Sohanganj, Near Clock Tower, Delhi-7, (India)

E-mail:*gurupawanbharti@rediffmail.com*

Other Important Titles by Editor-in-Chief:

1. **Advances in Biotechnology and Ecological Sciences**
   Bharti, P.K., Chauhan, A. and Ray, J. (eds.)
   (ISBN: 978-93-5056-358-8).
2. **Advances in Agriculture and Ecology**
   Bharti, P.K.; Chauhan, A. and Ezeaku Peter Ikemefuna (eds.)
   (ISBN: 978-93-5056-362-5).
3. **Agriculture and Environmental Biotechnology**
   Bharti, P.K. and Chauhan, A. (eds.)
   (ISBN: 978-93-5056-479-0).
4. **Agriculture Development and Sustainable Environment**
   Ray, J. and Bharti, P.K. (eds.)
   (ISBN: 978-93-5056-759-3).
5. **Agriculture Ecology and Environment**
   Bharti, P.K. and Olubukola O. Babalola (eds.)
   (ISBN: 978-93-5056-480-6).
6. **Agriculture Ecology, Sustainable Development and Agribusiness Management**
   Mehta Piyush; Sharma Pankaj; and 'Bharti' P.K. (eds.)
   (ISBN: 978-93-5056-851-4).
7. **Agriculture, Environment and Nano-science**
   Bharti, Pawan K. (ed.)
   (ISBN: 978-93-5056-760-5).
8. **Agricultural Practices and Crop Disease Control**
   Chauhan Alka and Sharma Anubhuti (eds.)
   (ISBN: 978-93-5056-859-0).

9. **Agro-biodiversity:** ***Conservation and Sustainable Development***
Sharma, Pankaj; Singh, Narayan; and Bharti, P.K. (eds.)
(ISBN: 978-93-505-782-1).

10. **Agro-forestry and Climate Change**
Bharti, Pawan K. and Singh, Narayan (eds.)
(ISBN: 978-93-5056-514-8).

11. **Agro-forestry and Sustainable Agriculture**
Sharma, Pankaj; Bharti, P.K. (eds.)
(ISBN: 978-93-5056-786-9).

12. **Air Pollution and Ecosystem Health**
Swami Abhishek and Bharti, P.K. (eds.)
(ISBN: 978-93-5056-877-4).

13. **Aquaculture and Fisheries Environment**
Gupta, S.K. and Pawan K. Bharti (eds.)
(ISBN: 978-93-5056-408-0).

14. **Aquatic Biodiversity and Pollution**
Bharti, P.K.; Chauhan, A. and Kaoud, H.A.H. (eds.)
(ISBN: 978-93-5056-359-5).

15. **Aquatic Ecology and Biotechnology**
Bharti, P.K. and Zaki, M.S.A. (eds.)
(ISBN: 978-93-5056-451-6).

16. **Aquatic Environment and Toxicology**
Bharti, Pawan K. (ed.)
(ISBN: 978-93-5056-236-9).

17. **Biodiversity, Biotechnology and Environmental Conservation**
Bharti, P.K. and Bhandari, G. (eds.)
(ISBN: 978-93-5056-750-0).

18. **Biodiversity of Aquatic Ecosystem:** ***Significance, Threat and Conservation*** **(2013)**
Bharti, P.K. and Kaoud, H.A.H. (eds.)
(ISBN: 978-93-5056-297-0).

19. **Biological Diversity and Ecology**
Arya, M.K.; Bharti, P.K. and Ritesh Joshi (eds.)
(ISBN: 978-93-5056-785-2).

20. **Bioremediation and Microbial Biotechnology**
Gupta, Sandeep; and Bharti, P.K. (eds.)
(ISBN: 978-93-5056-783-8).

21. **Biotechnological Approaches and Water Ecosystem**
Zaki, M.S.A.; and Bharti, P.K. (eds.)
(ISBN: 978-93-5056-779-1).

22. **Biotechnology, Agro-ecology and Environment**
Chauhan, Avnish and Bharti, P.K. (eds.)
(ISBN: 978-93-5056-757-9).

23. **Biotechnology and Environmental Management**
Arya Arun; Maheswari Raaz K., & Bharti, P.K (eds.)
(ISBN: 978-93-5056-862-0).

24. **Clean Technologies and Environmental Protection**
Chauhan, A.; Sharma, S. and Bharti, P.K. (eds.)
(ISBN: 978-93-5056-731-9).

25. **Climate Change and Agriculture**
Bharti, P.K. and Chauhan, Avnish (eds.)
(ISBN: 978-93-5056-148-5).

26. **Climate Change and Biodiversity**
Bharti, P.K. and Chauhan, Avnish (eds.)
(ISBN: 978-93-5056-360-1).

27. **Climate Change, Disaster Management and Environment**
Chauhan, Alka; Bharti, P.K. (eds.)
(ISBN: 978-93-5056-784-5).

28. **Conservation and Cultivation of Medicinal Plants**
Bharti, P.K. and Singh Narayan (eds.)
(ISBN: 978-93-5056-740-1).

29. **Crop Productivity and Plant Disease Management**
Chauhan, Alka; Bharti, P.K. and Sadana, Deepti (eds.)
(ISBN: 978-93-5056-791-3).

30. **Eco-toxicology and Eco-technology**
Bharti, P.K. and Zaki, M. (eds.)
(ISBN: 978-93-5056-313-7).

31. **Environmental Biotechnology and Application**
Bharti, P.K. and Chauhan, Avnish (eds.)
(ISBN: 978-93-5056-262-8).

32. **Environmental Conservation and Biotechnology**
Chauhan, A. and P.K. Bharti (eds.)
(ISBN: 978-93-5056-512-4).

33. **Environmental Health and Problems**
Bharti, P.K. and Gajananda, Kh. (eds.)
(ISBN: 978-93-5056-263-5).

34. **Environmental Pollution and Biodiversity**
Bharti, P.K.; Chauhan, Avnish and Kumar, P. (eds.)
(ISBN: 978-93-5056-149-2).

35. **Farming Techniques and Crop Production**
Chauhan Alka; Sharma Anubhuti; Ray Jaswant and 'Bharti' P.K. (eds.)
(ISBN: 978-93-5056-855-2).

36. **Fisheries and Toxicology**
    Zaki, M.S.A.; Bharti, P.K. and Chauhan, A. (eds.)
    (ISBN: 978-93-5056-452-3).
37. **Fish Habitat and Aquaculture**
    Bharti, P.K.; Gupta Kr. Sanjay (eds.)
    (ISBN: 978-93-5056-744-9).
38. **Forest and Biodiversity Conservation**
    Chauhan Alka; Bharti, P.K. (eds.)
    (ISBN: 978-93-5056-873-6).
39. **Food Processing, Management and Nanotechnology**
    Chauhan, Avnish; Bharti, P.K. (eds.)
    (ISBN: 978-93-5056-796-8).
40. **Freshwater Ecosystem and Xenobiotics**
    Bharti, P.K.; Zaki, M. and Chauhan, A. (eds.)
    (ISBN: 978-93-5056-299-4).
41. **Geospatial Technology and Water Management**
    Chauhan, Alka; Bharti, P.K. (eds.)
    (ISBN: 978-93-5056-885-9).
42. **Heavy Metals and Metalloids in Biosphere:** *Impacts & Assessment*
    Chauhan, Avnish, Gupta, Sandeep; and Bharti, P.K. (eds.)
    (ISBN: 978-93-5056-860-6).
43. **Limnology and Aquatic Science**
    Sharma, S., and Bharti, P.K. (eds.)
    (ISBN: 978-93-5056-735-7).
44. **Medicinal and Nutritional Values of Plants**
    Chauhan, Alka; Bharti, P.K. (eds.)
    (ISBN: 978-93-5056-883-5).
45. **Medicinal Plants:** *Distribution, Utilization and Significance*
    Sharma, P.; Bharti, P.K. and Narayan Singh (eds.)
    (ISBN: 978-93-5056-734-0).
46. **Microbial Applications and Environment**
    Bharti, Pawan K. (ed.)
    (ISBN: 978-93-5056-515-5).
47. **Microbial Ecology and Habitat**
    Bharti, Pawan K. (ed.)
    (ISBN: 978-93-5056-514-8).
48. **Microbial Environment and Bioremediation**
    Chauhan Alka; K. Rathoure Ashok; and K Maheshwari Raaz (eds.)
    (ISBN: 978-93-5056-856-9).
49. **Natural Ecosystem and Climate Change**
    Bharti, P.K., and Kh. Gajananda (ed.)
    (ISBN: 978-93-5056-745-6).

50. **Pest Management and Agro-Techniques**
Biswas, Asim; Bharti, P.K., Chauhan, Avnish (eds.)
(ISBN: 978-93-5056-794-4).

51. **Prakriti me Aushadhi (*in Hindi*)**
Singh, J.R.; Bharti, P.K. and Bharti, B.
(ISBN: 978-93-5056-200-0).

52. **Seed Technology, Plant Growth and Cropping System**
Tyagi, P.K. and Bharti, P.K. (eds.)
(ISBN: 978-93-5056-738-8).

53. **Seed Treatment, Plant Heath and Agro-technology**
Chauhan, A. and Bharti, P.K. (eds.)
(ISBN: 978-93-5056-810-1).

54. **Soil Characteristics and Agro-ecology**
Avnish Chauhan and Bharti, P.K. (eds.)
(ISBN: 978-93-5056-758-6).

55. **Soil Contamination and Conservation**
Ezeaku, P.I. and Bharti, P.K. (eds.)
(ISBN: 978-93-5056-737-1).

56. **Soil Quality and Contamination**
Bharti, P.K. and Chauhan, Avnish (eds.)
(ISBN: 978-93-5056-361-8).

57. **Sustainable Aquaculture Management**
Gupta, S.K.; Bharti, P.K (eds.)
(ISBN: 978-93-5056-797-5).

58. **Waste Disposal and Management**
Bharti, P.K.; Tabassum, B. and Bajaj, P. (eds.)
(ISBN: 978-93-5056-729-6).

59. **Waste Generation and Utilization**
Bajaj Priya; Tabassum, B., and Bharti, P.K. (eds.)
(ISBN: 978-93-5056-792-0).

60. **Waste Management and Environmental Health**
Tabassum, B., Bajaj Priya, and Bharti, P.K. (eds.)
(ISBN: 978-93-5056-777-7).

61. **Water Resources:** ***Mapping Monitoring and Management***
Tyagi, P.K., Chauhan, Avnish and Bharti, P.K. (eds.)
(ISBN: 978-93-5056-861-3).

62. **Water Resources and Agriculture**
Bharti, P.K. and Ezeaku Peter Ikemefuna (eds.)
(ISBN: 978-93-5056-481-3).

63. **Waste Resources Management:** ***Monitoring and Assessment***
Gupta, Sandeep and Bharti, P.K. (eds.)
(ISBN: 978-93-5056-799-9).

Preface

Knowledge of biological diversity is essential because it boosts ecosystem productivity where each species, no matter how small, all have an important role to play. The number of species of microorganisms, plants, animals and the enormous diversity of genes in these species and the various ecosystems on the earth are all part of a biodiversity. In view of the rapid loss of biodiversity, conservation of sensitive biodiversity elements has become indispensable. For this, it has now been realized that inventorisation of plants occurring in such areas is absolutely necessary and so are the initiatives from the Ministry of Environment, Forest, & Climate Change, Government of India.

Plants as a medicine for the prevention and treatment of various metabolic and infectious disorders have been used since time immemorial. Their medicinal properties are due to their rich phytochemistry. Despite the fact that the world has made outstanding progress in allopathic medicine, herbal practice still plays an important role in management and curing various ailments in remote and rural areas of India. Similarly, the invasive plants are commonly recognized to have severe ecological impacts in a wide range of ecosystems throughout the world. They can alter ecosystem structure and function, tropic structure, resource availability and alter biodiversity of natural landscape. Therefore native species needs to be propagated in an area to sustain the regional ecosystem.

Microbes are the smallest living creature found on earth, which play an important role in the functioning of ecosystem like cycling of many essential elements. The variability among all the microorganisms that exist on earth is mainly found at three levels, within species (genetic), species number (species) and community (ecological) diversity.

Because of the rising health concerns of preservation of the food, the natural antimicrobials like bacteriocins seem more attractive. In the present scenario, biopreservatives like bacteriocins have been proven the safer preservatives and are getting popular day by day due to mode of their size free action for shelf stability. Similarly, keeping in view the harmful nature of anti nutritional factors in our daily diet, it is very important to get rid of anti nutrients from the food for the proper intake of nutrients.

In the light of the above research issues, suitable conservation and sustainable development studies and strategies have been attempted to inquire into the varied biodiversity concerns. Almost all cultures have in some way or form recognized the importance that nature, and its biological diversity has had upon them and the need to maintain it. Yet, power, greed and politics have affected the precarious balance. These issues are to be managed and addressed for the upcoming future generations.

In this issue, apart from the contributions of the researchers, to various aspects of biodiversity of Indian Himalaya, medicinal plants, ethnobatany, pharmacology and alien species, this volume also incorporates the studies done on the microbial diversity, their metabolites, biopreservation and their heath related aspects which are particularly the recommended future issues and priorities for the research. We hope that this publication will be of immense help to academicians, researchers, conservationists and policy makers.

–Editors
(envbooks@gmail.com)

Contents

Pages: 1-23

MICROBIOLOGICAL AND PHARMACOLOGICAL ASPECTS OF BIODIVERSITY

Edited by: **Dr. Pankaj Sharma; Dr. Neha Gautam Sharma & Dr. Pankaj Sharma**

ISBN: 978-93-5056-878-1

Edition: **2017**

Published by: **Discovery Publishing House Pvt. Ltd., New Delhi (India)**

A Clean and Green Technology for Bacteriocin Mediated Food Biopreservation

Nivedita Sharma* and Ranjana Sharma

ABSTRACT

Bacteriocins are described to exert antimicrobial effects against closely or non-closely related bacteria. Bacteriocins have attracted much research interest as novel antimicrobial agents based on its wide-range effectiveness on pathogenic or spoilage causing bacteria and due to its accredited safety potency of their origin. They are produced by the major producer group i.e. lactic acid bacteria (LAB) that are "Generally Recognized as Safe (GRAS)" by the US Food and Drug Administration. Although many research updates are available in this field, it is remarkable that there are still several gaps in this emerging area. Filling these gaps fundamentally requires a clear understanding on the nature of bacteriocins and carefully considered research strategies. Thus, the present study includes general understanding towards bacteriocin i.e. definition, classification, benefits against antibiotics, selection criteria, role as biopreservatives, health beneficial effects, applications in food preservation, etc.

Keywords: Bacteriocins, antimicrobial agent, lactic acid bacteria, antibiotics, biopreservation

INTRODUCTION

The preservation of food is still a debated issue in modern advances technology due to economic losses and undesirable effects on human health. The growing awareness of public and the health concerns regarding chemical preservatives make natural antimicrobials like bacteriocin more attractive.

* **Microbiology Research Laboratory, Department of Basic Sciences, Dr. Y.S. Parmar University of Horticulture and Forestry, Nauni, Solan - 173 230 (H.P.) (India)**

The area of current food research help in maintaining the nutritional properties of food products ensuring safety issues with the help of antibacterial metabolite (i.e. bacteriocin) secreted by wide range of lactic acid bacteria. Bacteriocin has the property of heat stability, wider pH tolerance and proteolytic activity. So, the supply of bacteriocin in food preservation refocuses the attention on food security and decreases the impact of biopatenting on poor communities.

In the present scenario, biopreservatives like bacteriocins have been proven the safer preservatives and are getting popular day by day due to mode of their size free action for shelf stability. Bacteriocins are biologically extracellularly derived, low molecular weight, primary or modified products of bacterial ribosomal synthesis, which can have an antibacterial activity and are rapidly digested by human protease in the digestive tract (Pirzada *et al.*, 2004). Bacteriocins are proteinaceous compounds lethal to bacteria other than the producing strain. These are mostly heat stable and wide pH tolerant, thus can withstand heat, acidity/alkinity of food during storage conditions. Bacteriocins are heterogeneous group characteristically selected for evaluation and use as specific antagonists against problematic bacteria. Among microorganisms, antagonistic properties of LAB and *Bacillus* allied to their safe history of use in traditional fermented products make them very attractive source of bacteriocin (Sharma *et al.*, 2006).

Classification of Bacteriocins

Bacteriocins are classified into four main groups which include class I that contains Bacteriocin (Lantibiotics). Nisin the most studied bacteriocin belong to Class I bacteriocin which are active against broad spectrum of food spoilage and pathogenic bacteria including *L. monocytogenes* (Maisnier *et al.*, 1992).

Class II bacteriocins are heat stable, low molecular weight membrane active protein. Class II bacteriocins are divided ino three subclasses i.e. subclass II-A, subclass II-B and Subclass II-C. The members of the subclass II-A are characterized by showing high antilisterial activity. The subclass II-B includes heterodimeric bacteriocins which consist of two peptides. Members of this subclass of the bacteriocins meet three criteria: (i) full antimicrobial activity needs both peptides and the individual peptides show little or no activity, (ii) one immunity protein is sufficient to get immunity, and (iii) the genetic organization of the bacteriocin system includes two sequential bacteriocin structural genes encoding the individual peptides and a single immunity gene. Lactococcin G is the first discovered bacteriocin of this group and its antimicrobial activity depends on both α- and β-peptides. Bacteriocins of subclass II-C uniquely have a circular structure associated with a covalent bond between C and N terminals that cause head to tail cyclic shape of the peptides. The main representative and the most studied example of this subclass is AS-48 from *E. faecalis* (Balciunas *et al.*, 2013).

Class III bacteriocin members are generally large heat labile proteins. Big peptides with molecular weight over 30 k Da. They have complex activity and protein structure that provide a totally different mechanism of action from rest other bacteriocins, in which they lyses the cell wall of the target microorganism (Balciunas *et al.*, 2013).

Whereas, Class IV bacteriocin are complex bacteriocins that require non-protein moiety for activity (Klaenhammer, 1993).

Bacteriocins Vs Antibiotics

Bacteriocins being antimicrobial in nature have emerged as candidates of interest for food preservation as well as health application. Sometimes bacteriocins are often confused in the literature with antibiotics (Hansen, 1993; Hurst, 1981). This would limit their use in food applications from a legal standpoint. In some countries, it is crucial to make the distinction between bacteriocins and antibiotics. The main differences between bacteriocins and antibiotics are summarized in Table 1.1. Bacteriocins, which are clearly distinguishable from clinical antibiotics, should be safely and effectively used to control the growth of target pathogens in foods.

Table 1.1: Difference between bacteriocins and antibiotics

Characteristic	Bacteriocins	Antibiotics
Synthesis	Ribosomal	Secondary metabolite
Activity	Generally narrow spectrum	Varying spectrum
Host cell immunity	Yes	No
Mechanism of target cell	Usually adaptation affecting cell	Usually a genetically transferable
Resistance or tolerance	Membrane composition determinant affecting different sites	Depending on the mode of action
Interaction requirements	Sometimes docking molecules	Specific targets
Mode of action	Mostly pore formation	Cell membrane or intracellular targets cases possibly cell wall biosynthesis
Toxicity	Side effects	None

Modern medicine is faced with a drastic increase in the count of antibiotic- resistant pathogens. On the other hand, undesirable effects of new-generation antibiotics with highly toxic features have forced the consideration of alternative methods. Bacteriocins have a great potential in human health applications when compared to the traditional antibiotics. Their low toxicity, high target-specific affect mechanism, presence of various types in nature and effectiveness at nanomolar concentrations are the main advantages of bacteriocins (Riley and Wertz, 2002).

Role of Bacteriocins in Biopreservation of different Foods

Preservation of food and beverages resulting from fermentation has been an effective form of extending the shelf life of food for millennia. Traditionally foods were preserved through naturally occurring fermentations. However modern large scale production generally now exploits the use of defined strain starter system to ensure consistency and quality in the final product (Ross *et al.*, 2002). Biopreservation system in food is of increasing interest for industry and consumers. Biopreservation means the application of biopreservatives at low concentration having GRAS (Generally Regarded as Safe) status and not imparting any deleterious effect to the food in which it is used (Bizani and Brendelle, 2002). Among the biopreservatives, antimicrobial peptides i.e. bacteriocin are interesting group of biomolecules catching rapid attention in food preservation. The spreading of bacterial antibiotic resistance and the demand for product with fewer chemicals create the necessity of exploiting new alternatives in order to reduce the abusive use of therapeutic antibiotics. In this context, bacteriocins are indicated to prevent the growth of undesirable bacteria in a food grade and more natural way which is convenient for health and accepted by the community (Parada *et al.*, 2007).

Criteria for Selection of Bio-preservatives

Recently bacteriocin production and its mode of action has become main focal point of preservation studies. Any bio preservative which is to be used commercially should comply the following requirements:

1. It should be non-toxic and must be acceptable by recognized authorities.
2. It should not have any deleterious effect on the organoleptic properties of product.
3. It should be economical to industries.
4. It should have strong stability if being stored.
5. It should be effective at relatively low concentration.
6. It should not be used for any medicinal purpose.

Different Food Sources of Himachal Pradesh to Explore their Bacteriocin Potential

In India, a wide variety of traditional fermented foods made from milk, cereals, pulses and vegetables etc have been developed for the benefit of human health since ancient times. Its Trans Himalayan state - Himachal Pradesh is also well known for its traditional fermented food items viz. chhang, angoori, bhaturu, siddu, chilra, marchu, manna, dosha, pinni/ bagpinni and seera, etc. Since these traditional fermented food items are least explored, and supposed to be the rich repositories of bacteriocin producing strains with a high probability of yielding desirable bacteria upon isolation. Many fermenting microorganisms i.e. *Bacillus*, LAB and some yeasts have been reported to produce broad spectrum bacteriocin to control food borne illness/pathogenicity. *Bacillus* and *Lactobacillus sp.* are important food grade organisms recognized for their fermentative ability as well as their health and nutritional benefits.

Microorganisms from naturally occurring life/metabolic processes have always been the most powerful means for obtaining useful cultures for scientific and commercial purposes as shown in Table 1.2. The different food sources have been proven to be a good source of food grade lactic acid bacteria with probiotic potential and bacteriocin producing capabilities.

Bacteriocins and their producer organisms have vast potential in food, feed as well as in pharmaceutical industry as rich source of biopreservatives and probiotics (Raja *et al.*, 2010).

Table 1.2: Potential bacteriocinogenic bacteria from ethnic Indian fermented foods and their sources

Producer Organism	Name of Bacteriocin	Source	AU/ml	Reference
B. lentus	Lacticin	Dough	4×10^6	Sharma *et al.*,2006
L. brevis	Brevicin	KandalVari	4×10^6	Gautam and Sharma, 2009
Bacillus sp. A12	Bacicin A12	Whey	4×10^6	Sharma *et al.*, 2011
B. subtilis	Subtilin R75	Mung Bari	5×10^6	Sharma and Gautam, 2007
B. mycoides	Mycosin	Whey	2.6×10^6	Sharma *et al.*, 2009
Lactobacillus sp. A75	Lacticin A75	Dal Bari	4×10^6	Sharma *et al.*, 2008
Lactobacillus spicheri G2	Lacticin G2	Gundruk	2×10^3	Gautam and Sharma, 2015
Lactobacillus brevis UN	Lacticin UN	Dhulliachar	2×10^3	Gautam *et al.*, 2013
Brevibacillus borstelensis AG1	Brevicin AG1	Marcha	3×10^6	Gupta *et al.*, 2015
Lactobacillus plantarum L2	Lacticin L2	Luske	2.6×10^6	Sharma, 2014
Pediococcus acidilactici L1	Pediocin L1	Luske	2×10^3	Sharma, 2014
Lactobacillus pentosus S6	Lacticin S6	Siddu	4×10^6	Sharma, 2014
Bacillus licheniformis A3	Licheniocin A3		Angoori	2.6×10^6 Sharma, 2014
Lactobacillus reuteri F8	Lacticin F8	Jalebi Batter	4×10^6	Handa, 2012
Lactobacillus crustorum F11	Lacticin F11	Human Milk	2.6×10^6	Handa, 2012
Lactobacillus acidophilus F14	Lacticin F14	Lassi	2.6×10^6	Handa, 2012
Lactobacillus delbreuckii subsp. *bulgaricus* F18	Lacticin F18 Butter	Homemade	2×10^3	Handa, 2012
Lactobacillus plantarum F22	Lacticin F22	Chhang	2.6×10^6	Handa, 2012

It is well studied that lactic acid bacteria play an important role in food fermentation process and impart beneficial effect to the host. In India and particularly in hilly state, viz. Himachal Pradesh fermented foods are regularly being consumed by the people since ages (Kore *et al.*, 2012).

Health Beneficial Effects of Bacteriocin

In comparison to present chemotherapeutic products, most of bacteriocins have a high specific activity against different clinical targets such as antibiotic resistant strains as well as distinctive mechanisms. Bacteriocins have a great potential in human health applications when compared to the traditional antibiotics. Bacteriocins represent a new area of research in dental medicine, where the bacterial pathogens are killed by natural products. Dental caries is one of the most common diseases in the world, second only to the common cold (Islam *et al.*, 2007) and can lead to pain, infection and tooth loss and in severe cases, even death. Nisin is the most promising bacteriocin in the treatment of dental caries. Nisin was also applied in the treatment of respiratory tract infections. Bacteriocins produced by *S. mutans* are called mutacins. Although there is a biological war existing between mutacins and disease causing pathological bacteria in the mouth, many in vivo studies confirm the surrender of viable salivary pathogens to mutacins/bacteriocins. Mutacins inhibit the production of dental caries and sucrose formation. It may be used as a preventive agent in the control of dental caries by mouthwashes (Ikeda *et al.*, 1988; Fukushima, 1985; Hirasawa, 1984).

Staphylococcus aureus and methicillin-resistant *S. aureus* (MRSA) are the most prevalent organisms in skin infections and have become a serious problem, especially in hospitals (Guggenheim *et al.*, 2009; Lesseval and Hadjiiski, 1996; Taylor *et al.*, 1992). Many antibiotics such as oxacillin, nafcillin, quinopristin–dalfopristin, rifampicin, ciprofloxacillin, teichoplanin, cefazolin, and cephalothin A are used to treat *S. aureus* infection (Gould and Chamberlain, 1995; Lowy, 1998) but with limited success. In many cases, vancomycin is used as the last resort but also with limited success (Dicks *et al.*, 2009). Mersacidin, a lantibiotic produced by *Bacillus* sp. strain HIL Y-85, 54728 (Sass *et al.*, 2008), inhibits the growth of MRSA strains in vivo in mice (Kruszewska *et al.*, 2004) and may be considered an alternative treatment.

Bacteriocins are explored for the treatment of juvenile acne due to their specific and potent activity against *Propionibacterium acnei* (Van Kraaij *et al.*, 1999). Bacteriocins from *Bacillus subtilis* named mersacidin inhibit methicillin-resistant *Staphylococcus* with a killing efficiency similar to vancomycin (Bierbaum and Sahl, 1987). This way, harmful side effects caused by the antibiotics and risk of development of antibiotic resistance can be avoided.

MATERIALS AND METHODS

Isolation Procedure of different Bacteriocin Producing Strains

Different ethnic fermented food samples of India viz. dough, sepu vari, dangal vari, goat meat, chur saag, salori, gundruck, nimboosat, chillipickle, nashasta, dried shrimp, marcha, kandal bari, angoori, dried fish, rice beer, chaang (wheat fermented), chaang (rice fermented), chilra, lugri, luske, siddu, Ingra, siddu, tharda, chur saag, sauerkraut and dhuliachar was collected for isolation of potential bacteriocin producing isolates. All samples was collected in clean and sterilized polythene bags or test tubes and stored in refrigerator until further use. The samples were homogenized followed by serial dilution in the range of 10^{-1} to 10^{-9}. The samples from each dilution were mounted by spread plate method on sterilized petriplates containing Man, Rogosa, Sharpe (MRS), Nutrient agar for isolation of bacterial colonies (HiMedia, Mumbai). Plates were incubated at 37° C for 48 h under aerobic and anaerobic conditions in a jar by using anaerobic gas packs (HiMedia, Mumbai). After incubation, individual colonies were purified using streak plate technique on the same medium.

Identification of Bacteriocins Producing Isolates

Tentative identification of bacteriocin producing isolates was done by observing following characteristics:

(i) Morphological characteristics (Aneja, 2003)

1. Cell morphology
2. Gram's reaction
3. Spore staining
4. Colony size
5. Shape
6. Culture conditions

(ii) Biochemical tests (Aneja, 2003)

1. Catalae test
2. Carbohydrate fermentation

Inhibitory Effects of Bacteriocins against different Pathogenic/Spoilage causing Microorganisms

Various isolated microbes were further tested for their antagonistic activity against selected food borne/spoilage causing microorganisms viz., *Listeria monocytogens* MTCC 839, *Clostridium perfringenes* MTCC 1739, *Staphylococcus aureus* IGMC, *Bacillus cereus* CRI, *Enterococcus faecalis* MTCC 2729, *Rhizoctonia solani*, *Aspergillus niger*, *Rhizopus* sp. and *Fusarium* sp. Antagonistic activity of isolates was studied by the Bit/Disc method (Barefoot and Klanhammer, 1983). 1 ml of inoculums of each indicator bacteria (1.0 OD) was swabbed properly on pre-poured sterilized petriplates using sterilized cotton bud. Then with the help of sharp, sterilized borer bit of 10 mm diameter were cut. The bit of isolates was kept on lawn of indicator tested strains with the help of sterilized inoculating needle and the plates were checked for the appearance of clear inhibition zones.

Wide halos clearances (12 mm) by the isolates showed strong antimicrobial activity against their corresponding indicators. Antagonistic pattern of different isolated probiotic potential microorganisms varied against test pathogens (Figs. 1.1, 1.2 and 1.3) and the inhibitory action is mainly due to antimicrobial compound- bacteriocin secreted by them.

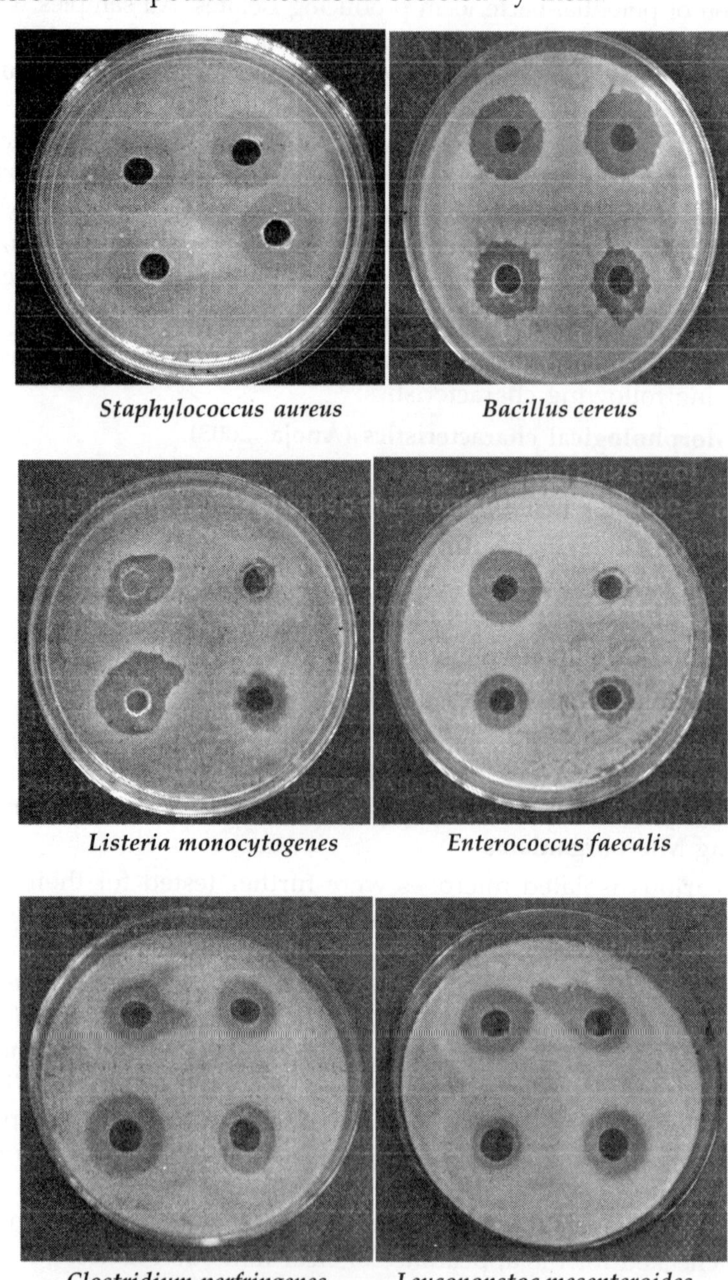

Fig. 1.1: Inhibitory Spectrum of Fermenting Microbes Present in Traditional Fermented Food against Challenging Food Borne Pathogens by well Diffusion method

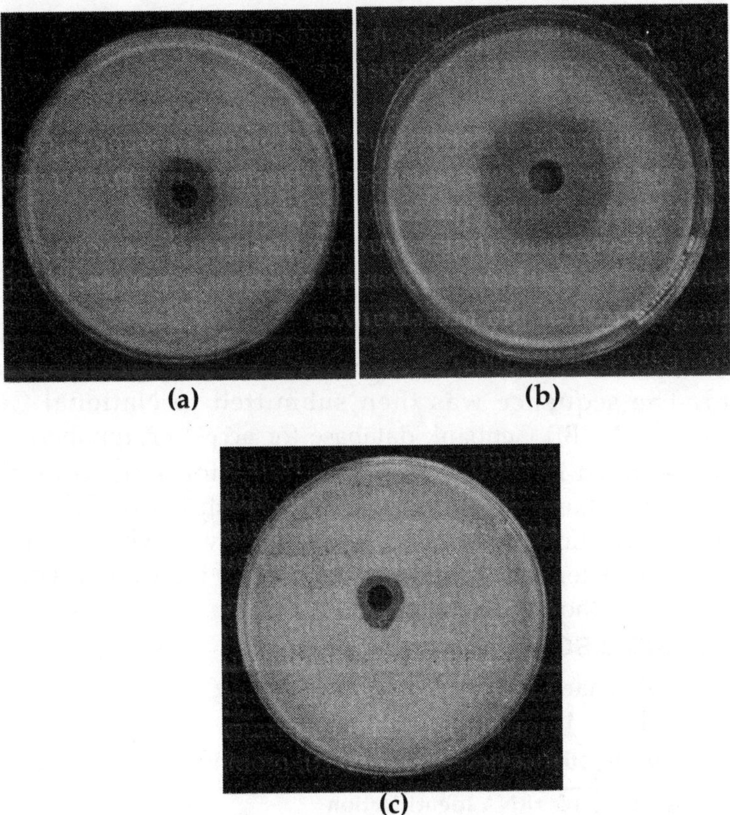

Fig. 1.2: Antimicrobial Activity of Bacteriocin (a) Lacticin (b) Bacicin (c) Brevicin against *L. monocytogenes*

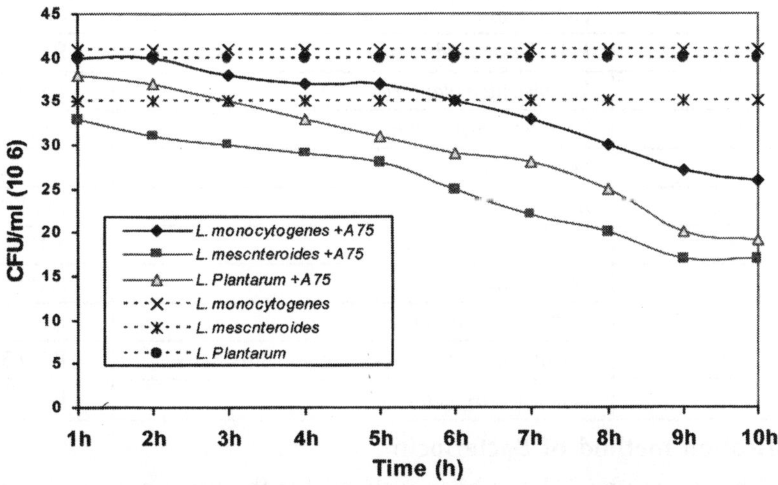

Fig 1.3: Bactericidal Effect of Purified Bacteriocin of *Bacillus subtilis* against Test Indicators

Protocol for Molecular Characterization using 16S rRNA Technique

The screened isolates were genetically identified using 16S rRNA gene technique. Genomic DNA of isolates was isolated using the protocol of Rodriguez and Tait, (1983). 1200 bp long fragment of the 16S rRNA gene were amplified from the extracted DNA using eubacterial universal primers [Forward primers: (5'AGAGTTTGATCMTGGCTCAG3') and Reverse primers: (5'ACCTTGTTACGACTT3')]. The PCR analysis was carried out with a volume of 25 µl mixture in a thermocycler (Eppendrof, make). The procedure consisted of 35 cycles of 92° C for 1 min, 55° C for 1 min, 72° C for 1 min. The partial genome sequence of approximately 700 bp long 16S rRNA gene was sequenced by the services provided by Xceleris, Ahmedabad, India. Pvt. Ltd. The sequence was then submitted to National Centre for Biotechnology (NCBI) Genbank database for accession numbers.

The identified isolates were then checked for bacteriocin production after neutralizing the effect of acids and H_2O_2 with 1 N NaOH and Catalase. Bacteriocin production was studied during its growth cycle. The antibacterial activity of the bacteriocin produced against test indicator was checked by well diffusion method of Kimura *et al.*, (1998).

RESULTS AND DISCUSSION

Genotypic characterization was done using 16S rRNA technique and presented in Table 1.3.

Table 1.3: Identification of finally screened bacteriocin producing isolates

Name of Isolates	16s rRNA Identification	Accession No.
UN	*Lactobacillus brevis*	JX046150
G2	*Lactobacillus spicheri*	JX048191
F3	*Lactobacillus fermentum*	KC242235
L1	*Pediococcus acidilactici*	KM251713
L2	*Lactobacillus plantarum*	KM251714
A3	*Bacillus licheniformis*	KM251712
S6	*Lactobacillus pentosus*	KU921222
AGI	*Brevibacillus borstelensis*	JX129162
F8	*Lactobacillus reuteri*	KT865222
F11	*Lactobacillus crustorum*	KT865221
F14	*Lactobacillus acidophilus*	KT865225
F18	*Lactobacillus delbreuckii* subsp. *bulgaricus*	KT865224
F22	*Lactobacillus plantarum*	KT865223

Purification method of Bacteriocin

Various methods have been utilized for the purification of bacteriocin from the bacterial screened isolates (Table 1.4 and Fig. 1.4). Ammonium sulphate precipitation, direct lyphophilized bacteriocin, gel exclusion chromatography and finally SDS page to confirm the purification process.

Table 1.4: Purification and recovery of bacteriocin produced by *L. brevis* UN (Gautam *et al.*, 2013)

	Volume (ml)	Activity unit (AU/ml)	Total* activity (AU)	Protein** (mg/ml)	Specific*** activity (AU/mg)	Purification• Fold	Recovery♦♦
Crude (Culture supernatant)	100	2×10^3	2×10^5	0.47	4,255.3	1	100
Lyophilized bacteriocin	20	6×10^3	1.2×10^5	0.371	16,172.5	3.8	78
Gel exclusion chromatography	2	8×10^3	1.6×10^4	0.174	45,977.0	10.80	37

* Total activity was determined by the multiplication of volume and activity

** Protein concentration was determined by Lowry's method

*** Specific activity is the activity unit/protein concentration

• Purification fold is increase in the specific activity

♦♦ Recovery % is remaining protein concentration as % of the initial protein concentration

Bacteriocin produced was then purified to homogeneity by ammonium sulfate precipitation (50% salt saturation) followed by gel exclusion chromatography. Purity of bacteriocin was checked by SDS-PAGE (Sharma *et al.*, 2011). The activity of culture supernatant, partially purified and purified bacteriocin was calculated by serial two fold dilution method. Two-hundred ìl of sample was poured into the wells cut on the lawns of indicators in nutrient agar plates. The plates were then incubated at 35°C for 24 h and the zones of inhibition formed around the wells were measured. After incubation at 35°C for 24 h clear inhibition zones were evaluated and expressed in arbitrary units (AU/ml) (Barefoot and Klaenhammer, 1983).

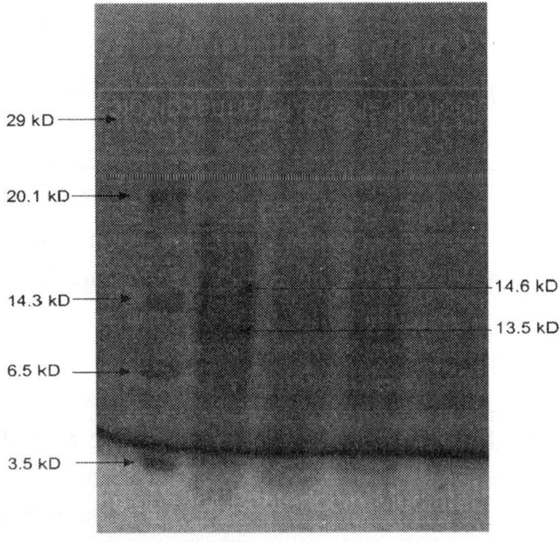

Fig. 1.4: SDS PAGE of *Bacillus* sp. A_{75}

Effect of different Parameters on Bacteriocin Production

(i) Effect of growth phases

Bacteriocin production is growth associated. Bacteriocin is produced at a particular time of growth phase so it is necessary to find out that period of growth cycle where bacteriocin is produced (Fig. 1.5). The length of time for which a culture is maintained is very important. Ideally cell will enter exponential phase fairly rapidly and reach stationary phase by 12 to 16 h. This can limit destruction of bacteriocin by intracellular proteolytic enzyme released in growth medium by dead cells and destruction caused by several proteolytic enzymes. In general, under optimum growth condition, high bacteriocin production was obtained within 16-18 h (Ray, 2001). The growth curve of the isolates followed a sigmoid curve pattern based on measuring bacterial turbidity level OD_{540} nm. The bacterial cultures were incubated at 37° C in MRS broth (6.5 pH) for different interval of time (24 to 60h). Optical density and inhibition zones of bacterial culture were measured after 2h of interval at 540 nm. The decrease in bacteriocin production at the end of stationary phase may due to protein aggregation, proteolytic degradation by specific or nonspecific enzymes and re-adsorption of bacteriocin to the producer cell surface at low pH (Sparo *et al.*, 2006; Gupta *et al.*, 2010).

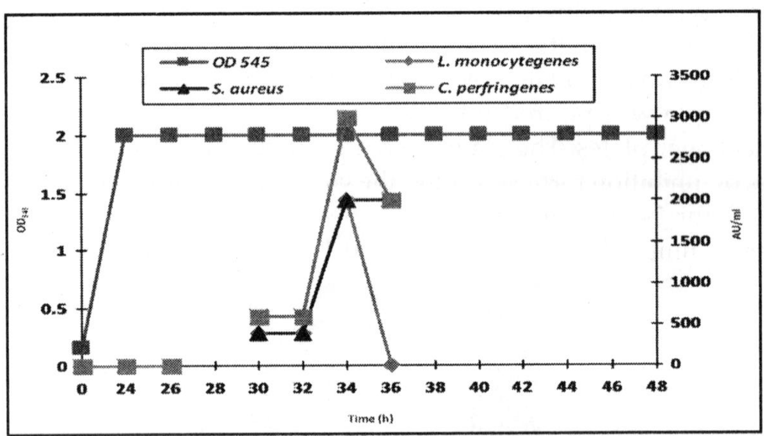

Fig 1.5: Growth Curve of *L. spicheri* G2 showing Production Pattern of Bacteriocin

The results indicated the bacteriocin produced during early stationary phase of the growth cycle of the isolates (Gautam and Sharma, 2015; Gautam *et al.*, 2013).

(ii) Effect of proteolytic enzymes

The purified bacteriocin of screened isolates was studied for effect of proteolytic enzymes i.e trysin, pepsin and proteinase K and this revealed that when treated with these three enzymes at the concentration of 0.25 mg/ml in the ratio 1:1 (Enzyme reaction) no zone formation was formed against *L. monocytogenes* in case of enzyme treated bacteriocin only, while bacteriocin treated with their respective indicators (EC_2) zones of 11mm, 14mm were formed for *L. monocytogens* respectively (Fig 1.6). Thus, confirming the proteolytic nature of the bacteriocin.

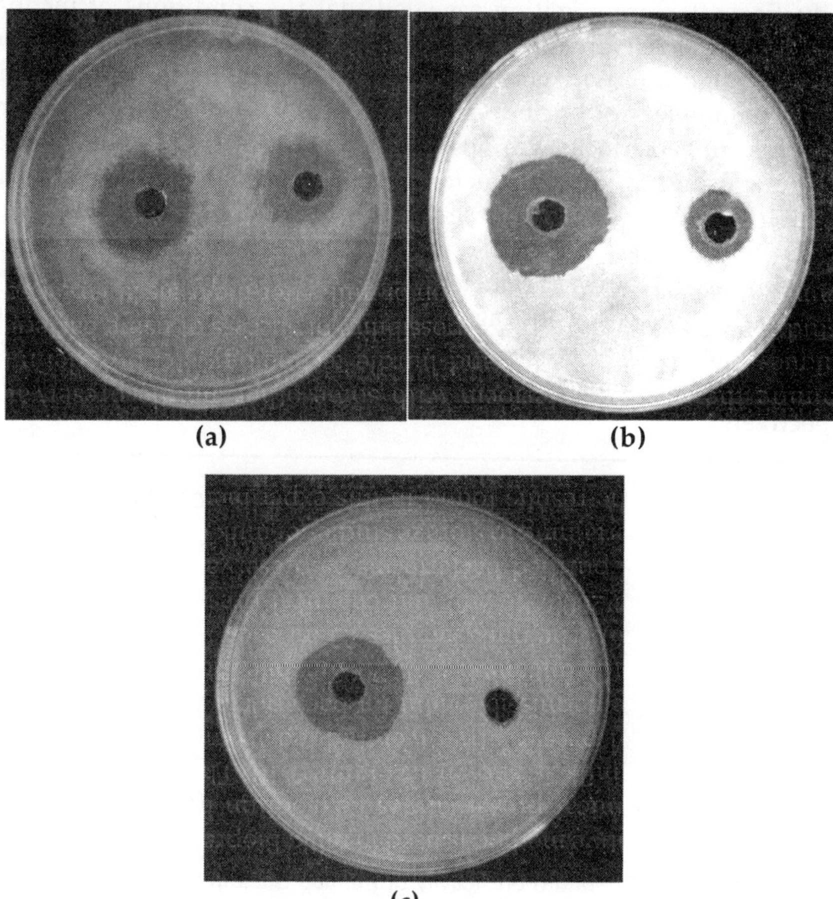

Fig. 1.6: Effect of (a) Trypsin (b) Proteinase K (c) Papain on activity of Purified Bacteriocin Lacticin against *Listeria monocytogenes*

(iii) Effect of temperature, pH and inoculums size

An incubation temperature at which growth rate is optimum is also important for obtaining high yield of bacteriocin. In *Pediooccus acidolactici* maximum cell mass and pediocin production occur at 30 and 37° C, respectively and reduction in cell mass and pediocin production above 40° C. A statistical interaction of temperature and agitation observed affecting microbial growth (Santoyo *et al.*, 2001). pH is also one of the factor which affect activity of bacteriocin. The screened isolates were then characterized based on various parameters viz. temperature, pH and inoculum size. for the effective production of the bacteriocin (Figures 1.7 and 1.8). All isolates showed different optimized conditions for the bacteriocin production. The increase in size of zones of inhibition after optimization is directly associated with the increase in bacteriocin production. The increase in bacteriocin production after optimization revealed that the conditions of incubation particularly temperature, pH and inoculum size influence the yield of active bacteriocin significantly. Therefore, it becomes necessary to optimize various process parameters of bacteriocin producing isolate to achieve maximum production of bacteriocin. Various studies are cited where optimization has been done using classical one factor at a time. (Gautam *et al.*, 2013; Gautam and Sharma, 2015), studied these factors where, the zone of inhibition of bacteriocin of *L. brevis* UN and *L. spicheri* G2 against test indicators increased after optimizing various parameters. The inhibitory zone size of bacteriocin of *L. brevis* UN increased 40% against *L. monocytogenes*, 20% against *S. aureus* and 70% against *C. perfringens*. Whereas in case of bacteriocin of *L. spicheri* G2 increase was 70%, and 41.17% against *L. monocytogens* and *C. perfringens* respectively.

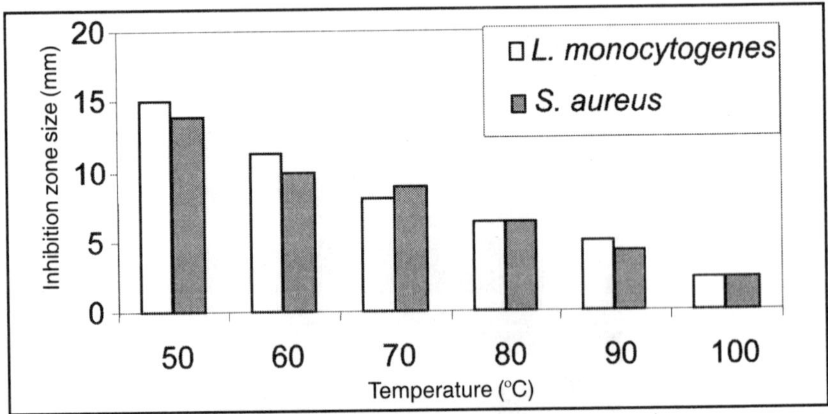

Fig. 1.7: Effect of Temperature on Activity of Purified Bacteriocin (In Terms of Inhibition Zones)

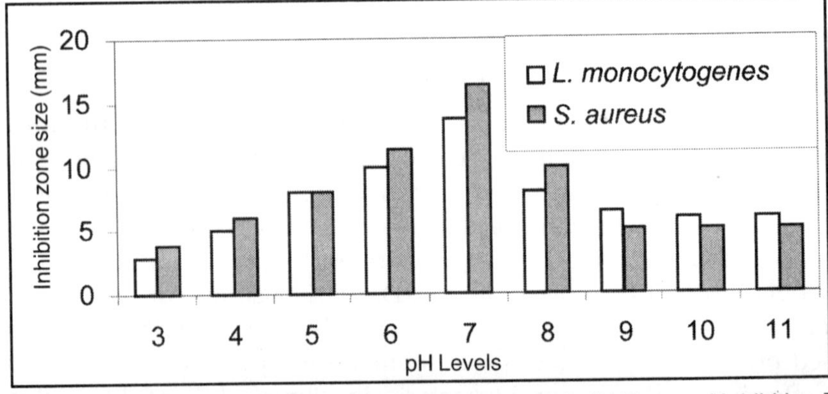

Fig. 1.8: Effect of pH on the Activity of Purified Bacteriocin (In Terms of Inhibition Zones)

Applications of Bacteriocin as a Food Biopreservative

Bacteriocin as food preservatives may be applied either by using the bacteriocinogenic strain as a starter culture and/or a protective culture or by using the isolated bacteriocin as a food additive (Calo-Mata *et al.*, 2008). The use of the Generally Recognized as Safe (GRAS) *Bacillus* sp. and lactic acid bacteria (LAB) and the antimicrobial compounds they produce i.e. bacteriocins is a promising ongoing development in food preservation and hence different preservative effect of purified bacteriocin was studied for checking its efficiency.

(i) In tomato paste

The purified bacteriocin (Bacicin) from *Brevibacillus borstelensis* AG1 was studied for nine days in tomato paste inoculated with food borne pathogens and was compared to commercial biopreservative – nisin and chemical preservative – sodium benzoate (Gupta *et al.*, 2015). The indicator strains i.e. *Listeria monocytogenes* MTCC839, *Bacillus subtilis* CRI and *Clostridium perfringens* MTCC1739 were used at the amount 8.16, 8.13 and 8.18 log cfu/ml. Viable cells were counted periodically and a consistent reduction in number of viable cells of each tested pathogen was observed. It was found antagonistic against *L. monocytogenes* MTCC839, *B. subtilis* CRI and *C. perfringes* MTCC1739 which are the most challengeable and food borne pathogens found in processed vegetables products. Purified bacteriocin was found active over a wide pH range i.e. 3.0 to 11.0 and was able to withstand temperature up to 100ÚC. It showed a better preservative potential by reducing pathogenic load of the tested strains (by 2.02, 2.05 and 2.02 log cycles (cfu/ml) of *L. monocytogenes* MTCC839, *B. subtilis* CRI and *C. perfringes* MTCC1739, respectively) in tomato paste as compared to control (without bacteriocin) (Fig. 1.9).

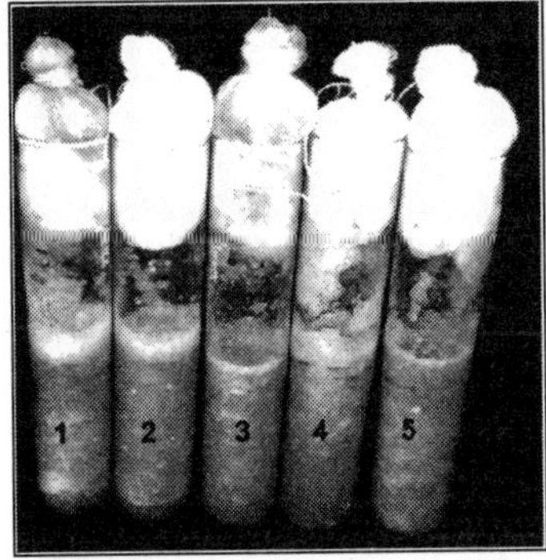

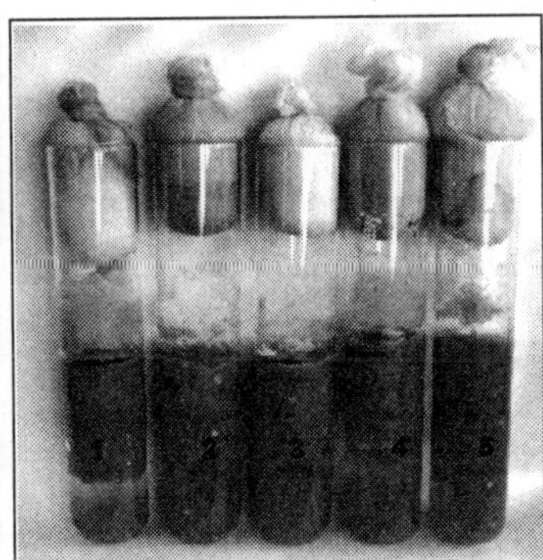

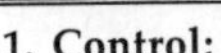

1. Control;
2. Partially purified bacteriocin
3. Purified bacteriocin
4. Sodium benzoate
5. Nisin

Fig 1.9: Efect of Partially Purified Bacteriocin and Purified Bacteriocin in Tomato Paste Inoculated with *L. monocytogens* at 4º C as Compared to Nisin, Sodium Benzoate and Control

(ii) In milk

Another preservative method is used in milk. Biopreservation compared with commercial chemical preservatives i.e. sodium benzoate in milk to evaluate its effect in milk is shown in Figure 1.10. The preservatives i.e. bacteriocins/chemical preservative were added in milk samples within permissible limits. The permissible limit for bacteriocin to be added in food is below 5000 AU/ml (Ogunbanwo *et al.*, 2003) while for sodium benzoate it is 0.2% (Lal *et al.*, 1986). The milk samples 25 ml each was inoculated with purified bacteriocin @ 2000 AU/ml and chemical preservative @ 0.2 % to study the potential of purified bacteriocins as preservation of milk during storage at 4° C. Data pertaining to storage studies of milk have been presented in (Figs. 1.11, 1.12). The results found in this experiment for application of bacteriocin as biopreservative in milk are quite encouraging and satisfactory. However, these findings could be refined and used meticulously after combining the use of bacteriocin with some other simple preservation techniques, viz. pasteurization and hurdle technology etc. But, definitely this study has indicated the strong possibility of success of using bacteriocin at commercial level for biopreservation of milk after the trials at larger scale.

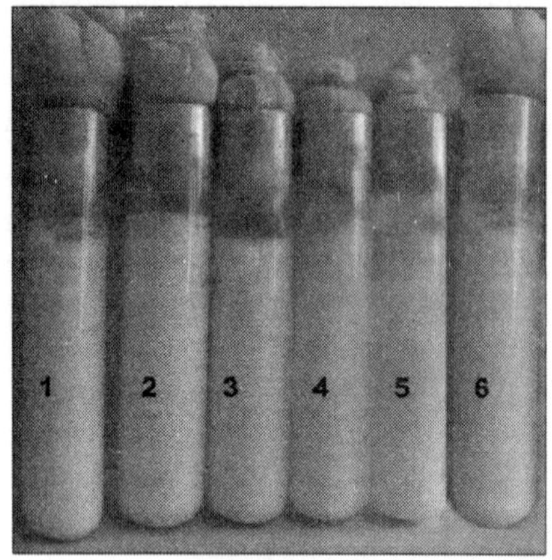

Day 0

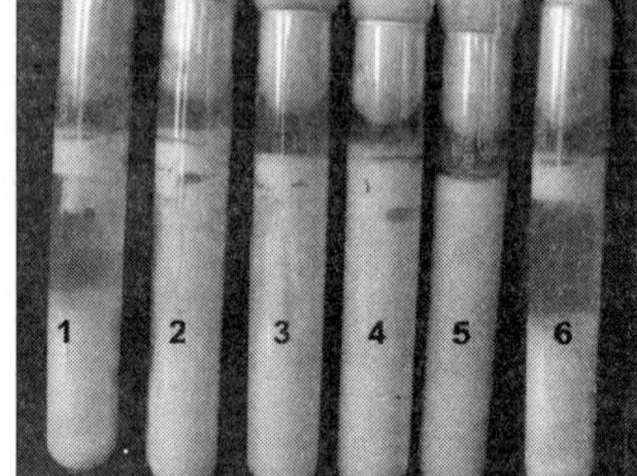

Day 4

1. Control
2. Cell culture
3. Partially purified bacteriocin
4. Purified bacteriocin
5. Nisin
6. Sodium benzoate

Fig 1.10: Effect of Cell Culture, Partially Purified Bacteriocin and Purified Bacteriocin in Milk Inoculated *C. perfringens* at Room Temperature as Compared to Nisin, Sodium Benzoate and Control

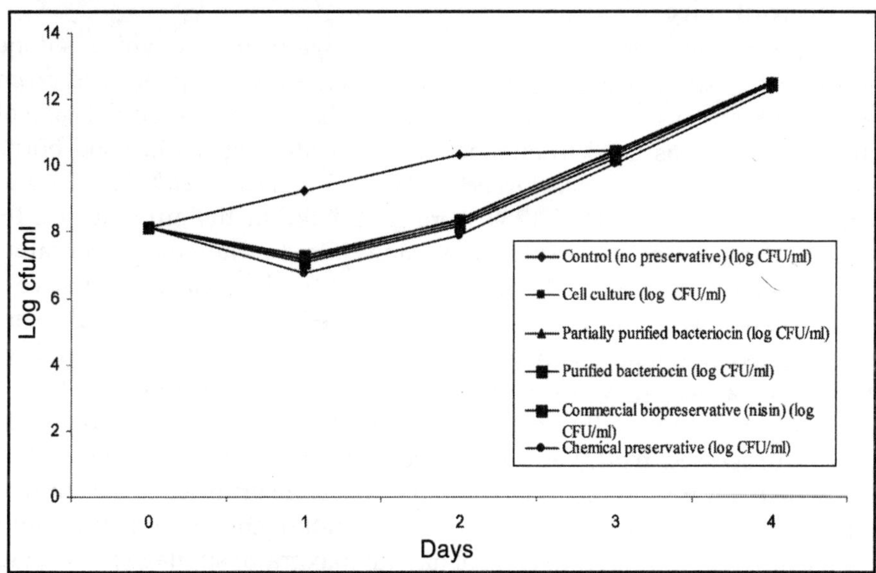

Fig. 1.11: A Comparative Study to use Biopreservative (*nisin*) with Chemical Preservative (Sodium benzoate) against *S. aureus* to Enhance Storage of Milk (4°C)

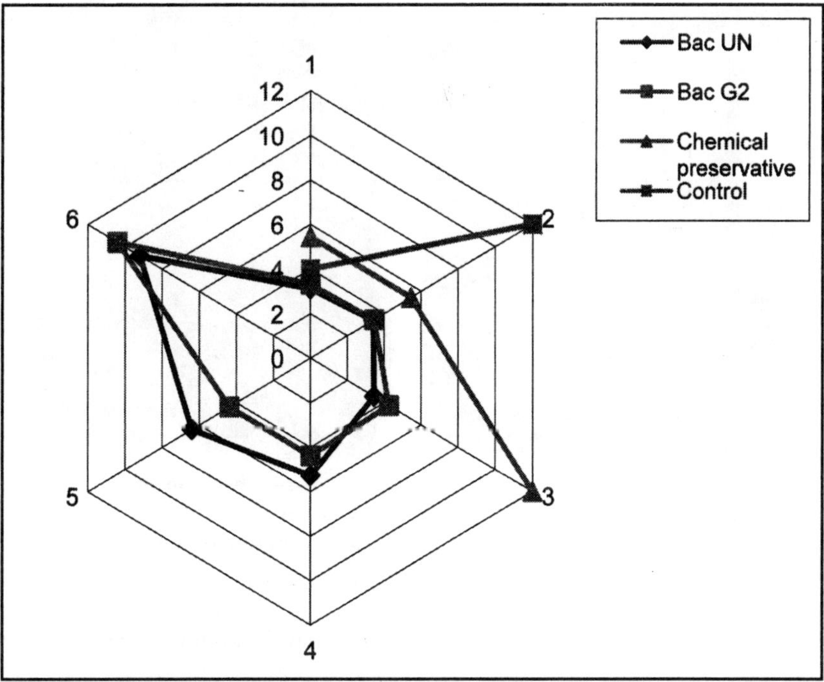

Fig. 1.12: Comparison between Bacteriocin and Chemical Preservative to Enhance the Shelf Life of Milk

(iii) In fruit juice

The third biopreservation product was orange fruit juice which is done to enhance the shelf life and microbial safety. Brevicin produced from *Brevibacillus borstelensis* AG1 isolated from Marcha – a natural herbal cake of North East India was used to enhance the shelf life (Fig. 1.13). Food borne pathogens viz. *Listeria monocytogenes* MTCC 839, *Bacillus subtilis* CRI and *Clostridium perfringens* MTCC 1739 were inoculated at the amount of 8.16, 8.13 and 8.18 log cfu/ml, respectively in orange juice to study the preservative effect of bacteriocin against them as compared to chemical preservative – sodium benzoate and commercial biopreservative i.e. nisin. Viable cells were counted periodically and a consistent reduction in number of viable cells of each tested pathogen was observed. Brevicin when tested was found antagonistic to most challengeable and serious food borne pathogens to control in processed fruit/vegetables products. Brevicin was found active over a wide pH range i.e. 3.0 to 11.0 and thermostable upto 100ÚC. It showed better preservative potential by reducing the pathogenic load of indicators in orange juice as compared to control having maximum spoilage proving its potential as a natural preservative to enhance microbial safety and shelf life of different food items (Gupta *et al.*, 2015).

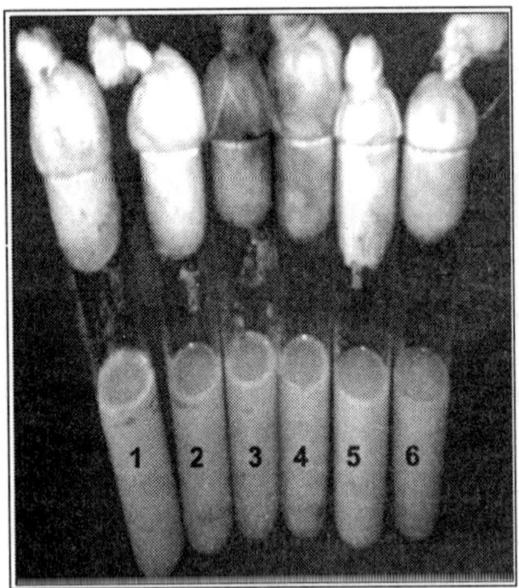

1. Control
2. Cell culture
3. Partially purified bacteriocin
4. Purified bacteriocin
5. Nisin
6. Sodium benzoate

Fig. 1.13. Effect of Cell Culture, Partially Purified Brevicin and Purified Brevicin in Enhancing the Shelf Life of Orange Fruit Juice Inoculated with *L. monocytogens* at Room Temperature as Compared to Nisin, Sodium Benzoate and Control

(iv) In cheese

The comparative study of use of lenticin against sodium benzoate was done for cheese inoculated with a mixed inoculum of *L. monocytogenes* and *S. aureus* (8.80 log cfu/ml), (1.0 OD). The initial log cfu/ml was found to be 8.80

and the pH was 6.0, 5.6 and 5.5 for lenticin, sodium benzoate and control respectively. The log cfu/ml on 1st day was found to be 6.80, 7.00, 9.20 for lenticin, sodium benzoate and control. The mean was found to be 7.67. The lowest log cfu/ml was found for lenticin on 2nd day and was 6.60 while the log cfu/ml was 7.50 and 10.30 for sodium benzoate and control respectively. The 2nd day mean was found to be 8.13. The log cfu/ml was 7.50, 8.10 and 11.60 for the respective comparisons and the mean was 9.07 for 3rd day. The 4th day log cfu/ml for lenticin was 9.20, 10.60 for sodium benzoate and 12.40 for control. The mean was 7.78 for lenticin, 8.40 for sodium benzoate and 10.46 for control. The final pH was 6.0, 5.6 and 5.5 for lenticin, sodium benzoate and control respectively (Fig. 1.14) (Sharma, 2012).

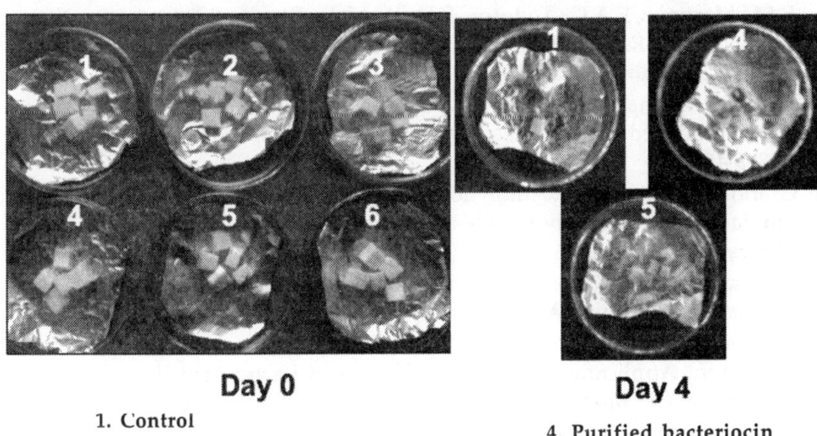

Fig. 1.14: Effect of Cell Culture, Partially Purified Bacteriocin and Purified Bacteriocin in Cheese Inoculated with *Listeria monocytogens* at 4º C as Compared to Nisin, Sodium Benzoate and Control

Concusion

Results obtained in this study showed that the strains isolated from traditional fermented food items of India are a potential bacteriocin producing strains. The results found in this experiment for application of bacteriocin as biopreservative in food products are quite encouraging and satisfactory. However, these findings could be refined and used meticulously after combining the use of bacteriocin with some other simple preservation techniques, viz. pasteurization and hurdle technology etc. But, definitely this study has indicated the strong possibility of success of using bacteriocin at commercial level for biopreservation of food after the trials at larger scale. With this result, main aim of our present study is successfully fulfilled, i.e. the isolation of potent bacteriocin producing bacteria, purification of bacteriocin and its application as food biopreservative in food to avoid spoilage and enhance its shelf life and the success in efficacy. Thus we may conclude from present piece of work that, that day is not far off when chemicals could be eradicated from the preserved food totally or partially and their place would be taken by biopreservatives and probiotics thus providing the consumers safer and healthier food which would lead to a revolution in the food unit/food processing industry.

REFERENCES

Aneja, K.R. (2003): In: Experiments in Microbiology, Plant Pathology and Biotechnology. Biochemical Activities of Microorganisms, 4th edn, New Age International Publishers, New Delhi.

Balciunas, E.M., Martinez, F.A.C., Todorov, S.D., de Melo, Franco. B.D.G., Converti, A., de Souza, Oliveira. R.P. (2013): Novel Biotechnological Applications of Bacteriocins: A Review. *Food Control*, 32: 134-142.

Barefoot, S.F. and Klanhammer, T.R. (1983): Detection and Activity of Lactacin B: A Bacteriocin Produced by *Lactobacillus acidophilus*. *Applied and Environment Microbiology*, 45(6): 1808-1815.

Bierbaum, G. and Sahl, H.G. (1987): Autolytic System of *Staphylococcus simulans* 22: Influence of Cationic Peptides on Activity of N-acetylmuramoyl-L-alanine amidase. *Journal of Bacteriology*, 169: 5452-5458.

Bizani, D. and Brandelli, A. (2002): Characterization of a Bacteriocin Produced by a Newly Isolated *Bacillus* sp. strain 8A. *Journal of Applied Microbiology*, 93: 521-519.

Calo-Mata, P., Aslindo, S., Boehme, K., de Mignel, T., Pascoal, A. and Barros-velazquez, J. (2008): Current Applications and Future Trends of Lactic Acid Bacteria and their Bacteriocin for the Biopreservation of Aquatic Food Products. *Food Bioprocess Technology*, 1: 43-63.

Dicks, L.M.T., Todorov, S.D. and Franco, B.D.G.M. (2009): Current Status of Antibiotic Resistance in Lactic Acid Bacteria. In: Antibiotic Resistance: Causes and Risk Factors, Mechanisms and Alternatives (Eds: Bonilla AR, Muniz KP), Nova Publications, pp: 379-425.

Fukushima, H. (1985): Characterisation and Mode of Action of a Purified Bacteriocin from the Oral Bacterium *Streptococcus mutans* RM 10. *Archives in Oral Biology*, 30: 229-34.

Gautam, N. and Sharma, N. (2009): Purification and Characterization of Purified Bacteriocin of *Lactobacillus brevis* Isolated from Traditional Fermented Food of H.P. *Indian Journal of Biochemistry and Biophysics*, 46: 337-341.

Gautam, N. and Sharma, N. (2015): A Study on Characterization of New Bacteriocin Produced from a Novel Strain of *Lactobacillus spicheri* G2 Isolated from gundruk- A Fermented Vegetable Product of North East India. *Journal of Food Science and Technology*, 52(9): 5808-16.

Gautam, N., Sharma, N. and Ahlawat, O.P. (2013): Purification and Characterization of Bacteriocin Produced by *Lactobacillus brevis* UN Isolated from Dhulliachar: A Traditional Food Product of North East India. *Indian Journal of Microbiology*, 54(2): 185-189.

Gould, D.J. and Chamberlain, A. (1995): *Staphylococcus aureus:* A Review of the Literature. *Journal of Clinical Nursing*, 4:5-12.

Guggenheim, M., Zbinden, R., Handschin, A., Gohritz, A., Altintas, M.A. and Giovanoli, P. (2009): Changes in Bacterial Isolates from Burn Wounds and their Antibiograms: A 20-year Study (1986-2005) *Burns*, 35: 553-560.

Gupta, A., Sharma, N. and Handa, S. (2015): Natural Preservation of Orange Juice to Enhance its Shelf Stability and Microbial Safety using Purified Bacteriocin of *Brevibacillus borstelensis* AG1. *American Journal of Pharmacy and Techonological Research,* 5(3): 168-179.

Gupta, H., Malik, R.K., De, S. and Kaushik, J.K. (2010): Purification and Characterization of Enterocin FH 99 Produced by a Faecal Isolate *Enterococcus faecium* FH 99. *Indian Journal of Microbiology,* 50: 145-155.

Handa, S. 2012. Isolation of Lactic Acid Bacteria and to Study their Potential as Probiotics [M.Sc Thesis]. Nauni, Solan, Himachal Pradesh, India: Dr Y S Parmar UHF, pp: 151.

Hansen, J.N. (1993): Antibiotics Synthesized by Post Translational Modification. *Annual Review of Microbiology,* 47: 535-564.

Hirasawa, M. (1984): Effect of Mouth Rinse Containing a Bacteriocin from *Streptococcus mutans* on Plaque Micro Flora. *Journal of Dental Research,* 63: 1146.

Hurst, A. (1981): Nisin. *Advances in Applied Microbiology,* 27: 85-123.

Ikeda, T., Kurita, T. and Hirasawa, M. (1988): Suppression of *S. sobrinus* 6715 (g) in the Plaques by *S. mutans* 32 K(c). *Journal of Oral Pathology,* 17; 471-4.

Islam, B., Khan, S. and Khan, A. (2007): Dental Caries: From Infection to Prevention. *Medical Science Monitoring,* 13(11): 196-203.

Kimura, H., Sashihara, T., Mastsuki, H., Sanamota, K. and Ishizaki, A. (1998): Noval Bacteriocin of *Pediococcus* sp. 15K-1 Isolated from Well Aged Bed of Fermented Rice Bran. *Annals of New York Academy of Science,* 864: 345-348.

Klaenhammer, T.R. (1993): Genetics of Bacteriocin Produced by Lactic Acid Bacteria. *FEMS Microbiological Review,* 12: 39-86.

Kore, K.B., Pattanaik, A.K., Sharma, K. and Mirajkar, P.P. (2012): Effect of Feeding Traditionally Prepared Fermented Milk Dahi (curd) as a Probiotics on Nutritional Status, Hindgut Health and Haematology in Dogs. *Indian Journal of Traditional Knowledge,* 11(1): 35-39.

Kruszewska, D., Sahl, H.G., Bierbaum, G., Pag, U., Hynes, S.O. and Ljungh, A. (2004): Mersacidin Eradicates Methicillin-resistant *Staphylococcus aureus* (MRSA) in a Mouse Rhinitis Model. *Journal of Antimicrobial Chemotherapy,* 54: 648-653.

Lal, G., Siddappa, G. S. and Tondon, G. L. (1986): *Chutneys,* Sauces and Pickles. In: Preservation of Fruits and Vegetables, Indian Council Agricultural Research, New Delhi, p 235-269.

Lesseval, M.I. and Hadjiiski, G. (1996): Staphylococcal Infections in the Sofia Burn Centre, Bulgaria. *Burns,* 2: 279-282.

Lowy, F.D. (1998): *Staphylococcus aureus* Infections. *New England Journal of Medicine,* 339: 520 532.

Maisnier, P.S., Deschamps, N., Tatini, S.R. and Richard, J. (1992): Inhibition of *Listeria monocytogenes* in Commembert Cheese made with a Nisin Producing Starter. *Lait,* 72: 249-263.

Ogunbanwo, S.T., Sanni, A.I. and Onilvde, A.A. (2003): Characterization of Bacteriocins Produced by *Lactobacillus plantarum* F_1 and *Lactobacillus bervis* OG 1. *African Journal of Biotechnology,* 2(8): 219-227.

Pal, V., Jamuna, M. and Jeevratanam. (2005): Isolation and Characterization of Bacteriocin Producing LAB from a South Indian special Dosa Batter. *Journal of Culture Collection,* 4(1): 53-60.

Parada, J.L., Caron, C.R., Medeiros, A.B.P. and Soccol, C.R. (2007): Bacteriocin from LAB: Purification Properties and use as Biopeservatives. *Brazilian Archives of Biology and Technology,* 50(3): 521-542.

Pirzada, Z.A., Ali, S.A., Khan, B.M. and Rasool, S.A. (2004): Production and Physico-chemical Characterization of Bacteriocin-like Inhibitory Substances from Marine Bacterium ZM 81. *Pakistan Journal of Biological Sciences*, 7(12): 2026-2030.

Raja, N.B., Ravi, P., Shyamsunder, A. and Mallikarjum. (2010): Isolation and Characterization of Bacteriocins from Fermented Foods and Probiotic. *International Journal of Pharma and Bioscienecs*, 1: 1-5.

Ray, B. (2001): Sublethal Injury Bacteriocins and Food Microbiology. *ASM News*, 59: 285-291.

Rilley, M.A. and Wertz, J.E. (2002): Bacteriocins: Evolution, Ecology and Application. *Annual Reviews in Microbiology*, 56: 117-137.

Rodriguez, R.L. and Tait, R.T. (1983): Recombinant DNA Techniques. An Introduction. Adisson Wesely, London.

Ross, R.P., Morgan, S. and Hill, C. (2002): Preservation and Fermentation: Past, Present and Future. *International Journal of Food Microbiology*, 79(1-2): 3-16.

Santoyo, C., Mondoza, Gsrcia. P.G., Garcia, Alvarado. M.A. and Escudero, Abarca. B.I. (2001): Effect of Physical Factors on the Production of Bacteriocin from Pediococcus Acidilactici ITV 26. *Journal of Industrial Microbiology and Biotechnology*, 26: 191-195.

Sarkar, S.P., Mandal, M. and Chahrabory, C. (2007): Beneficial Effect of Probiotics used as Food. *Beverages and Food World*, 40-42.

Sass, P., Jansen, A., Szekat, C., Sass, V., Sahl, H. G. and Bierbaum, G. (2008): *BMC Microbiology*, 8:186.

Sharma, N. (2012): Food Biopreservative Potential of Purified Antimicrobial Bacteriocins Produced from Bacteria Isolated from Fermented Food of India. In Proceedings on Antimicrobial Resistance: A Cause for Global Concern SHIATS, Allahabad.

Sharma, N. and Gautam, N. (2007): Use of Bacteriocin as Potential Biopreservative in Milk, Cheese and Apple Juice. *Beverages and Food World*, 34: 44-47.

Sharma, N., Attri, A., Gautam, N. and Gupta, R.K. (2012): Role of Lenticin-A Bacteriocin as Biopreservative in Different Food Products to Enhance their Safety. *Beverages and Food World*, 39(2): 23-27.

Sharma, N., Gargi, K. and Neopaney, B. (2006): Characterization of a New Bacteriocin Produced from a Novel Isolated Strain of *Bacillus lentus* NG 121. *Antonie van Leeuwenhock*, 89: 337-343.

Sharma, N., Gautam, N. and Sharma, H.K. (2009): Bacteriocin: Food Preservative. *Food Science and Technology*, 137-167.

Sharma, N., Kapoor, G. and Neopaney, B. (2006): Characterization of a New Bacteriocin Produced from a Novel Isolated Strain of *Bacillus lentus* NG121. *Antonie Van Leeuwenhoek*, 89: 337-343.

Sharma, N., Kapoor, R., Gautam, N. and Kumari, R. (2011): Purification and Characterization of Bacteriocin Produced by *Lactobacillus* sp. A75 Isolated from Fermented Chunks of *Phaseolus radiate*. *Food Technology and Biotechnology*, 49(2): 169-17.

Sharma, N., Kapoor, R., Gautam, N. and Neopaney, B. (2008): Purification and Characterization of Natural Food Biopreservative Produced from *Lactobacillus* sp. A75 Isolated from Traditional Fermented Food of India, Presented in Natural Product Discovery and Production, Whistler BC Canada.

Sharma, R. (2014): Isolation and Screening of Potential Microorganisms from Traditional Fermented Foods and to Study their Probiotic Attributes [M.Sc Thesis]. Nauni, Solan, Himachal Pradesh, India: Dr Y S Parmar UHF, pp: 166.

Sparo, M.D., Castro, M.S., Andino, P.J., Favigne, M.V., Ceriani, C., Gutierrez, G.I., Fernandez, M.M. and De Marzi, M.C. (2006): Partial Characterization of Enterocin MR99 from a Corn Silage Isolate of *Enterococcus faecalis*. *Journal of Applied Microbiology*, 100: 123-134.

Taylor, G.D., Kibsey, P., Kirkland, T., Burroughs, E. and Tredget, E. (1992): Predominance of Staphylococcal Organisms in Infections Occurring in a Burns Intensive Care Unit. *Burns*, 18: 332-335.

Van, Kraaij. C., de Vos, W.M., Siezen, R.J. and Kuipers, O.P. (1999): Lantibiotics: Biosynthesis, mode of Action and Applications. Natural Product Report, 16: 575-587.

Vescovo, M., Torriani, S., Orsi, C., Macchiorolo, F. and Solari, G. (1996): Application of Antimicrobial Producing Lactic Acid Bacteria to Control Pathogens in Ready to use Vegetables. *Journal of Applied Biotechnology*, 81(2): 113-119.

Pages: 24-36

MICROBIOLOGICAL AND PHARMACOLOGICAL ASPECTS OF BIODIVERSITY

Edited by: Dr. Pankaj Sharma; Dr. Neha Gautam Sharma & Dr. Pankaj Sharma

ISBN: 978-93-5056-878-1

Edition: 2017

Published by: Discovery Publishing House Pvt. Ltd., New Delhi (India)

Conservation of *Ginkgo biloba* L. through in- vitro Techniques and its Molecular Characterization

Lalit M. Tewari*[1]; Brij M. Upreti[2]; Neetu Bohra[2]; Mamta Bharti[2] Naveen Pandey[2]; Neha Chopra[2]; Geeta Tewari[3] and Tapan Nailwal[4]

INTRODUCTION

Due to legal and illegal exploitation of important plant species from wild, anthropogenic pressure and lack of knowledge about sustainable harvesting of useful bio resources particularly medicinal ones as many of them has been listed under the categories of rare, threatened, endangered or at the verge of extinction. A central problem is a continuing loss of biodiversity, but our knowledge about human dimension of biodiversity is still relatively limited. However, there are several plant species growing in this earth but has not still given priority for conservation due to lack of awareness about their usefulness, economic potential and applicable multiplication technology package. This remarkable order of great antiquity is represented in the present age by a sole survivor *Ginkgo biloba* Linn. (Family Ginkgoaceae) which by many palaeobotanists is regarded as a "living fossil". It is the native of China. It came in to existence during the Permian and achieved worldwide distribution and luxuriance during the Triassic and Jurassic periods of Mesozoic age. It is gradually thinned and fading out of existence and has spread in the modern period due to the interest of human taken in this plant. *Ginkgo* is one of the oldest living tree species. *Ginkgo* is known to have occurred in rocks as old as Triassic or even much earlier. Fossils of its leaves have been identified in the Permian and probably also in the carboniferous. In the words of Professor A.C. Seward from University

[1] Department of Botany, D.S.B. Campus, Kumaun University, Nainital - 263 002 (Uttarakhand) (India)

[2-4] Research Scholar, Department of Botany, D.S.B. Campus, Kumaun University, Nainital - 263 002 (Uttarakhand) (India)

of Cambridge, *Ginkgo biloba* is *"an assemblage of changelessness, a heritage from worlds of an age, too remote for our human intelligence to grasp, a tree whichhas in its keeping the secrets of an immeasurable past"*. The name ginkgo comes from the Chinese words sankyo or yin-kuo, which means a hill apricot or silver fruit, due to their apricot shaped mature fruits and yellow colour (McKenna and others, 2001).

Ginkgo biloba also known as Maiden hair tree, is extremely resistant to pollution and disease, and is often planted as an ornamental tree. Because of its hardiness, Ginkgo trees can live as long as 1,000 years and grow to a height of 120 feet. Ginkgo seeds and leaves have been used in traditional Chinese medicine for over 5,000 years. In modern botanical medicine, extracts are made from the distinctive, fan-shaped leaves. Active Constituents *Ginkgo biloba* extracts utilized in clinical trials are standardized in a multi-step procedure designed to concentrate the desired active principals from the plant. These extracts contain constituents include proanthocyanadins, glucose, rhamnose, organic acids (hydroxykinurenic, kynurenic, protocatechic, vanillic, shikimic), D-glucaric acid and ginkgolic acid, and related alkylphenols. Mechanisms of Action Ginkgo biloba extracts exhibit potent antioxidant activity, and are capable, in vitro, of scavenging various reactive oxygen species, and inhibiting or reducing the functional and morphological impairments observed after lipoperoxide release. Animal and human studies note that Ginkgo extracts reduce clastogenic (chromosome-breaking) activity in the plasma after radiation exposure. It is also possible that a large part of Ginkgo's anti-ischemic effect involves inhibition of free radical formation. One of the components of Ginkgo biloba, ginkgolide B, is a potent platelet-activating factor antagonist. It is also likely that the flavonoid fraction, containing free radical scavengers, is important in this respect. Extracts from the leaves of Ginkgo biloba are reported to be effective at increasing vascular relaxation via a nitric oxide pathway. Ginkgo extracts (specifically the bilobalide component) can suppress hypoxia-induced membrane breakdown in the brain. *Ginkgo* has various uses in traditional medicine and as a food. *Ginkgo* has been used and is still used for a numerous amount of health complaints and diseases. It is found to show antibacterial, antifungal, antioxidant, antitussive, astringent, circulatory stimulant, expectorant, kidney tonic, rejuvenative and sedative. The most powerful effect of *Ginkgo* is on the circulatory system. *Ginkgo* flavnoids directly dilate the smallest segment of the circulating system, the micro capillaries, which increase blood circulation and oxygen levels in the body.

History and Traditional Uses of *Ginkgo biloba*

Englbert Kaempfer, a German surgeon, first used the term "Ginkgo" in 1712, but it was Linnaeus who termed it Ginkgo biloba in 1771 (Gertz and Kiefer, 2004). Both the leaves and the nuts of this tree have been in use for the past several centuries in traditional Chinese medicine. In fact, the nuts are known to have a longer history of usage, being first mentioned in herbals in the Yuan dynasty [1280 to 1368 AD], published in1350 AD (GohandBarlow, 2002). For over 5000 years, the seeds (nuts) have been known to treat pulmonary disorders (like asthma, cough, and enuresis), alcohol abuse, and bladder inflammation while the leaves have been mainly used to treat heart and lung dysfunctions and skin infections (Mahady, 2002; Smith and Luo, 2004). Other uses of this tree include the fruit, prepared by fermentation and cooking, being a delicacy in weddings and feasts (McKenna and others, 2001; Bilia, 2002). The roasted or boiled ginkgo seeds are also considered a gourmet delicacy in Japan, China, Korea, and Malaysia. The tree is also grown in many parts of Europe and the United States mainly for its ornamental value. It grows well in most places due to such properties aspect, pollution, and disease resistance (McKennaand others, 2001).

In central Himalayan Mountains of India, there are very few spots in Uttarakhand (i.e. Ranikhet, Nainital and Dehradun) where the individuals of this species are found growing naturally and require immediate conservation measures. Due to poor regeneration, only few individuals exists in the nature particularly in diverse climatic conditions in different places and facing serious threat of extinction from central Himalayan mountains of India. Ginkgo has a long reproductive cycle and it takes two years to complete it. Due to its high medicinal value the tree has been exploited indiscriminately so facing a high risk of extinction and was listed as a rare species in the 1997 IUCN red list of threatened plants and listed in the red list of endangered plant species. Vegetative propagation via stem cuttings offers true-to type plants and availability of superior individuals in a short period of time for large scale commercial plantation. This method has been tried in many gymnosperms (Nandi *et al.*,1996, 2002; Tamta *et al.*, 2007). There are only few reports on its essential oil composition extract composition and antimicrobial activities (Tewari *et al.*, 2015).Due to high medicinal value and economic importance of *G. biloba*, its cultivation could not only play a major role to uplift the socio-economic status of people of this area, its propagation via stem cuttings would also help in the conservation of this rare and endangered species.

MATERIAL AND METHODS

Site visit was done during 2013to 2015 to assess *Ginkgo biloba* population in Kumaun region.

Phenological Assessment

Basic components of phenological responses include the timing of the ending of a biological event and details of intermediate stages, such as the timing and magnitude of peak of abundance or activity. The task of plant-phenology is to observe and record the periodically recurring growth stages and to study the regularities and dependency of the yearly cycles of development on environmental conditions.

Collection of Plant Material

Branch cuttings (semi-hardwood) were excised in the morning and brought to the laboratory in polythene bags in order to prevent desiccation. The semi hard stem cutting was collected from Snow view (Lat: 29° 23′41.5″N, Long: 79°27;40.5″E, 2203m asl), Glenthorn (Lat: 29°28′49.6″, Long: 79°26′49.8″, 2068m asl) and Botany Department (Lat: 29°21′ to 29°24′ N and Long: 79°25′ to 79°20′ E, 2150 m asl). Cuttings were 19.00±1.52 cm long and 9.00±1.52 mmin diameter with 12.00±1.15 nodes. The stem cuttings were collected in the last week of February 2013.

Explants Treatment

Some growth hormones IBA (Indol-3-butyric acid), NAA (α- naphthalene acetic acid) and IAA (Indole-3-acetic acid) were obtained from Hi-media Laboratory Pvt. Ltd, Mumbai, India were selected for rooting experiment. In the rooting experiments the selected branch were dipped separately in different concentrations 10µM, 50 µM, 100 µM, 200 µM and 500 µM of each of hormones including control the.The cuttings were treated with test compounds by dipping their basal 3.0 cm portions in various test solutions for 0h, 6h, 12h, 24h, and 48h at room temperature (20 ± 1°C). One untreated set of cuttings served as control. Hormones were dissolved in 1.0% NaoH; untreated cuttings were dipped in distilled water. Each treatment consisted of 25 cuttings.

Rooting Conditions

The experiments were carried out inside the playhouse, made up of semitransparent polyethylene sheet (thickness: 162.5 M, UV stabilized), established at Department of Botany, Kumaun University, Nainital. The mean temperature and relative humidity inside the playhouse were 25±2 C during the experiment. Semi hard stem cuttings were planted vertically in sand trays (length18.00±1.52 cm and width 9.00±1.32 cm).The cuttings were watered regularly.

Data Recording

Based on random observations, root initiation in majority of cuttings was first noticed during 7th weeks, and therefore the final data were recorded during 10th week after plantation of cuttings. After data recording, these plantlets were re-transplanted in polythene bags (20 cm height×12 cm diameter) containing sieved oak forest soil and kept inside the polyhouse to monitor the growth and survival of rooted cuttings.

Growth and Survival of Rooted Cuttings

All the rooted cuttings were kept inside the polyhouse from May, 2013 experiment to the end of November, 2013. To record percentage survival of *Ginkgo biloba*, shoot height, diameter of shoot, number of nodes per cutting, number of leaves/node, and numbers of branches per cutting were recorded. To see the effect of hormones treatment we were concentrated on those plantlets which were raised via IBA (Stock solution 5.0 M) NAA (Stock solution 5.0 M) and IAA (Stock solution 5.0 M) treatments and then compared these with the rooted plantlets raised via control. After that the plantlets were shifted from polythene bags to earthen pots (24 cm height×24 cm diameter) containing the same sieved oak forest soil and kept inside the mist chamber (25±2°C mean temperature) until the end of June 2015. Then they were transferred to their natural habitat.

Molecular Characterization

Electrophoresis was performed as described by Maniatis *et al.* (1982). One percent agarose gel was prepared in Tris-Acetate-EDTA (TAE) buffer(1X) at pH 8.0 and stained with 2 µL of ethidium bromide (0.5 µg/mL).Samples obtained from DNA fragmentation were loaded with gel loadingbuffer (2 µL of loading dye is used). Electrophoresis of DNA fragents was done at 50 volts. DNA fragents were visualized in the UV transilluminator and the details were recorded.

Callus Induction

Plantlets of *Ginkgo biloba* were obtained from Nainital, Uttarakhand. All the explants were taken from these donor plants for present investigation. Leaf explants was kept for 2 hours in systemic fungicide Bavistin (VIMCO pesticides, Gujarat) and Tween-80, an antimicrobial agent, prior to surface sterilization. For surface sterilization, chemicals such as $HgCl_2$ (0.1%), NaOCl (1%), H_2O_2 (1%) and ethanol (70%) was used. Juvenile leaves were washed thoroughly in running tap water for 30 minutes and then with distilled water three times. Leaves were treated with bavistin solution for 15 minutes, and then rinsed thoroughly with sterile distilled water. The leaves were subjected to 0.1% $HgCl_2$ for 30 seconds, washed with distilled water and then placed in 70% ethanol for 1 minute and again washed with distilled water, followed by addition of three drops of antibiotic solution (cefotaxime) in laminar airflow cabinet. In the antibiotic solution, all leaves were dissected into small pieces and treamed so that maximum part can be exposed to media. All the chemicals used were purchased from Hi-media.

Culture Media and Grout Condition

The medium comprised of macro and micro elements according to Murashige and Skoog (1962) with mesoino- sotol (100 mg/L), thiamine-HCl (0.5 mg/L), pyridoxine- HCl (1 mg/L), nicotinic acid (0.5 mg/L) and sucrose (30 g/L), solidified with 0.6% agar. The plant growth regulators used were 6-benzyl-aminopurine (BAP), α-naphthalene acetic acid (NAA). All experiments were carried out in culture tubes (150 × 25 mm) containing 30 mL of culture medium. The pH of media was adjusted to 5.8 prior to autoclaving at 121° C at 15 lbs pressure for 20 minutes. Cultures were incubated under 16 hours/8 hours light/dark cycles (artificial light, 80 µM per $2^{m}/s$).

RESULTS AND DISCUSSION

Population of *Ginkgo biloba* L. in Kumaun

*Ginkgo*was recorded at D.S.B. Campus, Nainital, Old Governor House, New Governor House, Chaubatia, Almora, Kalika Forest, Ranikhet, G.B.Pant National Institute of Himalayan Environment and Sustainable Development, Kosi-Katarmal, Almora, HBG, Nainital, Snow-view, High court, Nainital and Glenthorn, Nainital. The plants were recorded with a single individual population (Table 2.1).

Table 2.1: Population of *Ginkgo biloba* L. in Kumaun

Places	Location	Number of Trees
Nainital	D.S.B. Campus	1
	Snow-View	1
	Governor house	1
	High court	1
Almora	S.S.J. Campus	1
Bhimtal	Biotechnology Campus	1
Ranikhet	Kalaka	1

Phenological Study

Phenological observations showed first leaf initiation in *Ginkgo biloba* on 14th march 2014 and after seven months of leaf period first leaf fall starts on 6th October 2014 and deciduas period of three months from December to February was recorded. (Table 2.2, Plate 1)

Table 2.2: Phenological study of *Ginkgo biloba* L.

Biological Events	Timing
First leaf initiation	14 th March 2014
Last leaf initiation	20 th April 2014
Leaf period	21April 2014 -5th Oct 2014
Leaf fall initiation	6th Oct 2014
Total leaf fall	30th December 2014
Deciduas period	31st Dec 2014-13th March 2015

Mass Propagation of Seedling

The effect of treatments on callus and rooting ability of stem cuttings of *Ginkgo biloba* has been observed. The higher concentration of 500µm IBA and IAAresulted maximum rooting 66%, 63% and 64% (Table 2.3).

Table 2.3: Percentage of survival in rooting experiment

Concentration	Experiment	Percentage of Survival in Experiment Time (48 h)
	Control	44%
10μm	IAA	48%
	NAA	52%
	IBA	60%
50 μm	IAA	64%
	NAA	68%
	IBA	72%
100 μm	IAA	72%
	NAA	80%
	IBA	84%
200 μm	IAA	80%
	NAA	84%
	IBA	88%
500 μm	IAA	88%
	NAA	92%
	IBA	96%

The highest concentration (500 μm) of IAA, NAA and IBAresulted in maximum rooting *i.e.*, 66%, 63% and 64% respectively in *Ginkgo biloba* (Figure 2.1). Percentage of survival for 48 hr treatment was also maximum under highest concentration (500 μm) condition. The survival rate was highest in case of IBA (96%) followed by NAA(92%) and IAA(88%) (Table 2.3, Figure 2.1).

Molecular Characterization of *Ginkgo biloba* L.

Evaluation of Genetic Fidelity of Micro Propagated Plants of Ginkgo biloba *L.*

Random amplified polymorphic DNA (RAPD) analysis was performed to check the genetic fidelity of plantlets found in different locations. Around 5 random primers produced satisfactory amplification products in term of quality, quantity and reproducibility of banding pattern out of the 10 decamer RAPD primers used, while the rest of the primers resulted in either no amplification or smeared profiles. Based on this, they were selected to carry out RAPD fingerprinting of the three randomly selected plants. The maximum number of bands (12) were obtained in OPR-12 whereas, minimum numbers of bands (7) were obtained in OPI-18. A total of 46 bands were produced (Table 2.4). The bands obtained using all 5 primers were found to be monomorphic across the and the size of the amplified products separated by electrophoresis in two percent agarose gel ranged from 100 to 3000 bp. The RAPD profile exposed no variation in plants and they were found to be genetically stable. The representative RAPD profile obtained with different primers are shown in Table 2.4.

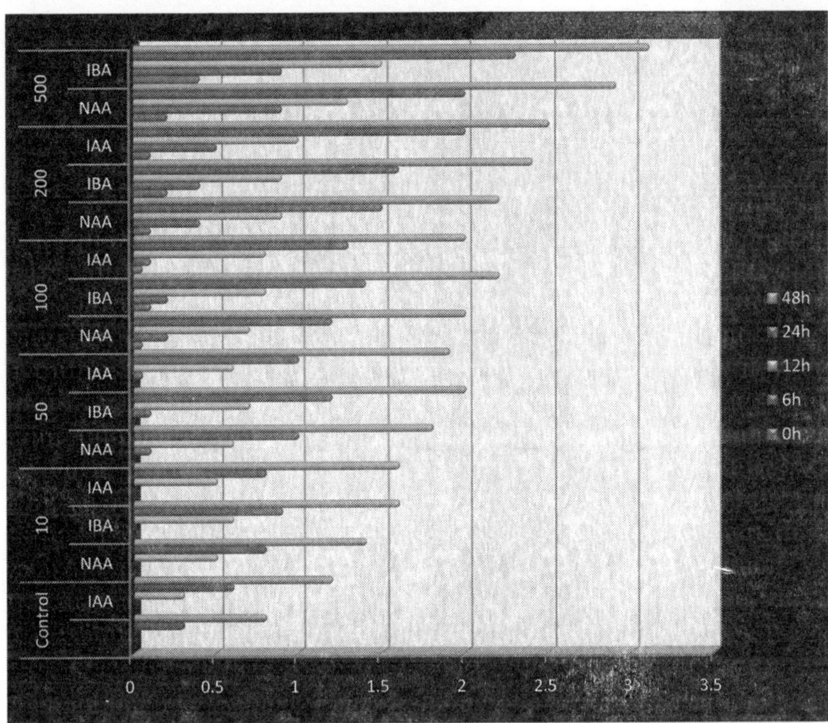

Fig. 2.1: Graphical Representation of Root Length in Different Rooting Hormones

Table 2.4: RAPD profile obtained with different primers of *Ginkgo biloba* L.

Sl. No.	Primer Name	Primer Sequence (5′-3′)	Annealing Temp.	Number of Total Amplicon	Approximate Size Range (bp)
1.	OPH O7	5′-CTGCATGGTG-3′	32°C	8	2500- 250
2.	OPR 12	5′-ACAGGTGCCT-3′	32°C	12	3000-350
3.	OPM 19	5′-CCTTCAGGCA-3′	32°C	10	900-250
4.	OPI 18	5′-AATGCGGGAG-3′	32°C	7	1000-300
5.	OPR 06	5′-GTCTACGGCA-3′	32°C	9	1500-750
	Number of total bands		=	**46**	

100bp DNA Ladder

The 100bp DNA ladder consists of 13 double stranded DNA fragments ranging from 100bp to3000bp in increments; 10 fragments from size 100 to 1000bp with an increment of 100bp and three larger fragments with 1500bp, 2000bp and 3000bp (Figure 1.2). The amounts of 500, 1000, 2000bp fragments are adjusted, so that their increased intensities upon staining serve as easy references after gel electrophoresis. The ladders are supplied pre-mixed with loading buffer (Figure 2.3).

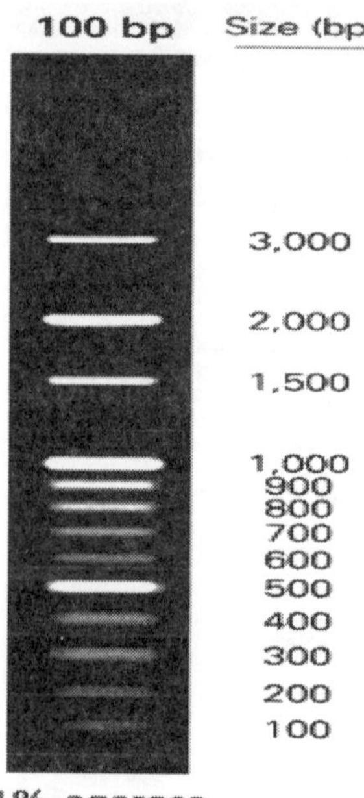

Fig. 2.2: 100bp DNA Ladder

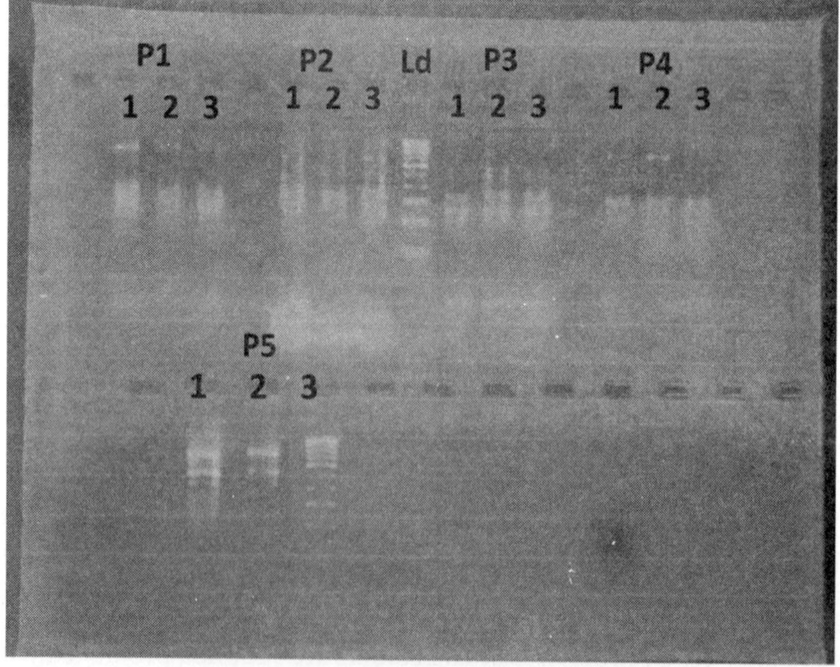

Fig. 2.3: Gel Electrophoresis (P1, P2, P3 and P4 are Primers and Ld Representing DNA Ladder)

Callus Induction

For callus induction juvenile leaf section (3-5 mm in length) with cut end surface in contact with culture medium were placed on MS medium supplemented with various concentrations of PGRs BAP (7.5 mg/L) and NAA (2mg/L). After 20 days of culture, the leaves cultured on MS basal medium supplemented with 3% (w/v) sucrose, BAP (1.0 ppm) and IAA (0.5 ppm) were found to give profuse callusing and when callusing was observed in entire explants, the callus was cut into small pieces transferred to MS media having BAP and IAA in same concentration as for callus induction. Sub culturing was done after every 1-2 weeks. After 3-4 weeks of sub culturing first shooting is observed in callus (Table 2.5 and Plate 4 a, b, c).

Table 2.5: Concentrationof PGR for callus induction of *Ginkgo biloba*

Sl.No.	PGR(mg/L)		Intensity of Callus Induction	Nature of Callus
	NAA	BAP		
1.	2mg/L	7.5mg/L	++	Light green coloured, fragile

Plate 1: Phenological Assessment

Plate 2: Laboratory and Field Experiments

Plate 3: Rooting Experiment

Plate 4: Showing Various Experiments in Laboratory, (a) Explants in Test Tubes, (b) Callus Induction, (c) Explants Placed in Laboratory

REFERENCES

Bilia A.R. 2002. *Ginkgobiloba* L. Fitoterapia 73: 276-9.

D.J. McKenna, K. Jones, K. Hughes, Altern. Ther. Health Med. 2001, 7, 70.

Gertz HJ, Kiefer M. 2004. Review about *Ginkgo biloba* Special Extract EGb 761 (Ginkgo). CurrPharmDes10: 261-4.

GohLM, Barlow PJ. 2002. Antioxidant Capacity in Ginkgobiloba. Food Res Int 35: 815-20.

Jacobs BP, Browner WS, Ginkgo Biloba: A Living Fossil. American Jour. of Medicine 2000; (108) 4: 341-342.

Mahadevan S, Park Y (2008). Multifaceted Therapeutic Benefits of Ginkgo biloba L.: Chemistry, Efficacy, Safety, and Uses. J. Food Sci., 73(1): 9-14.

Mahady GB. 2002. Ginkgo Biloba for the Prevention and Treatment of Cardiovascular Disease: Are View of the Literature. JC ardiovasc Nurs 16: 21-32.

Masood E. Medicinal Plants Threatened by Over Use. Nature 1997; 66: 570.

Murashige T, Skoogs F.A Revised Medium for Rapid Growth and Bio-assays with Tobacco Tissue Cultures. Physiol Plant 1962; 15: 473-9.

Murray F.G. Biloba Therapeutic and Antioxidant Properties of the Tree of Health. A Keats Good Herb Guide 1996, 7, 58.

Nandi SK, Palni LMS, Rikhari HC. Chemical Induction of Adventitious Root Formation in Taxus baccata Cuttings. Plant Growth Regulation 1996; 19: 117-122.

Nandi SK, Tamta S, Palni LMS. Adventitious Root Formation in Young Shoots of Cedrus Deodara. Biologia Plantarum 2002; 45(3): 473-476.

Neinhuis C, Barthlott W. Seasonal Changes of Leaf Surface Contamination in Beech, Oak, and Ginkgo in Relation to Leaf Micromorphology and Wettability. New-phytologist. 1998; 138(1): 91-98.

Sharma GK. Modification in G. biloba L. in Response to Environmental Pollution. J-Tenn-Acad-Sci. Hixon, Tenn.: The academy. 1989; 64(1): 26-28.

Smith JV, Luo Y. 2004. Studies on Molecular Mechanisms of Ginkgo biloba Extract. Appl Microbiol Biotechnol 64: 465-72.

Tamta S, Palni LMS, Nandi SK (2007). Adventitious Root Formation in Shoot Cuttings of Himalayan Cedar (Cedrus deodara Roxb. Ex. Lamb) G. Don under Mist Chamber Conditions. J. Non-Timber For. Pro. 14(3): 231-238.

Tewari, G., Mohan, B., Kishor, K., Tewari, L.M. and Nailwal, T.K. (2015). Volatile Constituents of Ginkgo biloba L. Leaves from Kumaun: A Source of (E)nerolidol and Phytol. Journal of Indian Chemical Society, Vol. 92. pp. 1583-1586.

Tewari, G., Mohan, B., Kishor, K., Tewari, L.M. and Nailwal, T.K. (2015). Comparative Phytochemical Composition and Antimicrobial Potential of Leaf and Twig Extracts of Ginkgo biloba L. from India.G- Journal of Environmental Science and Technolog, 2(6) pp. 97-100.

Pages: 37-44

MICROBIOLOGICAL AND PHARMACOLOGICAL ASPECTS OF BIODIVERSITY

Edited by: Dr. Pankaj Sharma; Dr. Neha Gautam Sharma & Dr. Pankaj Sharma

ISBN: 978-93-5056-878-1

Edition: 2017

Published by: Discovery Publishing House Pvt. Ltd., New Delhi (India)

Study on Nutritional Profiles of Working and Non-working Women and its Impact on their Health

Neha Gautam Sharma*[1]; Himani Mehta[1] and Pankaj Sharma[2]

INTRODUCTION

Health is an energetic and active state of human being. It depends upon genetic endowments, psychosocial atmosphere and surrounding environmental conditions. Nutrition is most important factor influencing the health of human being. Good health cannot be achieved without good food, this statement is true. Women play remarkable roles in the family that affect the health and well being of all family members. Nutrition of women is a critical part of their overall health status. It is related to other things i.e. the nourishment they received before birth, food intake during lifetime, work load, energy output and their roles in food chain. Women are usually vulnerable to malnutrition for both social and biological reasons, throughout their life cycle Ronzio (2004). The modern Indian woman is biased to excessive stress at home and work. Under-resting, overworking and higher level of burden at work brings about greater aggression in quality of life. Working women especially in low socio-economic class are subjected to excessive workload supplemented by insufficient food and incomplete rest and so are exposed to a high health risk (Gupta *et al.* 2005). Non-working women are occupied with their household's works where as the working women are busy with their professional works in their particular field. Both groups of women had different fitness level and health status (Barna and Sil, 2013).

Neglect of women's health is clearly linked with her lower nutrient intake. Hypertension and other deficiency problems further aggravate many

[1] Department of Microbiology, St. Bede's College, Navbahar, Shimla - 171 002 (Himachal Pradesh) (India)

[2] ICAR-National Bureau of Plant Genetic Resources, Regional Station, Phagli, Shimla - 171 004 (Himachal Pradesh) (India)

diseases and reduce her body resistance. Thus, affects women's access to health information. It is unfortunate that her nutritional status and care issues usually have not emerged seriously in planning the nutritional programs and policies. Keeping these points in view, the purpose of this chapter is to judge nutritional status and health of working and non-working women.

NUTRITIONAL STATUS AND FOOD CONSUMPTION AMONG WORKING AND NON-WORKING WOMEN

Nutritional status is defined as the level to which the food eaten is used by the body and its effect on health of an individual. A balanced diet will provide necessary nourishment to the body, which will lead to a good nutritional status and therefore, good health. Nutritional status of women is important for good health and increased work capacity of themselves as well as for the health of their children (Black *et al.* 2008). It has been reported by various authors in their studies that working women do not take balanced diet.

A study was conducted to examine the nutritional status of working and non-working women of Shimla town of northwest Himalaya. The former summer capital of the British in India, and the present capital of Himachal Pradesh, Shimla has been blessed with all the natural bounties which one can think of. It has got a scenic location, it is surrounded by green hills with snow capped peaks. This town is the largest of the state and makes a perfect study site wherein people of all walks of life reside. Being the capital of the state it represents the whole state altogether. Here, a sample of 50 working and 50 non-working women was selected. Random sampling technique was used to select participants. Dietary intake of women of age group 25-60 years was determined by interviewing the subjects regarding their diet for three consecutive days. Balanced diet of working and non-working were analyzed and results reveal that 88% and 90% of working and non-working women are consuming adequate diet, while 12 and 10 per cent working and non-working women do not consume balanced diet respectively (Figure 3.1). The results of the present study also revealed prevalence underweight was more in working women as compared to non-working women. This may be due to work stress or time constrains. The high prevalence of underweight in working women could be due to the pressure of work at work place and as well as at home. On the other hand the non-working women enjoy a more relaxed and tension free life style which resulted in their normal nutritional status. Burden of work and family can interfere with nutritional status and health of women with a great extent and worries about work issues can also be exhibited in the family front. This, in turn, has a detrimental effect on women's health. The multifaceted challenges concerning women's health, which in turn influence and raise other issues like infant mortality, reproductive health, child health, nutritional status, mental health etc. are interwoven with the several psychosocial variables which are of grave relevance to the women's existence in developing countries (Paul *et al.* 2011; D'Souza *et al.* 2013). Diet of women should include all food groups such as cereals, pulses, milk and milk products, vegetables and fruits in recommended amounts.

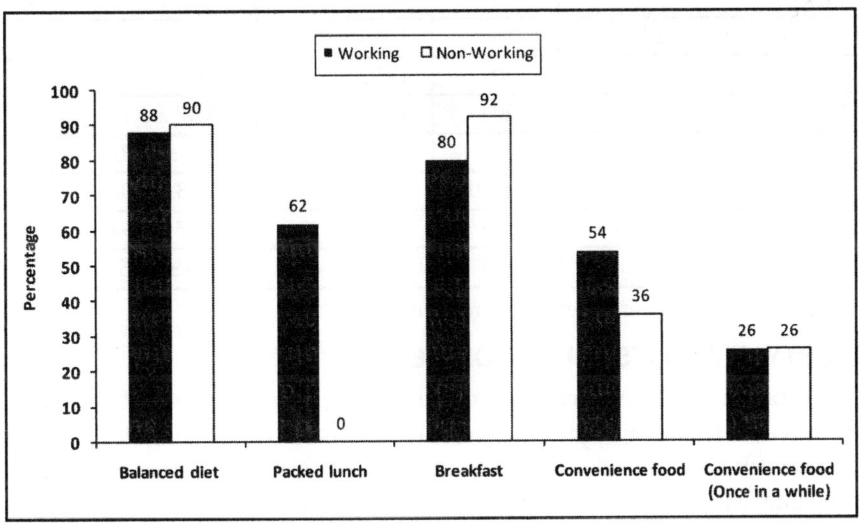

Fig. 3.1: Dietry Information of Working and Non-working Women of Shimla Town

In the present scenario with the increasing number of working women the convenience food consumption concept is becoming fast globally and in the Indian society also. The increasing level of affluence has changed the food consumption habits in society. Women of 21st century love to consume junk food (Mathur *et al.* 2015). Women prefer convenience food/junk food for saving time due to changes in life style. Outcome of consumption of such type of food is that more than half of the working women are suffering from obesity problem.

A comprehensive data of food intake (e.g. Cereals, pulses, green leafy vegetables, milk, fats, oils, sugar, egg, meat and fish etc.) of working and non working women of Shimla was recorded and presented in Table 3.1. To site few examples, the daily food intake of cereals was 170+10.06g and 137.2+10.71g by both the working and non working women. However, the Recommended Dietary Intake (RDI) of all the food products was lower in both the groups of women except of green vegetables and milk/products. For cereals it was significantly lower than RDI (i.e. 240g). Similarly, daily mean consumption of pulses by working and non-working women was 42.9 ± 2.30 g and 49.2 ± 3.06 respectively. The consumption was lower than the RDI (i.e. 60g). Many other studies also revealed similar results (Kaur and Chawla, 2015).

Table 3.1: Daily food intake of working and non-working women

Food Consumed (g/day)	RDA	Working	Non-Working	F-Test
Cereals	240	170 ± 10.06	137.2 ± 10.71	0.979
Pulses	60	42.9 ± 2.30	49.2 ± 3.06	0.568
Green leafy vegetables	100	108.5 ± 5.22	103.3 ± 5.03	1.073
Root and tubers	200	113.1 ± 6.92	90.7 ± 6.59	1.104
Other vegetables	200	103.1 ± 6.64	81.7 ± 5.14	1.701
Milk and milk products	300	400 ± 22.94	336 ± 27.10	0.695
Fats and oils	50-60	11.26 ± 0.81	10.8 ± 1.09	0.555
Sugar and jaggery	20	17.1 ± 1.31	12.7 ± 0.94	1.902
Egg, meat and fish	100	65 ± 27.45	53 ± 23.5	1.269

Values are mean ± standard error. Significant at 1

LIFESTYLE AND ITS IMPACT ON HEALTH

Women have ventured beyond the traditional roles of wife and mother, and have sought employment and career outside the home, and are actively participating in the growth and social development of the nation (Trama and Aggarwal, 2013). In present scenario employment is becoming increasingly significant in the lives of women. With the advancement of employment, more women are bringing marriage, home and career together. These multiple roles played by women in home and at workplace are often a source of stress. Lifestyle is pattern of living that one follow. Bad lifestyle worsens the quality of life. The main part contributing to lifestyle diseases is the sedentary lifestyle and poor food habits. Women found to be afflicted with lifestyle related health problems such as diabetes, depression, obesity, arthritis, angina and hypertension. Women who exert themselves in exercise have reported physically fit and lower level of depression, stress and anxiety and an improved outlook on life (Hanachi *et al.* 2010). Sedentary lifestyle is associated with increased risk of lifestyle disorder (Haskell *et al.* 2007; Lindstrom *et al.* 2006). Working women have increased body fat because of long working hours followed by allocation to household chores child rearing at home with limited chance to work out and get involved in leisure activities (Caruso *et al.* 2007). According to the survey of Associated Chamber of Commerce and Industry (ASSOCHAM), 68% of working women of age group 21-52 were affected by lifestyle ailments such as diabetes, arthritis, obesity, hypertension and depression.

Nonworking women are also susceptible to onset of diabetes and other health ailments because of sedentary lifestyle, lesser outdoor activities and opting lesser traditional methods of doing household chores (Sharma and Kahlon, 2015). Rapid social and traditional changes practices have reformed the food habits of the community. Equilibrium between life and work is essential for women to maintain good health. Lifestyle should be changed and workout plans need to be included in everyday life.

Women's are considered to be the emblems of the society are bestowed upon with duty of caring everyone before themselves. These caring responsibilities that working and non-working have lead to health problems specifically stress and nutritional deficiencies. When compared with one another non-working women were suffering from more health related problems.

Overeating may be another reason for the health related problems (Thilagamani and Mageshwari, 2010). Soomro *et al.* (2012), conducted research in Karachi, Pakistan to analyze the depression of working and non-working women. The research showed that the level of depression was much more in the non-working women. In another study done by Sanlier and Arpaci (2007), a relationship between stress and working status among working and non-working women was observed. Working women in subscales of immune system and susceptibility to stress scale have higher average score than that of non-working women. The results revealed that stress was associated with working status of women. Working women with high psychological job demands and long working hours suffer from depression than those whose psychological job demands less time (Nusrat, 2009).

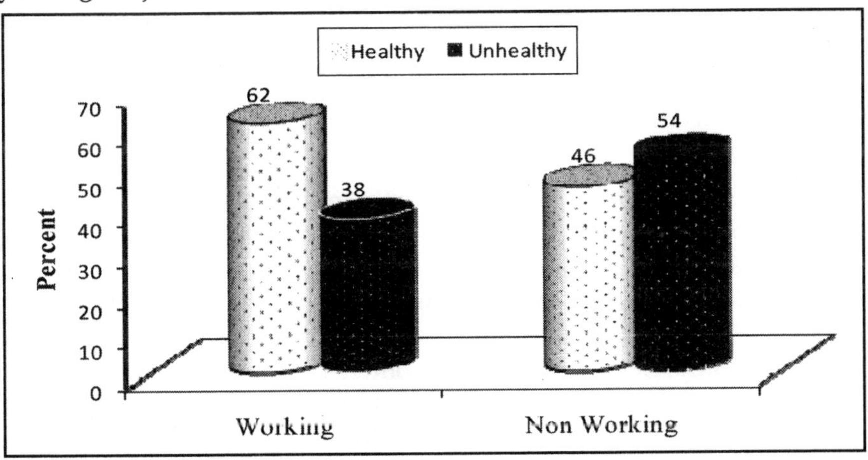

Fig. 3.2: Health Information of Working and Non-working Women (25-60 years)

In one of the study of Shimla town it was observed that working women had better health than non-working women. Out of 50 subjects 38% and 54% working and non-working women were having health problems and rest 62% and 46% working and non-working women were living healthy life as shown in figure 3.2. The disease condition seen in non-working women was higher as compared to working women. 63% working women were suffering from hypertension 15% were suffering from diabetes and 11% from heart disease and rest 11% suffering from gout. Whereas 37% non-working women were suffering from hypertension 29% from diabetes 26% suffering from heart disease and 4% from gout and rest 4 non-working women suffering from cancer figure 3.3.

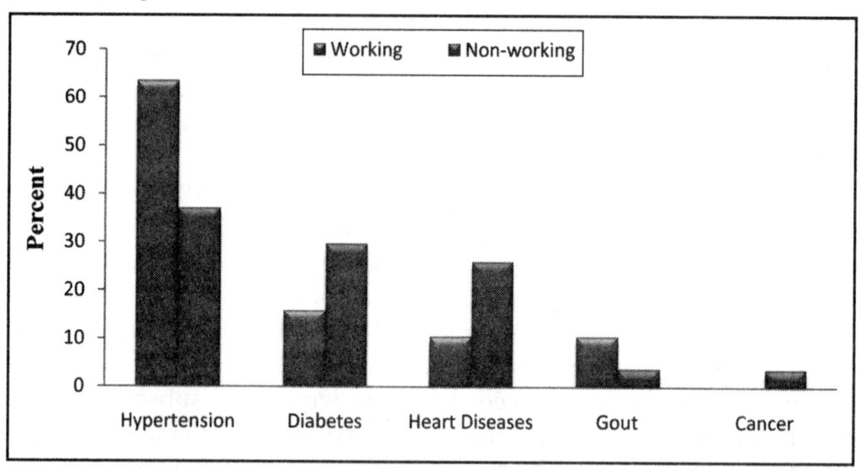

Fig. 3.3: Diseases in Working and Non-working Women (25-60 years)

Rout (2009), investigated nutritional status of rural and urban women in Orissa. Study revealed that 48.6% of rural women and 33% of urban women were falling in low body mass index group. Whereas, in urban women, mean height was slightly more than rural women. In study conducted by Girma and Genebo, (2002) in Ethiopia, non-working women had more possibility of being malnourished than working women doing manual work.

CONCLUSION

Women are usually susceptible to malnutrition for both biological and social reasons throughout their life process. There is a relationship between life stress and inclusion of personality among non-working and working women. It may be concluded that mean daily intake of energy, proteins, iron is low in both the groups and low intake of these nutrients is one of the reason of health related problems in women. If diet of women is not changed and the same pattern continues, it is most likely that women will suffer from many nutrient deficiencies. Nutrition education among working and non-working women can improve their eating habits and health. The concept of 'women as women,' responsible for their own health and nutritional status, needs to be advertised within nutrition programmes. The concept of improving a women's nutrition for their own sakes, rather than just as mothers, needs to be fostered. There is little doubt that a women whose basic nutritional and health needs are met, will be in a better position to meet the needs of her family. Women of this era can have a healthy quality of life only when work-life balance is maintained.

REFERENCES

Barna, S.R., and Sil, P. 2013. A Comparative Study of Health and Nutritional Status Among Housewives and Working Women of North Bengal, International J Behavioral Social and Movement Science, 2(4): 35-40.

Black, R.E., Allen, L.H., Bhutta, Z.A., Laura, E.C., Mercedes de Oris, MajidEzzati, Colin Mathers, Juan Rivera. 2008. Maternal and Child Under Nutrition: Global and Regional Exposures and Health Consequences. *The Lancet*, 371(9608): 243-260.

Caruso, C.C., Hitchcock, E.M., Dick, R.B. 2004. Overtime and Extended Work Shifts: Recent Findings on Illness, Injuries and Health Behaviours. Cincinnati: US Centers for Disease Control. *National Institute for Occupational Safety and Health.*

D'souza, M.S., Karkada, S.N., Somayaji, G. 2013. Factors Associated with the Health Related Quality of Life Among Indian Women in Mining and Agriculture. *Health and Quality of Life Outcomes*, 11(9). DOI: 10.1186/1477-7525-11-9.

Girma, W., Genebo, T. 2002. Determinants of Nutritional Status of Women and Children in Ethiopia. ORC Macro, Calverton, Maryland, USA. pp. 32.

Gupta, S.D., Mitra. S., Chatterjee, P.A. 2005. Comparative Study on Working Housemaids and Control Group. *Indian J. Comm. Med.*, 3(3): 87-88.

Hanachi, P., Ali, P.N., Rezayi, N., Latiff, A.L. 2010. Comparison of Physiological and Psychological well being in Physical Active and Sedentary Women in Iran. *Global Journal Health and Science*, 2(2). DOI: http://dx.doi.org/10.5539/gjhs.v2n2p249.

Haskell, W.L, Lee, I.M., Pate, R.R., Powell, K.E., Blair, S.N., Frankin, B.A., Macera, C.A., Heath, G.W., Thompson, P.D., Bauman, A. 2007. Physical Activity and Public Health: Updated Recommendation for Adults from American College of Sports Medicine and American Heart Association. *Med Sci Sports Exercise*, 39: 1423-1434.

Hossain, M.G., Bharti, P., Aik, S., Lestrel, P.E., Abeer, A., Kamarul, T. 2012. Body Mass Index of Married Bangladeshi Women: Trends and Association with Socio-demographic Factors. *J. Biosoc Sci*, 44(4): 385-399.

Kaur, G., Chawla, P. 2015. Impact of Nutritional Counseling on Nutritional Status of Postmenopausal Women. *Food and Nutrition Sciences*, 6(4): 429-436.

Lindstrom, J., Hanne, P.P., Peltonen, M., Sirkka, A., Johan, G.E., Katri, H., Halena, H., Pirjo, H., Sirkka, K., Mauri, L., Anne, L., Majro, M., Merja, P., Jouko, S., Timo, T.V., Matti, U., Jaako, T. 2006. Sustained Reduction in the Incidence of Type-2 Diabetes by Lifestyle Intervention: Follow up of the Finnish Diabetes Prevention Study. *The Lancet*, 368: 1673-1679.

Mathur, M., Harsh, M., Mathur, S. 2015. Diet Pattern and Nutritional Status of Women Working in Call Canters of India. *International Journal of Food Engineering*. 1(2): 127-133. DOI:10.18178/ijfe.1.2.127-133

Rout, N.R. 2009. Food Consumption Pattern and Nutritional Status of Women in Orissa: A Rural-urban Differential. *J. Human Ecol*, 25(3):179-185.

Nusrat, A. 2009. ASSOCHAM Business Barometer, ASSOCHAM Research Bureau. http//www.assocham.org/arb.

Paul, V.K., Sachdev, H.S., Mavalankar, D., Ramachandran, P., Sankar, M.J., Bhandari, N., Sreenivas, V., Sundaraman, T., Govil, D., Osrin, D., Kirkwood, B. 2011. Reproductive Health, Child Health and Nutrition in India: Meeting the Challenge. *The Lancet*, 377(9762): 332-349.

Ronzio, R. 2004. The Encyclopedia of Nutrition and Good Health. New Delhi: Viva Books Private Ltd.

Sanlier, N., Arpaci, F.A. 2007. Study into the Effects of Stress on Women's Health. *Humanity and Soc. Sci. J.*, 2(2): 104-109.

Sharma, S., Kahlon, N.R. 2015. Health Seeking Behavior of the Diabetic Women in Srinagar. *Indian Journal of Health and Wellbeing*, 6(9): 905-909.

Soomro, R.H., Riaz, F., Naveed, S., Soomro, F.H. 2012. Comparative Analysis of Depression Among Non-working Women in Bilal Colony of Kornagi Area Karachi. *Interdisciplinary Journal Contemporary Research in Business*, 3(11).

Thilagamani, S., Mangeshwari, U. 2010. Risk Appraisal for Cardiovascular Disease Among Selected Young Adult Women in Coimbatore India. *Indian J. Sci. and Technol*, 3(6): 672-675.

Trama, S., Aggarwal, N. 2013. A Study of Perceived Health of Working Women: Role of Fatigue and Psychological Distress. *Indian J. Health and Wellbeing*, 4(6): 1266-1271.

Pages: 45-66

MICROBIOLOGICAL AND PHARMACOLOGICAL ASPECTS OF BIODIVERSITY

Edited by: **Dr. Pankaj Sharma; Dr. Neha Gautam Sharma & Dr. Pankaj Sharma**

ISBN: 978-93-5056-878-1

Edition: **2017**

Published by: **Discovery Publishing House Pvt. Ltd., New Delhi (India)**

Ameliorative Effect of Quercetin on Sodium Azide Induced Alzheimers Disease in Rats

Possible Involvement of PPAR-γ Agonistic Property

Shivani Thakur*[1]; Atul Kabra[1]; Neha Aggarwal[2] and Chinu Kumari[1]

ABSTRACT

This study investigates the protective role of Quercetin in Sodium azide induced Alzheimer's disease and the role of PPAR-γ in Quercetin mediated protection has been explored. Donepezil served as the positive control in the study. Rat administered *i.p.* injection of SAZ. The morris water maze (MWM) test was employed for assessment of learning and memory. Various biochemical estimations, namely brain acetylcholinesterase (AChE) activity, Thiobatbituric acid reactive species (TBARS) activity, nitrite/nitrate activity, reduced glutathione (GSH) levels and myeloperoxidase (MPO) activity were also performed. The study showed that *i.p.* SAZ significantly impaired learning and memory of the animals along with a significant enhancement in brain AChE, MPO, TBARS, nitrite/nitrate levels and reduction in brain GSH levels. Treatments of Quercetin/ Donepezil significantly attenuated SAZ induced behavioral and biochemical changes. Pre-treatment with bisphenol-A-diglycidyl ether (BADGE), a selective PPAR-γ antagnost, significantly abolished the beneficial effect of Quercetin in *i.p.* SAZ treated animals. The results of this investigation document a potential role of PPAR-γ in the beneficial effects of Quercetin in *i.p.* SAZ Alzheimer's disease.

Keywords: Sodium azide, Querecetin, PPAR-gamma, Alzheimer's disease, BADGE, Mitochondrial Dysfunction.

[1] **School of Pharmacy, Abhilashi University, Mandi (Himachal Pradesh) (India)**

[2] **Chandigarh Group of Colleges, Landran, Mohali (Punjab) (India)**

INTRODUCTION

Alzheimer's disease, an age-related neurodegenerative disorder, is characterized clinically by a progressive loss of memory and cognitive functions, resulting in severe dementia (Katzman and Saitoh, 1991; Salmon *et al.*, 2002). The progressive loss of structure or function of neurons, including death of neurons is called as neurodegeneration (Abbas *et al.*, 1999). Mitochondrial defects particularly in Complex I occurs in neurodegenerative diorders. So, for this study Sodium azide is elicted as a chemical for inducing Alzheimer's disease because it is a mitochondrial toxin, which cause selective neuronal destruction and causes mitochondrial defects and inhibits mitochondrial key enzyme i.e cytochrome oxidase (Lalonde *et al.*, 1996). This enzyme is essential for respiratory chain that blocks mitochondrial complex-IV and deplete ATP levels which contributes to metabolic impairment and ROS production (Blass *et al.*, 1990; Davis *et al.*, 1997).

Sodium azide is rapidly acting chemical with a poorly understood mechanism of action (Gosselin *etal.*, 1984). Number of biological effects are common with cyanide and sulfide including an ability to inhibit cytochrome oxidase (Smith *et al.*,1977). When ROS production exceeds the antioxidant capacity ofmitochondria then the outcome of mitochondrial oxidation is the release of mitochondrial cytochrome c into thecytosol. Normally cytochrome c is bound to the inner mitochondrial membrane by an association with a phospholipidcardiolipin (Petrosillo *et al.*, 2003). Cardiolipin is particularly susceptible toperoxidation because of its high degree of unsaturation (Laganiere *et al.*, 1993).Peroxidation of cardiolipin leads to dissociation of cytochrome c and its release through the outermitochondrial membrane (Shidoji *et al.*, 1999). The mechanism by which cytochrome c is released through the outer membrane isnot clear. Some studies showed involvement of mitochondrial permeability transition (MPT) pore (Huang *et al.*, 2000). The MPT pore is a highconductance channel that is believed to be formed by the apposition of the voltage-dependent anion channel on the outer membrane and the inner membrane of Adenine Nucleotide Translocator (ANT) (Crompton *et al.*, 1999). It is also known as the ADP/ATP translocator that exports ATP from the mitochondria matrix and imports ADP into the matrix (Kaukonen *et al.*, 2000). The opening of the MPT pore causes asudden increase in the permeability of the inner mitochondrial membrane. This results in swelling of themitochondrial matrix followed by rupturing of the outer membrane and release of cytochrome C (Kroemer *et al.*, 1998). Cytochrome c released from mitochondria into the cytoplasm binds to Apaf-1 to initiate the formation of anapoptosome, which then binds pro-caspase-9 (Li,P *et al.*, 1997). The oligomerization of caspase-9 on the apoptosome activatesthe protease. The active caspase-9 cleaves 2 "executioner" caspases, caspase-3 and caspase-7, that goeson to cleave key substrates within the cell (Green *et al.*, 1998). This has been termed as intrinsic mitochondrial pathway ofapoptosis. Depending on the availability of intracellular ATP, the cell death pathway may switch from apoptosisto necrosis (Shimizu *et al.*, 1999). Due to disturbance in electron-transport chain electrons can escape from it and reduces oxygen to form reactive oxygen species (ROS) which results in oxidative damage (Sullivan *et al.*, 2005). Due to disturbance in the ROS-antioxidant balance superoxide anion radical does not convert into H_2O_2 by key mitochondrial enzyme, maganese superoxide dismutase (MnSOD) in mitochondria and (CuZn-SOD) in the cytosol that results in protein fragmentation and neuronal damage (Chio *et al.*, 1999). Further the metabolic impairment due to inhibition of cytochrome c oxidase (which results in superoxide anion formation) by sodium azide showed a increase in APPs production (AKA amyloid-beta, amyloid *ß*-protein, and A*ß*) which is one of the prime suspected protein risk factors for Alzheimer's. The presence of beta-amyloid leads to damage of the nerves and arteries of the brain. Beta amyloid can interact with certain RAGE receptors causing damage to the nerves and arteries of the brain and results in AD (Gasparini *et al.*, 1997).

The peroxisome proliferator activated receptor gamma exerts beneficial effects in patients with mild to moderate AD (Kaur *et al.*, 2009; Escribano *et al.*, 2010). PPAR-γ agonists could exert their salutary effects in treating AD by regulating multiple aspects involved in AD such as Aβ homeostasis, insulin sensitivity, energy metabolism, lipid metabolism and inflammation (Landreth *et al.*, 2008).The anti-inflammatory actions of PPAR-γ agonists have been proposed to account for their positive effects in a number of animal models of CNS disease including AD (Desvergne and Wahli 1999). PPAR-γ agonists have been reported to inhibit the expression of inflammatory cytokines, chemokines, Matrix metalloproteinases (MMPs), COX-2 and iNOS each of which is reliant upon NFB- dependent transcriptional effects (Combs *et al.*, 2000).

The purpose of the present study was to investigate the protective role of Quercetin in Sodium azide induced Alzheimer's disease. Moreover, the role of PPAR-γ in Quercetin mediated protection has been explored.

Experimental Animals

Wistar rats of either sex (150-200 g) were used in the present study (procured from Indian Institute of Intergrative medicine, Jammu, India) for behavioral paradigm of Alzheimer's disease and maintained in departmental animal house facility of Chandigarh College of Pharmacy Landran, Punjab in different polypropylene cages. Animals were maintained at standard laboratory pellet chow diet and water *ad libitum*. The mice were exposed to 12 hr light and 12 hr dark cycle. The animals were acclimatized to laboratory conditions prior to the experimental study. The experiment was performed between 09:30-17:30 hr in semi sound proof laboratory conditions. All the experiments were performed in accordance with the guidelines of Institutional Animal Ethical Committee (IAEC). Adequate measures were taken to minimize pain or discomfort with animal experimental procedures. The care of animals were carried out as per the guidelines of Committee for the Purpose of Control and Supervision of Experiments on Animals (CPCSEA), Ministry of environment and forest, Government of India (Reg. No. 1201/9/08 CPCSEA).

Drugs and Reagents

All reagents used in this study were of analytical grade and were freshly prepared. Sodium azide was purchased from Loba chemicals (Mumbai, India). DTNB (5, 5-dithiobis-2-nitrobenzoic acids), Folin-Ciocalteu phenol reagent, Bovine serum albumin, n-butanol, pyridine, reduced glutathione (GSH), Sulphanilamide, Hydrochloric acid, Sodium hydroxide, Sodium chloride, n-napthylethylene diamide dichloride and dipottasium hydrogen phosphate were purchased from Loba chemicals (Mumbai, India). Donepezil and Thiobarbituric acid were purchased from Magus Chemicals. Trichloroacetic acid was purchased from Nice Chem. Pvt.Ltd. (Cochin, India). EDTA was purchased from Thomas baker, India. Quercetin was purchased from Himedia laboratories (Mumbai). Glucose kit was purchased from Reckon diagnostic Pvt. Limited (Vodadara, India). Quercetin was dissolved in 0.05% DMSO solution and given by oral route. BADGE was dissolved in 0.05% DMSO solution and given by *i.p.* route. Sodium azide dissolved in normal saline was given by *i.p.* route.

LABORATORY MODELS

Interceptive Models

Sodium Azide Induced Alzheimer's Disease

In this model sodium azide was given at the dose of 12.5 mg/kg/day, *i.p.* in rats for 5 days followed by 10mg/kg/day *i.p.* for next 9 days (Megyeri *et al.*, 2008) for induction of chronic Alzheimer's Disease.

Exteroceptive Behavioural Models

Morris Water Maze Test

Morris water maze test was employed to access the learning and memory of mice (Morris, 1984; Saraf *et al.*, 2011). Morris water maze is a swimming based model where the animals learn to escape on to a hidden platform. It consists of large circular pool (150 cm in diameter and 45 cm in height, filled to a depth of 30 cm with water at 28 ± 1°C). The water was made opaque by using white non toxic dye or milk. The tank was divided in four quadrants with the help of two threads. The water pool was placed in illuminated light room. A submerged platform (10 cm^2) painted white was fixed at right angle to each other on the rim of the pool placed inside the target quadrant of this pool 1 cm below surface of water. The position of platform was kept unaltered throughout the training session. Each animal was subjected to four consecutive trials with the intertrial gap of 5 min. The mice was gently placed in the water between quadrants facing the wall of the pool with drop location changing for each trial and allowed 120 s to locate the platform. Then, it was allowed to stay on the platform for 20 s. When animal was failed to find the platform within 120 s, the experimenter guided the same to reach onto the platform and allowed to remain there for 20 s. The escape latency time (ELT) to locate the hidden platform inthe water maze on day 4 was noted as an index of acquisition or learning.

TRIALS

Acquisition (Training) Trial

Each mouse was subjected to four trials on consecutive days, during which the starting position was changed with each exposure as shown below while the target quadrant (Q4) was remained constant in all the acquisition trials.

Day 1	Q1	Q2	Q3	Q4
Day 2	Q2	Q3	Q4	Q1
Day 3	Q3	Q4	Q1	Q2
Day 4	Q4	Q1	Q2	Q3

Retrieval Trial

On day 5, the platform was removed and each mouse was allowed to explore the pool for 120 s. Mean time spent in all four quadrants was noted. The mean time spent in the target quadrant searching for the hidden platform was noted as an index of retrieval. The experimenter always stand at the same position. Care was taken to maintain the location of the water with respect to other objects in the laboratory. All the trials were completed between 09.00 and 17.00 hr.

COLLECTION OF SAMPLES

Animals were sacrificed by cervical dislocation, brains were removed and then homogenized in phosphate buffer (pH=7.4). The homogenates were then centrifuged at 3000 rpm for 15 min. The supernatant of homogenates were collected and used for biochemical measures such as acetyl cholinesterase (AChE)activity, brain total protein content, thiobarbituric acid reactive species (TBARS) level, reduced glutathione (GSH) level, nitrate/nitrite concentration, superoxide dismutase (SOD) level as per the methods described below. Blood samples were collected by retro orbital puncture just before sacrificing the animal. The blood was kept at room temperature (37° C) for 30 min after which it was centrifuged at 4000 rpm for 15 min to separate serum. Serum was used to estimate the level of total serum glucose levels.

BIOCHEMICAL PARAMETERS

Estimation of Acetylcholinesterase (AChE) Activity

AChE is a marker of loss of cholinergic neurons in the forebrain. The whole brain AChE activity was measured by method of Ellman *et al.* (1961) with slight modifications (Ellman *et al.*, 1991; Sain *et al.*, 2011). change in absorbance per min of the sample was read spectrophotmetrically at 420 nm (UV-1800 spectrophotometer, Shimadzu, Japan). AChE is calculated by the following formula.

$$R = \frac{\delta \text{ O.D.} \times \text{volume of assay}}{E \times \text{mg of protein}}$$

Where,

R = rate of enzyme activity in 'n' mole of acetylcholine iodide hydrolyzed/minute/mg protein

δ O.D = change in absorbance/min.

E = Extinction coefficient = (13,600/M/cm)

Estimation of Brain Total Protein Content

The brain total protein content was determined by the method of Lowry *et al.* (1931) with slight modifications using bovine serum albumin (BSA) as a standard. The protein content was determined spectrophotometrically at 750 nm.

Estimation of Thiobarbituric Acid Reactive Species (TBARS) Level

The whole brain TBARS level as an index of lipid peroxidation was described by Niehius and Samuelson, (1968). Finally the absorbance was measured at 532 nm (UV-1800 Spectrophotometer, Shimadzu, Japan).

Estimation of Reduced Glutathione (GSH) Level

The whole brain GSH level was estimated by method of Beutler *et al.* (1963). The absorbance was measured spectrophotometrically at 412 nm.

Estimation of Brain Nitrite/Nitrate Concentration Level

The accumulation of nitrite in the supernatant, was measured as an indicator of the production of nitric oxide, determined by the method of Green *et al.* (1982) using a colorimetric assay with the Griess reagent (0.1% N-(1-naphthyl) ethylenediamine dihydrochloride, 1% sulfanilamide and hydrochloric acid). The absorbance was measured at 540 nm using a (UV-1800 spectrophotometer, schimadzu).

Estimation of Brain Myeloperoxidase (MPO) Activity

The measurement of myeloperoxidase (MPO) activity was carried out as a marker of brain neutrophil infiltration i.e. inflammation (Green *et al.*, 2004) using a 0.5% hexadecyl trimethyl ammonium bromide (HETAB) in 10 mM EDTA, pH 6 at 25° and subjected to freeze with sonification between the cycles. The samples was centrifuged at 15000 rpm for 20 minutes at 4. 1ml of supernatant taken and 2.9 ml of 50 nM phosphate containing 0.167 ml/ml o-dianisidine dihydrochloride and 0.0005% hydrogen peroxide will be added. The absorption was read at 460 nm (UV-1800 Spectrophotometer, Shimadzu, Japan) and the MPO activity was normalized on the basis of grams of tissue wet weight.

$$\text{MPO Activity (U/G)} = \frac{X}{\text{Weight of piece of tissue}}$$

$$\text{Where, } X = \frac{10 \times \text{Change in absorbance per minute}}{\text{Volume of supernatent take in final reaction}}$$

Estimation of Serum Glucose Level

The total serum glucose level was estimated by glucose oxidase/ peroxidise method (Miksch and Wiedemann, 1973) using commercially available diagnostic kit.

HISTOPATHOLOGICAL STUDIES

H & E Staining

Haematoxylin and Eosin (H & E) staining was carried out as an marker of neutrophil infiltration. The method was described by (Banchroft *et al.*, 1996). Neutrophil infiltration pattern in brain was studied histologically as a marker of inflammation.

Experimental Protocol

Eleven groups of Wistar rats were employed in the study. Each group comprised of minimum 6 rats.

GROUP I (Normal Control, n=6): Normal untreated were exposed to acquisition trials conducted from Day 1 to Day 4 and retrieval trial conducted on Day 5 using Morris water maze (MWM) test.

GROUP II [Normal Saline control (0.9 %), n=6]: Rats were administered with normal saline (10 ml/kg, *i.p.*) for 14 days followed by exposure to Morris water maze (MWM) test. Animals were also administered with normal saline (10 ml/kg *i.p.*) 30 min before acquisition trials conducted from day 1 to day 4 and 30 min before retrieval trial conducted on day 5 using Morris water maze (MWM) test.

GROUP III [DMSO control (0.05%), n=6]: Animals were administered with DMSO [(0.05%) 10ml/kg: *i.p.*] for 14 days and then subjected to the Morris water maze (MWM) test. The DMSO was administered from day 1 to day 4 i.e. during acquisition trials and 30 min before retrieval trail conducted on day 5.

GROUP IV [Quercetin *per se* (50 mg/kg), n=6]: Animals were administered with (50mg/kg/day; *p.o.*) for 14 days and then subjected to the Moris water maze (MWM) test. The drug was also administered from day 1 to day 4 i.e. during acquisition trails. 0.9% normal saline (10 ml/kg, *i.p.*) was given 30 min before exposure to Morris water maze (MWM) on retrieval trial i.e. conducted on day 5.

GROUP V [Donepezil *per se* (0.1 mg/kg), n=6]: Animals were administered with Donepezil (0.1 mg/kg/day, *i.p.)* for 14 days and then subjected to Morris water maze (MWM) test. Animals were also administered with donepezil treatment from day 1 to day 4 during acquisition trails. 0.9% normal saline (10 ml/kg, *i.p.*) was given 30 min before exposure to Morris water maze (MWM) on retrieval trial i.e. conducted on day 5.

GROUP VI [BADGE *per se* (30 mg/kg), n=6]: Rats were administered with BADGE (30 mg/kg/day; *i.p.*) for 14 days and then subjected to the Morris water maze (MWM) test. Rats were also administered with BADGE treatment from day 1 to day 4 i.e. during acquisition trails. DMSO [(0.05%), 10 ml/kg, *i.p.*] was administered to the animals 30 min before the retrieval trial conducted on day 5.

GROUP VII (Sodium azide control, n = 6): Rats were administered with Sodium azide (12.5mg/kg/day; *i.p.* for 5 days and 10mg/kg/day; *i.p.* for next 9 days) for 14 days followed by exposure to Morris water maze (MWM) test. The sodium azide was given during acquisition trails conducted from day 1 to day 4. 0.9% normal saline (10 ml/kg, *i.p.*) was given 30 min before the retrieval trail conducted on day 5.

GROUP VIII [Sodium azide + Quercetin low dose (25 mg/kg), n= 6]: Sodium azide treated animals were co-administered with Quercetin (25mg/kg; *p.o.*) for 14 days 30 min before exposure to Morris water maze (MWM) test. The treatment was continued during acquisition trails i.e. day 1 to day 4 (day 15-day 19). On day 5 i.e. on retrieval trial DMSO [0.05%), 10 ml/kg, *p.o.*] was administered to the animals 30 min before exposure to the Morris water maze (MWM) test.

GROUP IX [Sodium azide + Quercetin high dose (50 mg/kg), n= 6]: Sodium azide treated animals were co-administered with Quercetin (50mg/kg; *p.o.*) for 14 days 30 min before exposure to Morris water maze (MWM) test. The treatment was continued during acquisition trails i.e. day 1 to day 4 (day 15-day 19). On day 5 i.e. on retrieval trial DMSO [0.05%), 10 ml/kg, *p.o.*] was administered to the animals 30 min before exposure to Morris water maze (MWM) test.

GROUP X [Sodium azide + Donepezil (0.1 mg/kg), n = 6]: Sodium azide treated rats were co-administered with donepezil (0.1 mg/kg/day, *i.p.*) for 14 days 30 min before exposure to Morris water maze test. Donepezil was also co- administered with sodium azide during acquisition trials conducted from day 1 to day 4 (day 15-day19). On day 5 i.e. on retrieval trial normal saline [10 ml/kg, *i.p.*] was administered to the animals 30 min before exposure to Morris water maze (MWM) test.

GROUP XI [Sodium azide + Quercetin (50 mg/kg) + BADGE (30 mg/kg), n=6): BADGE (30 mg/kg, *i.p.*) was administered to the animals 30 min before the administration of Quercetin (50 mg/kg, *p.o.*) for 14 days. After that Quercetin was administered to sodium azide treated rats followed by exposure to the Morris water maze (MWM) test. The treatment was continued during the acquisition trials i.e. conducted on day 1 to day 4 (day 15 – day 19). Vehicles were administered to animals 30 min before exposure to Morris water maze (MWM) test on retrieval trial conducted on day 5.

Statistical Analysis

The results were expressed as mean ± Standard error of means (S.E.M). The data obtained from various groups were statistically analyzed using one-way ANOVA followed by Tukey's Multiple Range test $p< 0.05$ was considered to be statistically significant.

RESULTS

Administration of Sodium azide (12.5 mg/kg/day) for 7 days and various pharmacological interventions did not show any significant effect on body weight. Further no mortality was observed.

Effect of Sodium Azide on Serum Glucose Level

Animals treated with sodium azide [(12.5mg/kg/day; *i.p.*) for 5 days followed by (10mg/kg/day; *i.p.*) for next 9 days] showed a significant increase in serum glucose levels when compared to serum glucose levels of control animals (Table 4.1).

Table 4.1: Effect of Quercetin on Serum glucose levels of Sodium azide treated Rats

Groups	Dose (mg/kg)	Serum Glucose Levels (mg/dl)
Normal control	–	80.65 ± 0.3
Normal Saline	0.9% NaCl, 10ml/kg; *i.p.*	80.88 ± 0.7
DMSO	0.05%, 10ml/kg; *p.o.*	80.79 ± 0.5
QA *per se*	50mg/kg; *p.o.*	81.79 ± 0.4
Don *per se*	0.1mg/kg; *i.p.*	82.23 ± 1.6
BADGE *per se*	30mg/kg; *i.p.*	79.16 ± 1.7
SAZ control	12.5mg/kg(9days), 10mg/kg (5days)	170.85 ± 2.2[a]
SAZ+ QA (LD)	SAZ + 25mg/kg	117.93 ± 0.6[b]
SAZ + QA (HD)	SAZ + 50 mg/kg	89.49 ± 0.7[b]
SAZ+ Don	SAZ + 0.1mg/kg	168.86 ± 0.8
SAZ+QA(HD)+BADGE	SAZ +50 mg/kg+ 30mg/kg	101.21 ± 0.2[c]

DMSO = Dimethyl sulphoxide, Don = Donepezil (0.1mg/kg; *i.p.*), SAZ = Sodium azide (12.5mg/kg; *i.p.*), Quercetin (LD) = Quercetin low dose (25mg/kg; *p.o.*), Quercetin (HD) = Quercetin high dose (50mg/kg; *p.o.*), BADGE= Bisphenol A diglycidyl ether (30mg/kg; *i.p.*) Values are expressed as mean ± Standard error of mean (S.E.M), n= 6, one way ANOVA followed by Tukey's multiple range test. Values are expressed as mean ± Standard error of mean (S.E.M), n= 6, one way ANOVA followed by Tukey's multiple range test.

[a] denotes $p<0.0.5$ versus Serum glucose levels in control group.

[b] denotes $p<0.05$ versus Serum glucose levels in Sodium azide treated group.

[c] denotes $p<0.05$ versus Serum glucose levels in SAZ+QA(HD) group.

Effect of Quercetin/Donepezil/BADGE on Serum Glucose Level of Sodium Azide Treated Animals

Administration of Quercetin (25mg/kg and 50mg/kg; *p.o.*) for 14 days to sodium azide treated animals showed a significant decline in serum glucose levels when compared to serum glucose levels of sodium azide treated animals (Table 4.1). Pretreatment with BADGE (30 mg/kg; *i.p.*) for 14 days abolished the protective effect of Quercetin (50mg/kg; *p.o.*) on sodium azide treated animals indicating by significant rise in serum glucose levels (Table 4.1). However, treatment with donepezil (0.1 mg/kg; *i.p.*) for 14 days did not show any effect on serum glucose levels when compared to serum glucose levels of sodium azide treated rats (Table 4.1). Neither *per se* nor vehicles (Normal saline, DMSO) groups did not show any effect on Serum glucose levels.

Effect of Vehicles on Escape Latency Time (ELT) and Mean Time Spent in Target Quardrant (TSTQ), using Morris Water Maze (MWM)

Control rats showed a significant drop in day 4 ELT when compared to day 1 ELT, reflecting normal learning (Table 4.2). However, on day 5 a significant rise in TSTQ was observed, reflecting normal memory (Figure 4.2). Administration of vehicles (Normal Saline, DMSO) did not show any significant effect on day 4 ELT (Table 4.2) and day 5 TSTQ (Figure 4.1) when compared to control group animals.

Table 4.2: Effect of Quercetin on Day 4 escape latency time (ELT) of Sodium azide treated rats using morris water maze

Groups	Dose (mg/kg)	Day 1 ELT (sec)	Day 4 ELT (sec)
Normal control	–	114.83 ± 1.4	61.5 ± 8.4[a]
Normal Saline	0.9% NaCl, 10ml/kg; *i.p.*	113.33 ± 1.3	60.83 ± 6.3[a]
DMSO	0.05%, 10ml/kg; *p.o.*	115.21 ± 1.4	62.33 ± 5.3[a]
QA *per se*	50mg/kg; *p.o.*	116.66 ± 2.1	61.16 ± 4.3[a]
Don *per se*	0.1mg/kg; *i.p.*	113.13 ± 3.6	63.16 ± 1.7[a]
BADGE *per se*	30mg/kg; *i.p.*	112.83 ± 3.3	61.23 ± 1.9[a]
SAZ	12.5mg/kg (9 days), 10mg/kg (5 days)	112.83 ± 5.3	92.45 ± 4.6[a,b]
SAZ+ QA(LD)	SAZ+ 25mg/kg.	109.66 ± 9.3	75.15 ± 1.0[a,c]
SAZ+ QA(HD)	SAZ + 50mg/kg	110.66 ± 3.2	66.16 ± 3.2[a,c]
SAZ+DON	SAZ + 0.1mg/kg	114.56 ± 3.5	63.83 ± 0.9[a,c]
SAZ+QA(HD)+BADGE	SAZ +30mg/kg+ 50mg/kg	109.22 ± 2.4	71.83 ± 1.9[a,d]

***Abbreviations*:** DMSO=Dimethyl sulphoxide, Don = Donepezil (0.1mg/kg; *i.p.*), SAZ = Sodium azide (12.5mg/kg; *i.p.*), Quercetin (LD) = Quercetin low dose (25mg/kg; *p.o.*),Quercetin (HD) = Quercetin high dose (50mg/kg; *p.o.*), BADGE= Bisphenol A diglycidyl ether (30mg/kg; *i.p.*).
Values are expressed as mean ± Standard error of mean (S.E.M), n=6, one way ANOVA followed by Tukey's multiple range test.

[a] denotes $p<0.05$ versus Day1 ELT in control group.

[b] denotes $p<0.05$ versus Day 4 ELT in control group.

[c] denotes $p<0.05$ versus Day 4 ELT in Sodium azide treated group.

[d] denotes $p<0.05$ versus Day 4 ELT in SAZ + QA (HD) treated group.

Effect of Sodium Azide on Learning and Memory using Morris Water Maze (MWM) Test

Animals treated with sodium azide [(12.5mg/kg/day; *i.p.*) for 5 days followed by (10mg/kg/day; *i.p.*) for 9 days] showed a significant increase in day 4 escape latency time (ELT) in comparison to the control group animals and decrease in day 5 time spent in target quadrant (TSTQ) indicating impairment of learning and memory respectively (Table 4.2, Figure 4.1).

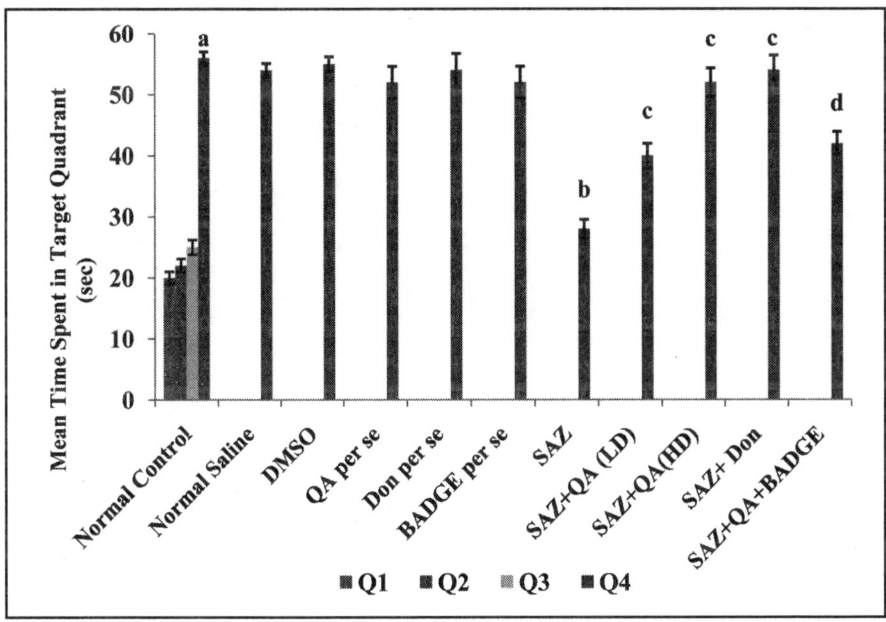

Fig. 4.1: Effect of Quercetin on Mean Time Spent in Target Quadrant (TSTQ) of Sodium Azide Treated Rats, using Morris Water Maze

Abbreviations: DMSO = Dimethyl sulphoxide, Don = Donepezil (0.1mg/kg; *i.p.*), SAZ = Sodium azide (12.5mg/kg; *i.p.*), Quercetin (LD) = Quercetin low dose (25mg/kg; *p.o.*), Quercetin (HD)= Quercetin high dose (50mg/kg; *p.o.*), BADGE= Bisphenol A diglycidyl ether (30mg/kg; *i.p.*)

Values are expressed as mean ± Standard error of mean (S.E.M), n=6, one way ANOVA followed by Tukey's multiple range test.

[a] denotes $p<0.05$ versus time spent in other quadrant in control group.

[b] denotes $p<0.05$ versus time spent in target quadrant in control group

[c] denotes $p<0.05$ versus time spent in target quadrant in Sodium azide treated group

[d] denotes $p<0.05$ versus time spent in target quadrant in SAZ+QA(HD) treated group

Effect of Quercetin/Donepezil/ BADGE on Sodium Azide Induced Impairment of Learning and Memory using Morris Water Maze Test (MWM) Test

Administration of Quercetin (25mg/kg and 50mg/kg; *p.o.*)/ Donepezil (0.1mg/kg; *i.p*) for 14 days to sodium azide [(12.5mg/kg/day; *i.p.*) for 5 days followed by (10mg/kg/day; *i.p.*) for 9 days] treated rats showed a significant fall in day 4 ELT when compared to sodium azide treated rats (Table 4.2). Further, a significant rise in the day 5 TSTQ was observed indicating reversal of learning and memory respectively (Figure 4.1). Pretreatment of BADGE (30 mg/kg; *i.p.*) for 14 days abolished the protective effect of Quercetin (50mg/kg; *p.o.*) on sodium azide treated animals as reflected by significant rise in day 4 ELT (Table 4.2) and decrease in day 5 TSTQ (Figure 4.1). However, administration of Quercetin/donepezil/ BADGE *per se* did not exhibit any significant effect on day 4 ELT and day 5 TSTQ indicating normal acquisition and retrieval (Table 4.2 and Figure 4.1).

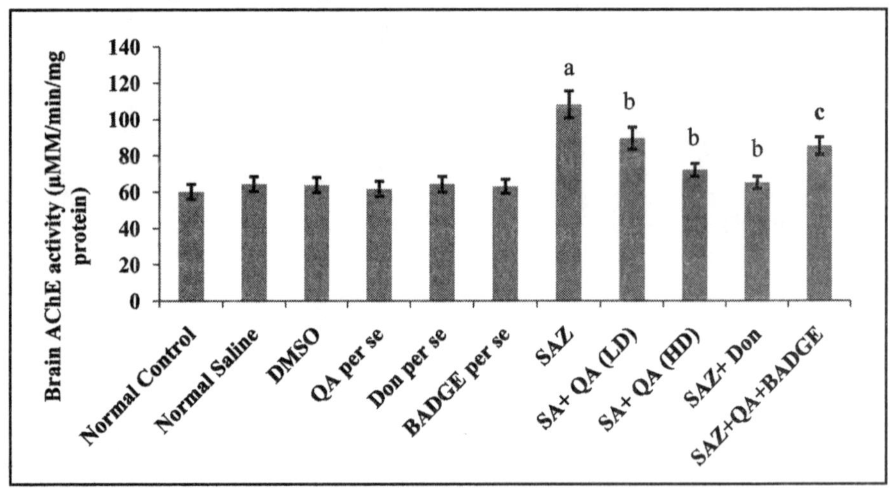

Fig. 4.2: Effect of Quercetin on Brain Acetyl Cholinesterase Level of Sodium Azide Treated Rats

Abbreviations: DMSO = Dimethyl sulphoxide, Don = Donepezil (0.1mg/kg; *i.p.*), SAZ = Sodium azide (12.5mg/kg; *i.p.*), Quercetin (LD) = Quercetin low dose (25mg/kg; *p.o.*), Quercetin (HD)= Quercetin high dose (50mg/kg; *p.o.*), BADGE= Bisphenol A diglycidyl ether (30mg/kg; *i.p.*)

Values are expressed as mean ± Standard error of mean (S.E.M), n= 6, one way ANOVA followed by Tukey's multiple range test.

[a] denotes $p<0.05$ versus brain AChE activity of control group.

[b] denotes $p<0.05$ versus brain AChE activity of Sodium azide treated group.

[c] denotes $p<0.05$ versus brain AChE activity of SAZ+QA(HD) treated group.

Effect of Quercetin/Donepezil/BADGE on Sodium Azide Induced Changes in Brain Acetylcholinesterase (AchE) Activity

Sodium azide treated animals [(12.5mg/kg/day; *i.p.*) for 5 days followed by (10mg/kg/day; *i.p.*) for next 9 days] showed a significant increase in brain acetyl cholinesterase activity when compared to control group animals (Figure 4.2). Administration of Quercetin (25mg/kg and 50mg/kg; *p.o.*)/Donepezil (0.1 mg/ kg *i.p.*) for 14 days to sodium azide treated rats showed a significant decline in brain acetyl cholinesterase activity when compared to sodium azide treated rats (Figure 4.2). Pretreatment with BADGE (30 mg/kg; *i.p.*) for 14 days abolished the protective effect of Quercetin (50mg/kg; *p.o.*) on sodium azide treated animals reflected by significant rise in AChE activity (Figure 4.2). However, administration of these drugs did not show any *per se* effect on brain AChE activity (Figure 4.2). Vehicles such as Normal saline, DMSO did not exhibit any significant changes in brain acetyl cholinesterase activity when compared with control group rats (Figure 4.2).

Effect of Quercetin/Donepezil/ BADGE on Sodium Azide Induced Changes in Brain Thiobarbituric Acid Reactive Species (TBARS) Level

Sodium azide [(12.5mg/kg/day; *i.p.*) for 5 days followed by (10mg/kg/day; *i.p.*) for next 9 days] treated rats showed a significant rise in brain thiobarbituric acid reactive species (TBARS) level when compared with control group animals (Figure 4.3). Administration of Quercetin (25mg/kg and 50mg/kg; *p.o.*)/ Donepezil (0.1 mg/kg; *i.p.*) for 14 days to sodium azide [(12.5mg/kg/day; *i.p.*) 5 days followed by (10mg/kg/day; *i.p.*) for 9 days] treated rats showed a significant reduction in brain thiobarbituric acid reactive species (TBARS) level in comparison with sodium azide treated animals (Figure 4.3). Moreover, pretreatment with BADGE (30 mg/kg; *i.p.*) for 14 days attenuated the beneficial effect of Quercetin (50mg/kg; *p.o.*) on sodium azide treated animals indicating by significant increase in TBARS levels (Figure 4.3). Neither the *per se* nor the vehicle (Normal saline and DMSO) treated groups did not show any significant change in brain TBARS levels when compared to control group animals (Figure 4.3).

Effect of Quercetin/Donepezil/BADGE on Sodium Azide Induced Changes in Brain Reduced Glutathione (GSH) Level

Adminstration of vehicles (Normal saline and DMSO) treated groups did not show any significant change in brain GSH levels when compared to control group (Figure 4.4). Sodium azide [(12.5mg/kg/day; *i.p.*) for 5 days followed by (10mg/kg/day; *i.p.*) for next 9 days] treated rats showed a significant decline in brain reduced glutathione (GSH) level in comparsion with control group animals (Figure 4.4). Administration of Quercetin (25mg/kg and 50mg/kg; *p.o.*)/Donepezil (0.1mg/kg;*i.p.*) for 14 days to sodium azide treated rats showed a significant increase in brain GSH levels in comparison with sodium azide treated animals (Figure 4.4). Moreover, pretreatment with BADGE (30 mg/kg; *i.p.*) for 14 days attenuated the beneficial effect of Quercetin (50mg/kg; *p.o.*)on sodium azide treated animals indicating by significant decrease in GSH levels (Figure 4.4). However, administration of these drugs did not show any *per se* effect (Figure 4.4).

Effect of Quercetin/Donepezil/BADGE on Sodium Azide Induced Changes in Brain Nitrite/Nitrate Levels

Sodium azide [(12.5mg/kg/day; *i.p.*) for 5 days followed by (10mg/kg/day; *i.p.*) for next 9 days] treated rats showed a significant rise in the brain nitrite/nitrate level when compared with control group animals (Figure 4.5). Administration of Quercetin (25mg/kg and 50mg/kg; *p.o.*)/Donepezil

(0.1mg/kg, *i.p.*) for 14 days to sodium azide treated rats showed a significant decrease in brain nitrite/Nitrate level in comparsion with sodium azide treated group (Figure 4.5). However, pretreatment with BADGE (30 mg/kg; *i.p.*) for 14 days abolished the protective effect of Quercetin (50mg/kg; *p.o.*)on sodium azide treated animals indicating by significant increase in nitrite/nitrate levels (Figure 4.5). Administration of vehicles (Normal Saline and DMSO) did not show any significant effect when compared to control group animals (Figure 4.5). However, administration of these drugs did not show any *per se* effect (Figure 4.5).

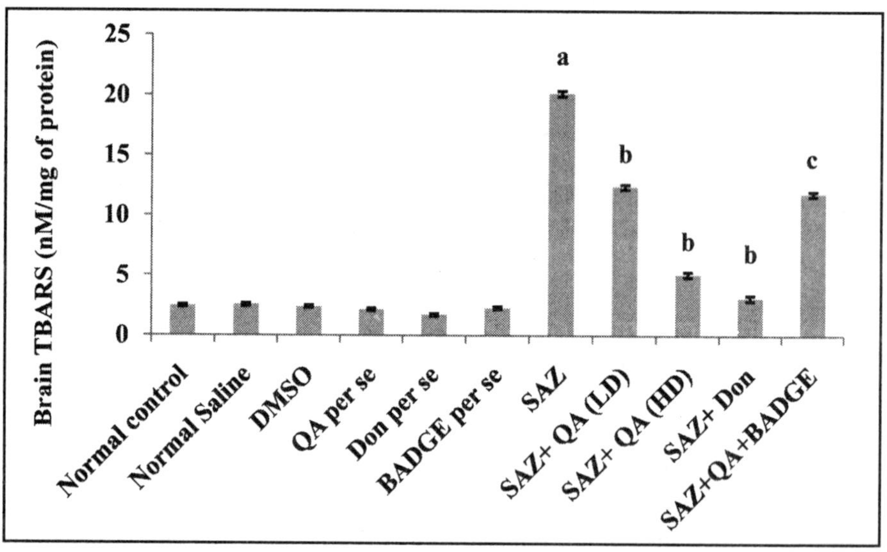

Fig. 4.3: Effect of Quercetin on Brain Thiobarbituric Acid Reactive Species (TBARS) Level of Sodium Azide Treated Rats

Abbreviations: DMSO = Dimethyl sulphoxide, Don = Donepezil (0.1mg/kg; *i.p.*), SAZ = Sodium azide (12.5mg/kg; *i.p*), Quercetin (LD) = Quercetin low dose (25mg/kg; *p.o.*), Quercetin (HD)= Quercetin high dose (50mg/kg; *p.o.*), BADGE= Bisphenol A diglycidyl ether (30mg/kg; *i.p.*)

Values are expressed as mean ± Standard error of mean (S.E.M), n= 6, one way ANOVA followed by Tukey's multiple range test.

[a] denotes $p<0.05$ versus brain TBARS level of control group.

[b] denotes $p<0.05$ versus brain TBARS level of Sodium azide treated group.

[c] denotes $p<0.05$ versus brain TBARS levels of SAZ+ QA(HD) treated group.

Effect of Quercetin/Donepezil/BADGE on Sodium Azide Induced Changes in Brain MPO Activity

Sodium azide [(12.5mg/kg/day; *i.p.*) for 5 days followed by (10mg/kg/day; *i.p.*) for next 9 days] treated rats showed a significant increase in the brain MPO level when compared with the control group animals (Figure 4.6). Moreover, a significant decrease in MPO activity on administration of Quercetin (25mg/kg and 50mg/kg; *p.o.*)/Donepezil (0.1mg/kg, *i.p.*) for 14 days was observed when compared with Sodium azide treated rats (Figure 4.6). Pretreatment with BADGE abolished the protective effect of Quercetin (50mg/kg; *p.o.*) on Sodium azide treated rats (Figure 4.6). However the administration of these drugs did not show any *per se* effect. Administration of vehicles (Normal Saline and DMSO) did not show any significant effect when compared to control group animals (Figure 4.6).

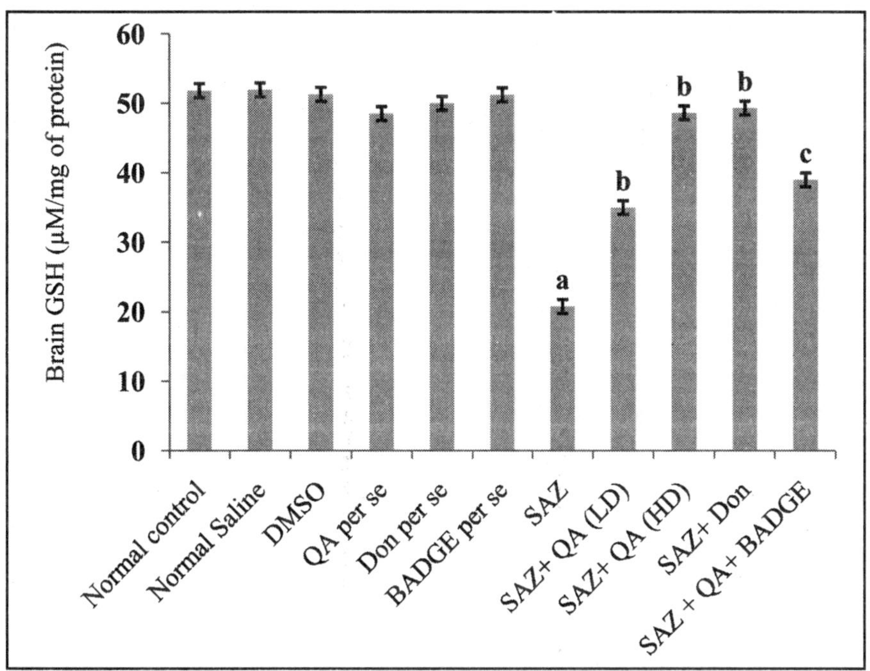

Fig. 4.4: Effect of Quercetin on Reduced Glutathione (GSH) Level of Sodiumazide Treated Rats

***Abbreviations*:** DMSO = Dimethyl sulphoxide, Don = Donepezil (0.1mg/kg; *i.p.*), SAZ = Sodium azide (12.5mg/kg; *i.p.*), Quercetin (LD) = Quercetin low dose (25mg/kg; *p.o.*), Quercetin (HD)= Quercetin high dose (50mg/kg; *p.o.*), BADGE= Bisphenol A diglycidyl ether (30mg/kg; *i.p.*)

Values are expressed as mean ± Standard error of mean (S.E.M), n= 6, one way ANOVA followed by Tukey's multiple range test.

[a] denotes $p<0.05$ versus brain GSH level of control group.

[b] denotes $p<0.05$ versus brain GSH level of Sodium azide treated group.

[c] denotes $p<0.05$ versus brain GSH level of SAZ+ QA(HD) treated group.

HISTOPATHOLOGICAL STUDIES

Effect of Quercetin/Donepezil/BADGE on Sodium Azide Induced Histopathological Changes in Rat Brain (Coronal Section)

Blue Color Indicates Neutrophil Infiltration as a Marker of Inflammation

Control group animals brain did not show any neutrophillic infiltration [Figure 4.7(A)]. Sodium azide [(12.5mg/kg/day; *i.p.*) for 5 days followed by

(10mg/kg/day; *i.p.*) for next 9 days] treated animals brain showed a significant neutrophil infiltration when compared to control group [Figure 4.7 (B)]. However administration of Quercetin (50mg/kg; *p.o.*)/Donepezil (0.1mg/kg, *i.p.*) for 14 days to sodium azide treated animals showed a significant reduction in neutrophillic infiltration [Figure 4.7 (C, D)]. Pretreatment with BADGE abolished the protective effect of Quercetin (50mg/kg; *p.o.*) on sodium azide treated rats indicating by a neutrophillic infiltration [Figure 4.7(E)].

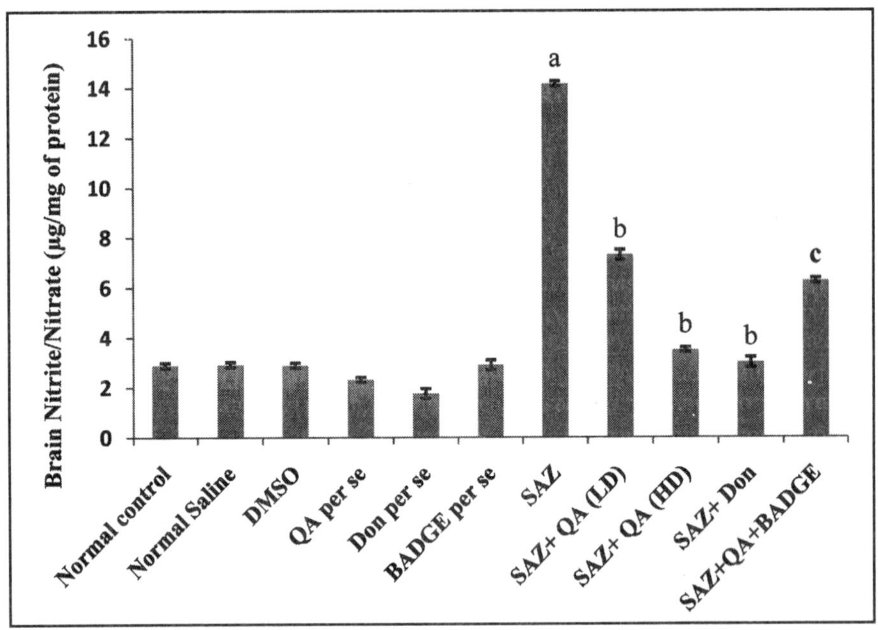

Fig. 4.5: Effect of Quercetin on Brain Nitrite/Nitrate Level of Sodium Azide Treated Rats

Abbreviations: DMSO= Dimethyl sulphoxide, Don = Donepezil (0.1mg/kg; *i.p.*), SAZ = Sodium azide (12.5mg/kg; *i.p.*), Quercetin (LD) = Quercetin low dose (25mg/kg; *p.o.*), Quercetin (HD)= Quercetin high dose (50mg/kg; *p.o.*), BADGE= Bisphenol A diglycidyl ether (30mg/kg; *i.p.*)

Values are expressed as mean ± Standard error of mean (S.E.M), n= 6, one way ANOVA followed by Tukey's multiple range test.

[a] denotes $p<0.05$ versus brain nitrite/Nitrate level of control

[b] denotes $p<0.05$ versus brain nitrite/nitrate level of Sodium azide treated group.

[c] denotes $p<0.05$ versus brain nitrite/nitrate level of SAZ+ QA(HD) treated group.

DISCUSSION

The Morris water maze (MWM) employed in the present study is one of the most widely used behavioral model to assess learning and memory in rodents (Morris, 1984; Parle and Singh, 2004). A significant decrease in day 4 ELT during acquisition trials by control animals showed normal acquisition of memory and an increase in TSTQ to locate the platform during the retrieval trial conducted on day 5 indicated retrieval of memory. These results are consistent with findings in other laboratories (Packard *etal.*, 1996). Vehicle such as normal saline did not show any effect in present study on acquisition and retrieval of memory. Further the administration of Querecetin/ donepezil and BADGE *per se* did not show any effect.

Sodium azide did not show any effect on body weight or serum cholesterol levels but showed significant increase in serum glucose levels. Sodium azide is a mitochondrial toxin, which cause selective neuronal destruction and inhibits mitochondrial key enzyme i.e cytochrome oxidase. This enzyme is essential for respiratory chain that blocks mitochondrial complex-IV and deplete ATP levels which contributes to metabolic impairment and ROS production (Blass *et al.*, 1990; Davis *et al.*, 1997). Due to disturbance in electron-transport chain electrons can escape from it and reduces oxygen to form reactive oxygen species (ROS) which results in oxidative damage (Sullivan *et al.*, 2005). Due to disturbance in the ROS-antioxidant balance superoxide anion radical does not convert into H_2O_2 by key mitochondrial enzyme, maganese superoxide dismutase (MnSOD) in mitochondria and (CuZn-SOD) in the cytosol results in protein fragmentation and leads to neuronal damage (Chio *et al.*, 1999). Further the metabolic impairment due to inhibition of cytochrome c oxidase (which results in superoxide anion formation) by sodium azide showed increase in APPs production (AKA amyloid-beta, amyloid *ß*-protein, and A*ß*), which is one of the prime suspected protein risk factors for Alzheimer's. The presence of beta-amyloid leads to damage of the nerves and arteries of the brain. Beta amyloid can interact with certain RAGE receptors causing damage to the nerves and arteries of the brain and results in AD (Gasparini *et al.*, 1997). Glucose is the major source of energy for the brain and is essential for the normal functioning of the central nervous system (Sandra *et al.*, 2001). Circulating glucose regulates memory storage under several conditions. Decreased glucose uptake coupled with reduced activity of cytochrome oxidase (complex IV) results in increased production of ROS by impaired mitochondria (Mutisya *et al.*, 1994). Increased levels of ROS in cells, such as H_2O_2 interfere with glucose metabolism, by inhibiting the activity of metabolic enzymes involved in this process (such as pyruvate dehydrogenase, alpha-ketoglutarate dehydrogenase enzyme complex and transketoloase) which results in AGE production and altered the protein function (Chinopoulos *et al.*, 1999; Gibson *et al.*, 2000; Gibson, 2002; Xu *et al.*, 2001,). AGE receptor, known as RAGE, is also a â-amyloid receptor. This discovery supports the idea of a relation between AGE and AD as well as between the production of free radicals and oxidative stress (Yan *et al.*,1996). Futher a general reduction in glucose uptake also increases ROS production (Behl *et al.*, 1994; Huang *et al.*, 1999).

Flavonoids comprise a large group of secondary metabolites occurring widely in fruits and vegetables (Ikizler *et al.*, 2007). Querecetin a natural flavonoids is a strong antioxidant and free radicals scavenger found in many edible plants (Saponara *et al.*, 2002). Querecetin has been reported to display anti-inflammatory effects and can pass the blood brain barrier (Youdim *et al.*, 2004). In additional Querecetin has protective effects on cell function in vitro and in vivo (Zhu *et al.*, 2007; Cho *et al.*, 2006). The mechanistic effects of Querecetin on the cognitive deficits and electrophysiological changes accompanying cerebral ischemia are not fully understood, and its effect on ion channels in hippocampal neurons has been investigated previously.

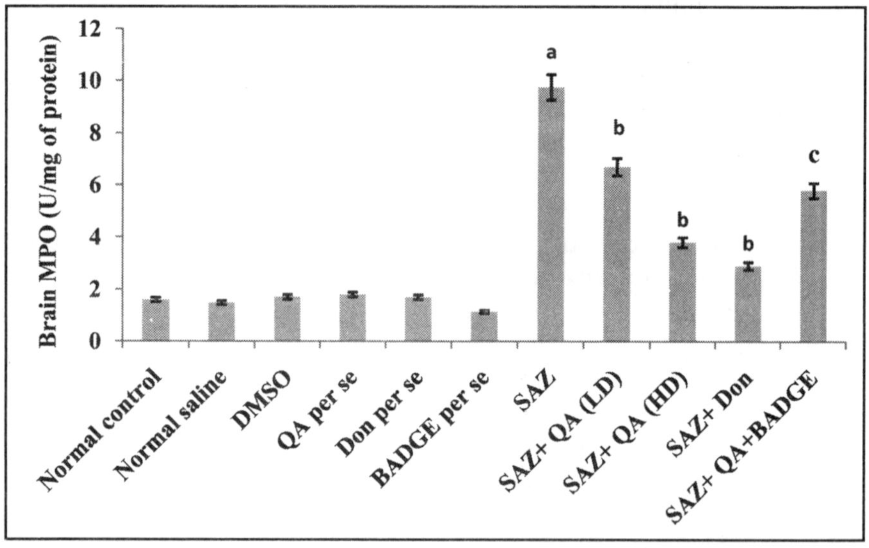

Fig. 4.6: Effect of Quercetin on Brain MPO Level of Sodium Azide Treated Rats

Abbreviations: DMSO = Dimethyl sulphoxide, Don = Donepezil (0.1mg/kg; *i.p.*), SAZ = Sodium azide (12.5mg/kg; *i.p.*), Quercetin (LD) =Quercetin low dose (25mg/kg; *p.o.*), Quercetin (HD)= Quercetin high dose (50mg/kg; *p.o.*), BADGE= Bisphenol A diglycidyl ether (30mg/kg; *i.p.*)

Values are expressed as mean ± Standard error of mean (S.E.M), n= 6, one way ANOVA followed by Tukey's multiple range test.

[a] denotes $p<0.05$ versus brain MPO activity of control group.

[b] denotes $p<0.05$ versus brain MPO activity of Sodium azide treated group.

[c] denotes $p<0.005$ versus brain MPO activity of SAZ+ QA(HD) treated group.

SUMMARY AND CONCLUSION

The study was designed to investigate the beneficial role of Quercetin in memory deficits and biochemical changes associated with Sodium azide induced Alzheimer's disease in rats. Memory impairment was assessed by using Morris water maze (MWM) test. Furthermore, brain biochemical parameters such as change in serum glucose level, brain acetyl cholinesterase (AChE) activity, brain total protein content, brain thiobarbituric acid reactive species (TBARS), brain glutathione (GSH) level, brain nitrite/nitrate and brain myeloperoxidase (MPO) activity were also evaluated. Histopathological studies were also carried out.

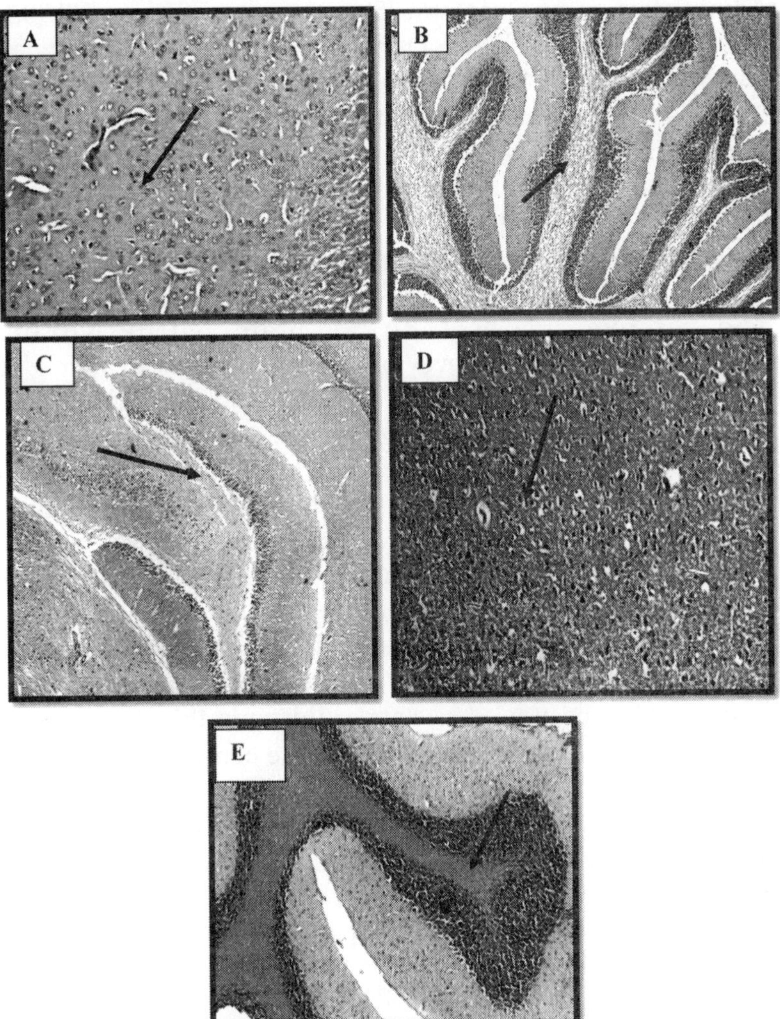

Fig. 4.7: Effect of Quercetin on Sodium Azide Induced Histopathological Changes by (H & E staining) in Rats Brain Coronal Section, (Microscope; X 40). (A) Control (B) Sodium Azide (SAZ) Control (C) SAZ + Quercetin (50mg/kg; *p.o.*) (D) SAZ + Donepezil (E) SAZ + QA (50mg/kg; *p.o.*) + BADGE (30 mg/kg; *i.p.*)

Following salient findings may be summarized on basis of results obtained in the present study.

- Control group animals showed a good performance on Morris water maze test as reflected by normal learning abilities and memory capacities.
- Vehicles (Normal saline, DMSO) used in the study did not show any significant effect on acquisition and retrieval using MWM test.

- Administration of Quercetin (50mg/kg; *p.o.*)/Donepezil (0.1mg/kg; *i.p.*)/BADGE (30mg/kg; *i.p.*) *per se* for 14 days did not show any effect on acquisition and retrieval using MWM test.
- Animals subjected to sodium azide (12.5mg/kg/day; *i.p.* for 5 days and 10mg/kg/day; *i.p.* for next 9 days) showed a significant impairment in learning and memory using MWM test.
- Sodium azide treated rats did not show any effect on body weight. However, Sodium azide showed a significant increase in serum glucose level, brain acetyl cholinesterase (AchE) activity, brain thiobarbituric acid reactive species (TBARS), brain Nitrite/Nitrate, brain myeloperoxidase (MPO) level followed by decrease in brain glutathione (GSH) level along with significant histopathological changes.
- Quercetin (25mg/kg and 50mg/kg; *p.o.* for 14 days) treated animals significantly attenuated sodium azide induced memory impairment. It showed a significant improvement in MWM performance. Furthermore, it also showed a significant decrease in serum glucose level, brain acetyl cholinesterase (AChE), brain thiobarbituric acid reactive species level (TBARS), brain Nitrite/Nitrate, myeloperoxidase (MPO) activity and increase in brain reduced glutathione (GSH) level. Histopathological changes were also reversed.
- Donepezil has been used as standard drug in this study.
- Pre-treatment with BADGE abolished the beneficial effect of Quercetin on Sodium azide treated rats.

On the basis of above findings, it may be concluded that Quercetin may reverse memory and cognitive disabilities, mitochondrial dysfunction and oxidative stress which contribute majorly in the pathogenesis of Alzheimer's disease and their PPAR-γ agonistic action is one of the prominent contributor.

REFERENCES

Abass N, Lucking CB, Ricard S, Durr A, Bonifati V, De Michele G, Bouley S, Vaugha JR, Gasser T, Marconi R (1999). A Wide Variety of Mutations in the Parkin Gene are Responsible for Autosomal Dominant Recessive Parkinsonism in Europe. *Hum Mol Gen*; 8: 567-574.

Banchroft AS, Turner DR (1996). Theory and Practice of Histopathological Techniques.

Behl, C, Davis JB, Lesely R, Schubert D (1994). Hydrogen Peroxide Mediates Amyloid Beta Protein Toxicity. *Cell*; 77: 817-827.

Beutler RG, Duron O, Kelly B (1963). Reduced Gluthathione Estimation. J. Lab. *Clinical Med*; 61: 82-82.

Blass JP, Baker AC, Ko L, Black RS (1990). Induction of Alzheimers antigen by an Uncoupler of Oxidative Phosphorylation. *Arch Neurol*; 47: 846-869.

Chader V, Singh D, Chopra K (2005). Reversal of Experimental Myoglobinuric Acute Renal Failure in Rats by Quercetin a Bioflavonoids. *Pharmacology* 73: 49-55.

Cho JY, Kim IS, Jang YH, Kim AR, Lee SR (2006). Protective Effect of Quercetin a Natural Flavonoids Against Neuronal Damage after Transient Global Cerebral Ischemia. *Neurosci Lett* 404: 330-335.

Combs CK, Jhonson DE, Karlo JC, Cannady SB, Landreth GE (2000). Inflammatory Mechanisms in Alzheimers Disease Inhibition of beta-amyloid Stimulated Proinflammatory Responses and Neurotoxicity by PPAR gamma Agonists. *J.Neurosci*; 20: 558-576.

Crompton M, Barksby E, Johnson N, Capano M (1999). Mitochondrial Intermembrane Junctional Complexes and their Involvement in Cell Death. *Biochem*; 84: 143-152.

Desvergne B, Wahli W (1999). Peroxisome Proliferator-activated Receptors Nuclear Control of Metabolism. *Endocr. Rev*; 20: 649-688.

Ellman GL, Courtney DK, Andres V, Feathstone RM (1961). A New and Rapid Colorimetric Determination of Acetylcholinesterase Activity. *Biochem Pharmacol*; 7: 88-95.

Escribano L, Simon AM, Gimeno E (2010). Telmisartan Rescues Memory Impairment in Alzheimers Transgenic Mice Mechanism Involving Reduced Amyloid and tau Pathology. *Neuropsychopharmacology*; 35: 1593-1604.

Forth Ed. Churchil Iivingestone, New York, London, San Francisco, Tokyo.

Gasparini L, Racchi M, Benussi L, Curti D, Binetti G, Bianchett A, Trabucchi M, Govoni S (1997). Effect of Energy Shortage and Oxidative Stress an Amyloid Precursor Protein Metabolism in COS Cells. *Neurosci Lett*; 231: 113-117.

Green DR, Reed JC (1998). Mitochondria and Apoptosis. *Sci*; 281: 1309-1312.

Green LC, Wanger DA, Glogowski J, Skipper PL (1982). Analysis of Nitrate, Nitrite and Nitrate in Biological Fluids. Ann Biochem; 126: 131-138.

Huang X, Zhai D, Huang (2000). Study on Relationship between Calcium induced Calcium Release from Mitochondria and PTP Opening. Mol Cell Biochem; 213: 29-35.

Ikizler M, Erkasap N, Dernek S, Kural T, Kaygisiz Z (2007). Dietary Polyphenol Quercetin Protects Rat Hearts during Reperfusion Enhanced Antioxidant Capacity with Chronic Treatment. *Anadolu Kardiyol Derg* 7: 404- 410.

Katzman R, Saitoh T (1991). Advances in Alzheimer's Disease. *FASEB J*. 5; 278-286.

Kaur B, Singh N and Jaggi AS (2009). Exploring Mechanism of Pioglitazone Induced Memory Restorative Effects in Experimental Dementia. *Fundam Clin Pharmacol*; 23: 557-566.

Kroemer G, Dallaporta B, Resche-Rigon M (1998). Mitochondrial Death Life Regulator in Apoptosis and Necrosis. *Annu Rev Physiol*; 60: 619-642.

Laganiere S, Yu BP (1993). Modulation of Membrane Phospholipid Fatty Acid Composition by Age Food Restriction. *Gerontol*; 39: 7-18.

Lalonde R, Joyal C, Beaudin S (1995). Effects of Sodium Azide on Motor Activity. Motor Coordination and Learning. *Biol*, 21. 43-45.

Landreth G, Jiang Q, Mandrekar S (2008). PPAR gamma Agonists as Therapeutics for the Treatment of Alzheimers Disease. *Neurotherapeutics*; 5: 481-489.

Li P, Nijhawan D, Budihardjo I (1997). Cyctochrome c and ATP-dependent Formation of Apaf 1 caspase -9 complex Initiates an Apoptotic Cascade. *Cell*; 91: 479-489.

Lowry OH, Rosebrough NL, Farr AL, Randall RJ (1951). Protein measurement with the Folin Phenol Reagent. *J Bio Chem*; 193: 265-275.

Megyeri K, Albert M, Kompagne H, Harsing LG, Gacsalyi I, Levay Gy (2008). A New Treatment Regime for Sodium Azide to Evoke Experimental Alzheimers Disease for Pharmacological Screening. *J Neurosci*; 17: 1046-1054.

Miksch, R, Wiedemann G (1973). Blood Sugar Determination with the GOD-POD-ABTS method using Uranylacetate for Deproteinization. *Z Med Labortech*; 14: 27-33.

Morris R (1984). Development of a Water Maze Procedure for Studying Spatial Learning in the Rat. *J Neurosci Methods*; 11: 47-60.

Niehius WG JR, Samuelsson B (1968). Formation of Malonaldehyde from Phospholipid Arachidonate during Microsomal Lipid Peroxidation. *European J Uiochem*; 6: 126-130.

Petrosillo G, Ruggiero FM, Paradies G (2003). Role of Reactive Oxygen Species and Cardiolipin in the Release of Cytochrome c from Mitochondria. *Fging and ASEB J*; 17: 2202-2208.

Rogerio AP, Kanashiro A, Fontanari C (2007). Antiinflammatory Activity of Quercetin and Isoquercitrin in Experimental murine allergic asthma. *Inflamm Res* 56; 402-408.

Salmon DP, Thomas RG, Pay MM, Booth A, Hofstetter CR, Thal LJ, Katzman R (2002). Alzheimer's Disease can be Accurately Diagnosed in very Mildly Impaired Individuals. *Neurology*; 59: 1022-1028.

Saponara S, Sgaragil G, Fusi F (2002). Quercetin as a Noval Activator of L-type Ca(2+) Channels in Rat Tail Artery Smooth Muscle Cells. Br J Pharmacol 135: 1819-1827.

Shidoji Y, Hayashi K, Komura S, Ohishi N, Yagi K (1999). Loss of Molecular Interaction between Cytochrome c and Cardiolipin due to Lipid Peroxidation. *Biochem Biophys ResCommun*; 264: 345-347.

Smith MA, Perry G, Richey PL (1977). Oxidative Stress Damage in Alzheimers Nat; 382: 120-121.

Sullivan PG, Browm MR (2005). Mitochondrial Aging and Dysfunction in Alzheimers Disease. *Progress in Neuro-Psychopharmaco & Biol Psycho*; 29: 407-410.

Yan SD, Chen X, Fu J (1996). RAGE and Amyloid beta Peptide Neurotoxicity in Alzheimers Disease. *Nat*; 382: 685- 691.

Youdim KA, Qaiser MZ, Begley DJ, Rice-Evans CA, Abbott NJ (2004). Flavonoid Permeability Across an *in situ* Model of the Blood Brain Barrier. *Free Radic Biol Med* 36: 592-604.

Zhu JT, Chio RC, Chu GK (2007). Flavonoids Possess Neuroprotective Effects on Cultured Phenochromocytoma PC12 cells: A Comparsion of Different Flavonoids in Activating Estrogenic Effect and in Preventing beta-amyloid Induced Cell Death. *J Agric Food Chem* 55: 2438-2445.

Pages: 67-103

MICROBIOLOGICAL AND PHARMACOLOGICAL ASPECTS OF BIODIVERSITY

Edited by: Dr. Pankaj Sharma; Dr. Neha Gautam Sharma & Dr. Pankaj Sharma

ISBN: 978-93-5056-878-1

Edition: **2017**

Published by: **Discovery Publishing House Pvt. Ltd., New Delhi (India)**

Ethno-medicinal Plants of Kumaun Himalaya

Deepika Bhatt*[1]; G.G.Joshi[2] and Lalit M. Tewari[3]

ABSTRACT

Inspite of remarkable advances in allopathic medicine, herbalpractice still plays an important role in management and curing various ailments in remote and ruralareas of India. However, traditional knowledge on the use of medicinal plants is eroding day by day andthere is a need to document such knowledge, before it is lost forever.Kumaun Himalaya, in the Indian Himalayan region has a rich diversity of medicinal plants which are widely used in traditional medicinal systems. The present study concludes the diversity, vernacular names, associated authorship, ethno-medicinal uses, and use pattern, life form; plant part used and accession number of the medicinal flora together. The paper describes distribution and local/ traditional uses of the 256 medicinal plants representing 96 families, in which pteridophytes were constitute 1%, trees were 18%, shrubs were 25% and herbs were 56%) in total. Various plant parts used in formulations, such as: underground part- 33%, leaves- 24%, whole plant- 11%, bark- 7%, seeds- 7%, resin/latex/oil- 4%, stem/shoot/wood- 4%, flowers and inflorescences- 5%, and fruits and nuts- 5% were used in the treatment of different ailments.

INTRODUCTION

The importance of plants used in therapy can be evaluated by the estimation of the World Health Organization (WHO) that the present demand for medicinal plants is about US$14 billion a year, and that the demand for medicinal plant-based raw materials is growing at the rate of 15-25% annually.Thus, there is a growing threat on the use of medicinal plants, their

1 **G.B. Pant National Institute of Himalayan Environment and Sustainable Development.**

2 **Regional Research Institute of Himalayan Flora, C.C.R.A.S., Ranikhet.**

3 **Departments of Botany, D.S.B. Campus, Nainital, Uttarakhand.**

products and the Indigenous medicinal practice as the deforestation and encroachment by people are rapidly leading to agriculture land and urbanization in the former jungle. As the result of the popularity of medicinal plants and their associated indigenous knowledge, the number of people and national and international institutions seeking information on these plants is increasing very rapidly. So there is an urgent need to consolidate and organize all available information on medicinal plants of the region.

The Kumaun Himalaya harbors a rich diversity of ethno-botanical species, which generate considerable benefits from social and economic perspectives. The region is well known for various forms of non- formal (traditional) medical treatments. Among the various tribal ethnic groups of the region, the Tharu, Bukshas, Rajis and Bhotiyas largely depend upon wild resources (Maikhuri *et al.*, 2000; Nautiyal *et al.*, 2000). Due to the extreme inhospitable conditions, tribal communities are dependent on collection and trade of medicinal plants, and they have gradually become familiar with the healing properties of the available plants. This has resulted in a traditional system of cure, which has remained non formal and undocumented. A consolidated account and analysis of the total use pattern with regard to ailments and traditional treatments is not available. Therefore, this study aims to (i) prepare an inventory of locally occurring important plant species (ii) document some of the major plant species with their use in various therapies (iii) to access the population structure of threatened plants.

STUDY AREA AND METHODS ADOPTED

To document the ethno-medicinalplants used in Kumaun thorough literature survey was done. To assess the distribution range, use pattern and formulations general interviews, gatherings and participatory rural appraisal were carried out in remote places of study area. To identify the plants field trips were made with practitioners and herbarium specimens were also prepared and submitted to R.R.I.H.F. herbarium, Tarikhet. To analyze the gathered data for the number of ailments treated by each plant species, the medicinal plants were arranged into fourteen broad classes of diseases:Dermatological Disorders, Digestive Disorders, Generalized Body Ache (GBA), Respiratory Disorders, Venereal and Urogenital Disorders, Reproductive problems, Liver and Billiary Disorders, Nervous Disorders, Cardio-vascular Disorders, Metabolic Disorders, Bone/Muscles/Joints Disorders, Anti poison/Antidote, Physical Irritant and Others. Various practitioners and Mandi (market) owners were also consulted to cross check the information.

RESULT AND DISCUSSION

The compiled inventory documents uses of 256 medicinal plant species (Table 5.1), which belong to 96 families out of which 8 major families (Asteraceae 23%, Lamiaceae 14%, Fabaceae 12%, Liliaceae 11%, Ranunculaceae

11%, Rosaceae 11%, Apiaceae10%, Euphorbiaceae 8%) (Figure 5.1). It is the result of a systematic treatment of the recorded taxa and presents the correct nomenclature and synonymus, distributional range, plant habits (Tree 18%, Shrub 25%, Herb 52% and Ferns 1%), plant parts used in formulations (Underground part 33%, Leaves 24%, Whole plant 11%, Bark 7%, Seeds7%, Resin/Latex/Oil 4%, Stem/Shoot/Wood 4%, Flowers and Inflorescences 5%, Fruits and Nuts 5%) (Figures 5.2 & 5.3).

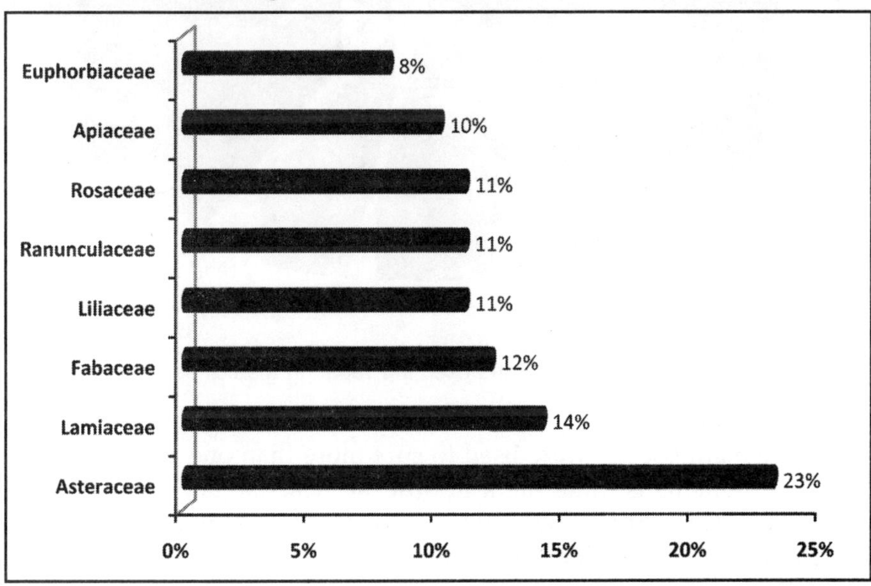

Fig. 5.1: Top Eight Families Supporting Ethno-medicinal Plants in Kumaun

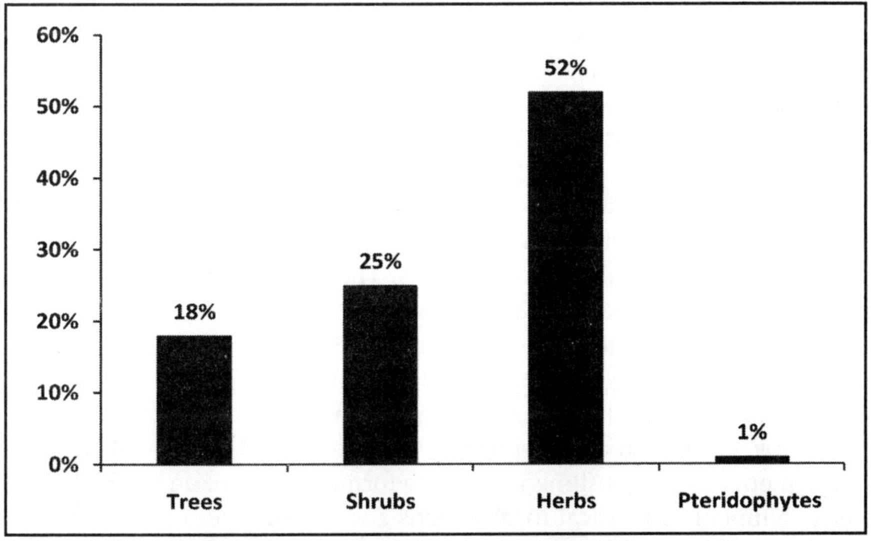

Fig. 5.2: Habit of Plants used in Ethno-medicinal Plants in Kumaun

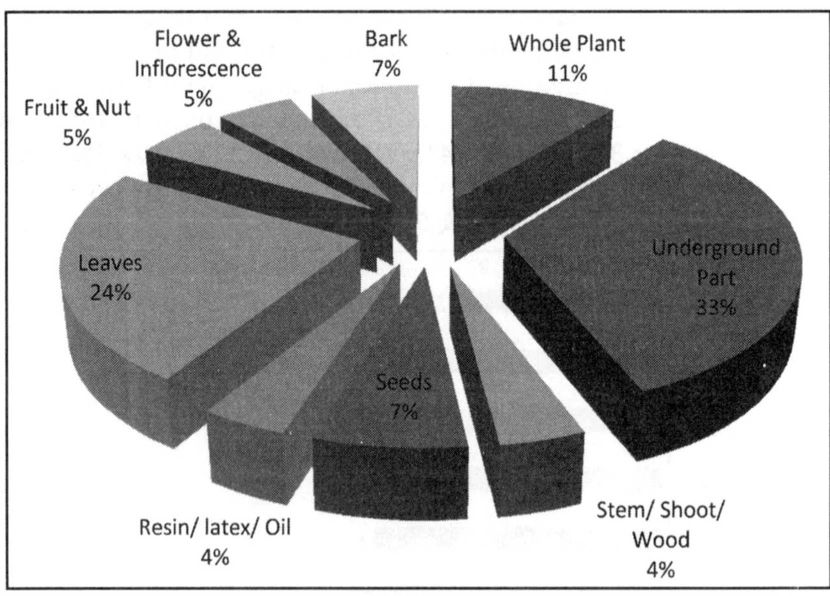

Fig. 5.3: Plant Parts used in Preparing Medicines

The recorded plant species were being used in curing about 108 ailments. Most of the plant species were used to cure more than one ailment. Since the number of ailments is quite high, in order to describe and to include all of them in the analysis, the ailments were categorized and grouped into fourteen broad classes of diseases. The highest number of plant species were documented to cure Dermatological problems (69 species, 18%), followed by Digestive disorders (63 species, 16%), Generalized Body ache (43 species, 11%), Reproductive Disorders (35 species, 9%), Bone/Muscles/Joints disorders (32 species, 8%), Venereal and Urinogenetial disorders (29 species, 8%), Respiratory disorders (25 species 6%), Nervous disorders (18 species, 7%), Others (16 species, 4%), Cardio vascular disorders (14 species, 4%), Liver and Billiary disorders (12 species, 3%), Antidotes (12 species, 3%), Metabolic disorders (7 species, 3%), Physical Irritants (3 species, 1%) (Figure 5.4). A total of 256 herbal medical formulations were documented during the survey/or interviews conducted among traditional *Vaidyas* in the Kumaun. Plants were the major ingredients in these medical formulations. The common ailments were cough and cold, followed by skin diseases, dysentery, Arthritis and cuts and wounds.

Despite the development of rural health services, villagers still use medicinal herbs to a large extant for treatment of common ailments like cough, cold and fever, headache and body ache, constipation, dysentery, cuts and burns, boils, ulcer, skin and respiratory diseases etc. The list of plants used in the treatment of various ailments and the formulations made by the *Vaidyas* is diverse. Number of medical formulations and the number of diseases treated were significantly correlated in the area ($r=0.46$, $n=256$, $P<0.01$).

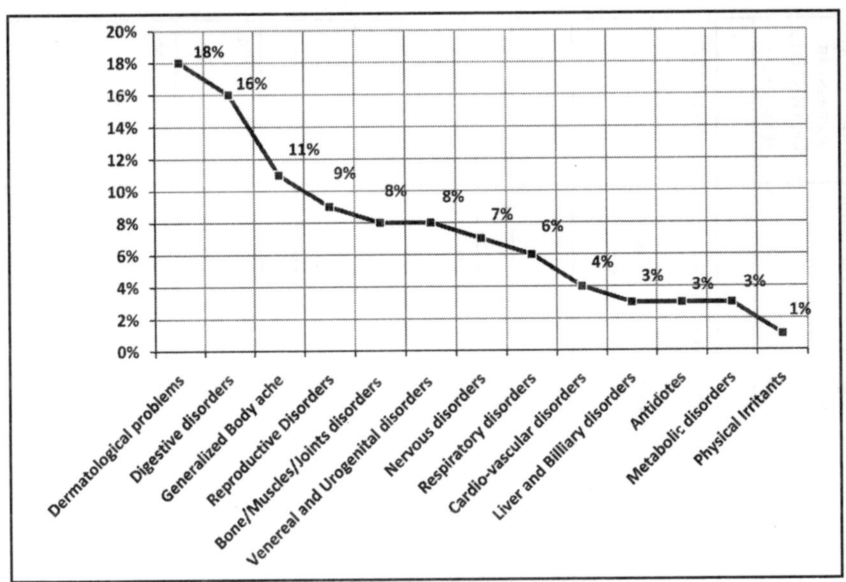

Fig. 5.4: Categories of Prevalent Diseases in Kumaun

Even within the minor altitudinal variations one can find diversified uses of the same plant species. Attempts have been made to explore, identify and prepare an inventory of plant resources of this region (Rawal and Pangtey, 1987; Bhatt, 1990; Datt and Lal, 1993; Dhar *et al.*, 1997; Pande *et al.*, 1999; Kala, 2000; Pande, 2000; Pande and Joshi, 2001; Tewari and Pande, 2010; Pant *et al.*, 2009, 2011). Such studies give an idea about the existing status of plant resources of a particular region. The present study provides comprehensive database on the diversity, distribution, and utilization pattern and plant part used for the medicines in traditional medicinal systems in Kumaun Himalaya. Such baseline information on the useful species is very much important to access the population in wild and identify their conservation and economic values. This information is useful in developing strategies for the conservation and management of the species that are under high anthropogenic pressure. About 90% of the plant species used in herbal industry and traditional systems of medicines are directly extracted from wild, majority of which comes from sub-alpine and alpine zones of theHimalaya (Uniyal *et al.*, 2002). *Aconitum heterophyllum, Angelica glauca, Arnebia benthamii, Dactylorhiza hatagirea, Nardostachys grandiflora, Picrorhiza kurrooa, Podophyllum hexandrum, Rheum australe, Rheum webbianum, Rhododen-dronanthopogon* are some of the alpine species which are facing excessive pressure on wild populations due to continuous extraction from wild for trade. Grazing is another factor that is putting pressure on these species by both migratory animals of transhumance *i.e.* sheep, horses and goats of the inhabitants of adjacent lower valleys during snow free period (Ram and Singh, 1994). These effects are described various workers (Sundriyal *et al.*, 1988; Kala *et al.*, 1998; Kala and Rawat, 1999).

Table 5.1: Diversity, distribution and utilization of ethno medicinal plants of Kumaun Himalaya

Sl. No.	Taxa	AR (m)	Local Name	LF	PU	Ethno-medicinal Uses	Accession No. (RRIHF, Tarikhet)
Family-Acanthaceae							
1.	***Adhatoda vasica* Nees** (*Justicia adhatoda* L.)	300-1600	Vasa	Sh	Lf, Fl	Decoction of flowers and leaves is given in coryza, cough and fever.	Rkt 2537
2.	***Barleria cristata* L.**	200-2000	Kala-bansa	H	Lf	Leaf paste is applied externally on cuts and wounds for healing purpose.Decoction of the leaves is given once a day to alleviate headache.	Rkt 2524
3.	***Dicliptera bupleuroides* Nees**	500-2000	Kuthi	H	Sd, WP	Seeds or whole plant decoction is useful in dysentery.	Rkt 2542
Family-Adiantaceae							
4.	***Adiantum lunulatum* Houtt.**(*A. philippense* L.)	1800-2600	Hansraj	Pt	Rt, WP	Root paste mixed with mustard oil is applied externally on skin patches and eczema.Whole plant is powdered and taken orally during old fever.	Rkt 14314
Family-Agavaceae							
5.	***Agave americana* L.**	500-1800	Rambansh	Sh	Lf, Sd	Warm leaf poultice is applied on syphilis to control further infection.Seeds are used as abortifacient.	Rkt 940
Family-Amaranthaceae							
6.	***Achyranthes bidentata* Blume**	1000-2200	Apmarga	H	Ld, Rt	Tablets made from the leaf paste of *A.bidentata* with jaggery are given during dog bite for three days. Root paste is applied on mouthblisters.	Rkt 25904
7.	***Amaranthus caudatus* L.**	1000-2300	Kedari chua	H	Sd	Seeds are ground and applied on abscess to get relief from pain.	Rkt 25885
Family-Alliaceae							
8.	***Allium stracheyi* Baker**	3500-4500	Jambu	H	Lf	A clean cloth dipped in the decoction of leaves is applied on wounds.Leaf decoction is given to cure diarrhoea and gastric trouble.	Rkt 24971

(Table Contd...)

Sl. No.	Taxa	AR (m)	Local Name	LF	PU	Ethno-medicinal Uses	Accession No. (RRIHF, Tarikhet)
Family-Anacardiaceae							
9.	***Rhus parviflora* Roxb.**	1000-2000	Samak Dana	Sh	Br, Lf, St	Decoction of bark and leaves is given at intervals during cholera and stomachache.Twig of stem is used to brush teeth.	Rkt 25151
Family-Apiaceae							
10.	***Angelica glauca* Edgew.**	3000-3700	Gandh-rayan	H	Rt	Roots boiled with water on moderate flame up to 15min. and kept for cooling. The liquid is drunk to cure vomiting and indigestion, dysentery, gastric complaints and stomach disorders.Roots dried in shadeare chewed directly to cure dyspepsia.	Rkt 25088
11.	***Bunium persicum* B.Fedtsch.**	2500-3200	Bhotia-jeera	H	Sd	Seeds are chewed to increase lactation among women. Same formulation is also given to cure abdominal pain, loss of appetite and inliver problems.	Rkt 24736
12.	***Carum carvi* L.**	2500-5100	Thoya	H	Sd	Seeds are boiled with roots of *Bergenia stracheyi*, and the decoction is given to cure rickets.	Rkt 24654
13.	***Centella asiatica* (L.) Urb.**	Upto-2100	Mandook-parni	H	Lf, Rt	Leaf juice is administered orally in mental disorders. Roots are ground and given to patient suffering from heat stroke.	Rkt 21873
14.	***Chaerophyllum villosum* Wall. ex DC.**	2100-3500	Ginjari	H	Rt	Root paste is applied on cuts and wounds.	Rkt 21840
15.	***Heracleum candicans* Wall. ex DC.**	2200-3800	Gandhraj	H	Fr, Rt	Fruits are used as aphrodisiac, nerve tonic, and for intestinal parasites. Root paste is applied on eczema, ring worm infection and leucoderma.	Rkt 23533
16.	***Pleurospermum angelicoides* (Wall. ex DC.) Benth. ex C.B. Clarke**	3100-3700	Chippi	H	Rt	Decoction of roots is given in dyspepsia, ascariasis, dysentery and gastric trouble.	Rkt 23230

(Table Contd...)

Sl. No.	Taxa	AR (m)	Local Name	LF	PU	Ethno-medicinal Uses	Accession No. (RRIHF, Tarikhet)
17.	***Selinum wallichianum*** **(DC.) Raizada & H.O. Saxena**	3000-3800	Bhutkesi	H	Rt	Roots are burnt with ghee and fumes work as insecticide. Root extract is applied on skin to get relief from muscles pain and Swelling.	Rkt 24080
Family-Apocynaceae							
18.	***Carissa opaca*** **Stapf ex Haines**	Upto-1200	Jangli-Karonda	Sh	Fr	Roots of *Raphanus sativus* and *Carissa opaca* are taken in raw form, orally to cure jaundice.	Rkt 25490
19.	***Catharanthus roseus*** **(L.) G. Don**	150-1500	Sadabahar	Sh	WP	Juice of whole plant is given to the patient of diabetes.	Rkt 25584
20.	***Holarrhena antidysenterica*** **(L.) Wall. ex A. DC.**	Upto-1500	Dhodhi	Sh	Ltx, St	Latex of plant is applied on urticaria and ring worm. Stem bark is chewed in stomachache and burning sensation.	Rkt 22622
21.	***Nerium indicum*** **Mill.**	600-1200	Kaner	Sh	Lf	A decoction of the leaves is applied externally in the treatment of scabies and to reduce swellings.	Rkt 23887
22.	***Plumeria acutifolia*** **Poir.**	600-1200	Akhia	Sh	Br, Ltx	Decoction of bark or latex is used as gargle to reduce dental pain.	Rkt 20649
23.	***Rauvolfia serpentina*** **(L.) Benth. ex Kurz**	1000-1400	Sarp-gandha	Sh	Rt	Powdered root is given internally for three days to cureulcers.Decoction of roots is given in malarial fever and to decrease the high blood pressure.Also used as antidote.	Rkt 24919
Family-Araceae							
24.	***Acorus calamus*** **L.**	1400-2300	Vach	H	Lf, Fl, Rt	Leaves and flower decoction is given in cough, fever and coryza.Root powder is used to cure worm infestation in children.	Rkt 23539
25.	***Arisaema flavum*** **(Forssk.) Schott**	2400-3800	Bang	H	Rh	Wounds are washed with decoction of rhizomes. Rhizome paste with water is applied on body part sting by snake or scorpion.	Rkt 14856

(Table Contd...)

Sl. No.	Taxa	AR (m)	Local Name	LF	PU	Ethno-medicinal Uses	Accession No. (RRIHF, Tarikhet)
Family-Asclepiadaceae							
26.	***Calotropis procera* (Aiton) R. Br.**	Upto-800	Aak	Sh	Lf, WP	Powder of dried leaves mixed with aiggery (gur) given orally before sunrise for 5 days to cure migraine. Juice of whole plant is administered orally, it acts as abortifacient.	Rkt 25586
27.	***Gymnema sylvestre* (Retz.) R. Br.**	300-1000	Gurmar	Sh	Lf	Leaf powder is given in diabetes mellitus.	Rkt 14205
28.	***Hemidesmus indicus* (L.) R. Br.**	500-1400	Anant-mool	Sh	Rt, Lf	Root of plant and cumin seeds are ground in equal quantities, some sugar is mixed and given internally to reduce body heat.Leaf juice mixed with some water is given in fever.	Rkt 22373
Family-Asparagaceae							
29.	***Asparagus adscendens* Roxb.**	1000-2200	Kairuwa	Sh	Rt	To cure redness in eyes, root is crushed slightly and used as eye pencil thrice a day.	Rkt 25155
30.	***Asparagus curillus* Buch.-Ham. ex Roxb.**	1800-3000	Shatavar	Sh	Rt	Root paste of *A.curillus*, *Cuscuta reflexa* and *Coleusbarbatus*is given to infant babies to cure Jaundice.	Rkt 23013
31.	***Asparagus filicinus* Buch.-Ham. ex D. Don**	1200-1800	Shatavar	Sh	Rt	Root juice is given to the patient to cure fever.Root is tied on naval region to facilitate delivery.	Rkt 24198
Family- Asteraceae							
32.	***Achillea millefolium* L.**	1800-3600	Gandan	H	Fl	Tea of flowers is given to treat urinary infection and for menstrual regularization.	Rkt 16883
33.	***Ageratum conyzoides* L.**	200-2000	—	H	Lf	Juice of the leaves is applied on cuts to stop bleeding and pus formation.	Rkt 24431
34.	***Anaphalis adnata* DC.**	800-3200	Poth	H	WP	Whole plant is made into paste and applied on cut & wounds.	Rkt 23997
35.	***Artemisia maritima* L.**	3000-4000	Pati	H	Rt	Fresh root juice is applied externally on skin to cure boils.	Rkt 23793

(Table Contd...)

Sl. No.	Taxa	AR (m)	Local Name	LF	PU	Ethno-medicinal Uses	Accession No. (RRIHF, Tarikhet)
36.	***Artemisia nilagirica* (C.B. Clarke) Pamp.**	Upto-1800	Pati	Sh	Rt, Lf	Fresh and washed roots/leaves are kept overnight in cold water and water drunk for 5-6 days before meal to get rid of intestinal worms.	Rkt 24767
37.	***Aster asteroides* (DC.) Kuntze**	3700-4900	—	H	Rt	Roots are given to check haemorrhage.	Rkt 17003
38.	***Aster thomsonii* C.B. Clarke**	—	—	H	Lf	Leaves are chewed during indigestion.	Rkt 25642
39.	***Bidens bipinnata* L.**	1000-2000	Arka-jhar	H	Lf	Leaves crushed and juice rubbed on itching feet during rainy season.	Rkt 25663
40.	***Eclipta prostrata* (L.) L.**	200-1200	Bhringraj	H	Lf	Paste of leaves is applied on wounds.	Rkt 25529
41.	***Galinsoga parviflora* Cav.**	800-3000	Khursani	H	Lf	2-3 drops of leaf juice are dropped in earache.	Rkt 14447
42.	***Inula cappa* (Buch.-Ham. ex D. Don) DC.**	Upto-2500	Pushkar-mool	Sh	Rt	Decoction of roots is taken orally to cure boils. Root paste is applied externally on boils.	Rkt 23456
43.	***Jurinea dolomiaea* Boiss.**	3400-4500	Dhoop-jhar	H	Lf	Leaf paste is taken orally as antiseptic, also to cure fever.	Rkt 23779
44.	***Saussurea costus* (Falc.) Lipsch.**	3000-4000	Kuth	H	Rt	Root paste is used for 10-12 days to cure leprosy. Root paste directly applied on skin to cure boils. Powdered root taken with water against dysentery.	Rkt 25097
45.	***Saussurea obvallata* (DC.) Edgew.**	3800-4600	Brahma-kamal	H	Sd, Fl	Seeds of plants are kept in a bowl made of bronze for overnight, and given to patient for 7 days to cure jaundice. Paste of flowers given with milk is said to cure "Dhatu Rog".	Rkt 25091
46.	***Senecio nudicaulis* Buch.-Ham. ex D. Don**	—	Rasdhaur	H	Rt	Root is ground with black pepper and given during the attack of epilepsy.	Rkt 23261

(Table Contd...)

Sl. No.	Taxa	AR (m)	Local Name	LF	PU	Ethno-medicinal Uses	Accession No. (RRIHF, Tarikhet)
47.	*Tagetes erecta* **L.**	1000-2000	Genda	H	Lf	Leaf paste is applied on wounds to check bleeding.	Rkt 1296
48.	*Tagetes minuta* **L.**	1000-2400	Hajari	H	Lf	Leaf paste is applied on wounds to check bleeding	Rkt 19610
49.	*Tanacetum tomentosum* **DC.**	300-4500	Guggul	H	WP	Decoction of whole plant is given before 5 days of starting menstruation to regulate it.	Rkt 1214
50.	*Taraxacum officinale* **Weber.**	1800-4000	Dudhi	H	Inf, Ltx	Decoction of inflorescence is taken orally to cure blisters. Latex is applied externally during skin eruption.	Rkt 21368
Family-Begoniaceae							
51.	*Begonia picta* **Sm.**	600-2800	Lalpatti	H	WP	Decoction of whole plant is taken in dyspepsia.	Rkt 25187
Family-Berberidaceae							
52.	*Berberis aristata* **DC.**	2000-3000	Kilmora	Sh	Rt	Root juice mixed with water is dropped in eyes to cure redness and infection.	Rkt 24881
53.	*Berberis lycium* **Royle**	1600-3000	Rasaut	Sh	Rt	Roots are kept in water for overnight and drunk early in the morning to cure diabetes.	Rkt 22818
Family-Betulaceae							
54.	*Betula utilis* **D. Don**	2700-4300	Bhojpatra	T	Rs	Resin and seed kernels of *Prunus persica* and *B. utilis* ground into paste, mixed with milk and drunk to conceive pregnancy and for internal strength.	Rkt 25093
Family-Bignoniaceae							
55.	*Kigelia pinnata* **(Jacq.) DC.**	—	Balam-kheera	T	Fr	Fruits in pieces are eaten to remove the kidney stones.	Rkt 24315
56.	*Oroxylum indicum* **(L.) Kurz**	400-1500	Pharkat	T	Br, Rt	Water extract of stem bark is given in stomachache. Root juice is given at intervals of 30 minutes until the patient regains consciousness.	Rkt 23903

(Table Contd...)

Sl. No.	Taxa	AR (m)	Local Name	LF	PU	Ethno-medicinal Uses	Accession No. (RRIHF, Tarikhet)
Family-Bombacaceae							
57.	***Bombax ceiba* L.**	200-1600	Semal	T	Rt, Br	Root decoction of *Bombax ceiba* . and*Curculigo orchioides* is filtered and given to the patient twice a day for a period of 10 -15 days to cure leucorrhoea.Poultice made through bark is plastered on fractured bones.	Rkt 25408
Family-Boraginaceae							
58.	***Arnebia benthamii* (Wall. ex G. Don) I.M. Johnst.Syn.** (*Macrotomia benthamii*) (Wall. ex D. Don) A. DC.	2800-3800	Balchar	H	Rt	Dry roots are soaked in mustard oil for more than one week and the warm oil is massaged on the affected part(s) at bedtime to cure arthritis. The dry roots are soaked in mustard oil for more than one week till the colour changes to reddish pink. The oil is massaged on scalp as hair tonic.	Rkt 15461
59.	***Cynoglossum zeylanicum* (Vahl ex Hornem.) Thunb. ex Lehm.**	1000-4100	Chitkuri	H	WP	Whole plant is ground and made into paste to heal the wounds.	Rkt 25176
Family-Caesalpiniaceae							
60.	***Bauhinia vahlii* Wight & Arnott**	200-1300	Malu	Sh	Br	Stem bark is pasted and applied on skin eruption.	Rkt 25351
61.	***Bauhinia variegata* L.**	Upto-1900	Kachnar	T	Br	Fresh stem bark is warmed on fire and the juice extracted is given in stomachache due to worms.	Rkt 25989
62.	***Cassia fistula* L.**	Upto-1500	Amaltas	T	St, Br	Fresh stem bark is warmed on gentle fire and juice extracted from it is given in stomachache due to worms.	Rkt 24812
63.	***Cassia tora* L.**	400-1300	Banar	H	Lf, Br, Rt	Leaves, bark and roots are applied externally on skin diseases such as ring worms, leprosy. Leaves are eaten raw to expel intestinal worms.	Rkt 24638
64.	***Saraca asoca* (Roxb.) De Wilde**	Upto-1400	Ashok	T	Br	Decoction of bark is used as cardio tonic. The decoction is also used to regulate menstruation and uterus problems	Rkt 23575

(Table Contd...)

Sl. No.	Taxa	AR (m)	Local Name	LF	PU	Ethno-medicinal Uses	Accession No. (RRIHF, Tarikhet)
Family-Cannabaceae							
65.	***Cannabis sativa* L.**	Upto-3000	Bhang	H	Sd, Lf	Oil extracted from dry seeds is applied to cure paralysis and joint pain. It is also used to cure fever caused by severe cold. Concentrated and dried sap extracted from the leaves is mixed with mustard oil and applied internally, as well as externally to cure piles.	Rkt 25601
Family-Celastraceae							
66.	***Celastrus paniculatus* Willd.**	1000-2000	Jyotismati	Sh	Fr	Oil extracted from seeds is applied to skin to get rid of itching locally called kandu.Fruits are boiled and this decoction is applied on rheumatoid arthritis.	Rkt 22150
Family-Clusiaceae							
67.	***Mesua ferrea* L.**	400-1000	Nagkesar	T	Rt, Fl, Sd	Root paste is given orally as antidote to snake bite. Stamens of flowers are given before 5 days of menstruation to control menorrhagia.The seed oil is considered for healing of sores, wounds and rheumatism.	Rkt 248
Family-Combretaceae							
68.	***Terminalia arjuna* (Roxb. ex DC.) Wight & Arn.**	Upto-800	Arjun	T	Br	Spermatorrhoea is relieved by the decoction of bark of *Terminalia arjuna*. This decoction works as heart stimulant.	Rkt 11759
69.	***Terminalia bellirica* (Gaertn.) Roxb.**	300-1300	Bahera	T	Fr	Powdered fruits of *Terminalia bellirica* and *Terminalia chebula* are mixed in equal amount and taken with ghee in cough.	Rkt 25575
70.	***Terminalia chebula* Retz.**	150-1500	Harar	T	Fr	Fruits, *Piper nigrum* and *Zingiber officinale* are taken in equal quantity, powdered and given with honey in asthma.	Rkt 20030
Family-Convolvulaceae							
71.	***Ipomoea nil* (L.) Roth**	500-2000	Bharar	Sh	Sd	Crushed seeds are considered as abortifacient when taken in heavy doses.	Rkt 8903

(Table Contd...)

Sl. No.	Taxa	AR (m)	Local Name	LF	PU	Ethno-medicinal Uses	Accession No. (RRIHF, Tarikhet)
72.	***Ipomoea purpurea*** **(L.) Roth**	900-2400	—	H	WP	Whole plant is ground and poultice is applied on venereal infection called Syphilis.	Rkt 25523
Family-Corylaceae							
73.	***Corylus jacquemontii*** **Decne.**	2400-2800	Bhotiya-badam	T	Fr	Nuts are eaten as tonic to get rid from weakness.	Rkt 2807
Family-Costaceae							
74.	***Costus speciosus*** **(Koen.) Sm.**	800-1500	Keva	H	Rh	Roasted roots are ground and mixed with *Piper nigrum*, made into tablets and taken orally to cure arthritis. Fried rhizome is administered orally with jaggery (gur), is said to work as abortifacient.Rhizome is made into paste and eaten in anorexia due to intestinal worm.	Rkt 25180
Family-Crassulaceae							
75.	***Bryophyllum pinnatum*** **(Lam.) Oken**	—	Bishkapru	H	WP	Juice of whole plant is used over cuts.	Rkt 20473
76.	***Kalanchoe integra*** **(Medik.) Kuntze (*****K.spathulata*** **DC.)**	1000-1800	Boi	H	Rt	Root paste is applied in deep septic wounds to remove the poisonous material.	Rkt 20115
Family-Cucurbitaceae							
77.	***Trichosanthes bracteata*** **(Lam.) Voigt**	Upo-1200	Indrayan	H	Rt, Fr	Decoction of Roots is administered orally in fever. Rind of dried fruit pounded with water is applied on swollen neck glands.	Rkt 23909
Family-Cupressaceae							
78.	***Juniperus communis*** **L.**	3000-3800	Dhoop	Sh	St, Oil	Smoke of green wood is inhaled to cure vomiting. The heartwood oil is used regularly to cure boils, skin eruption and itching.	Rkt 24815

(Table Contd...)

Sl. No.	Taxa	AR (m)	Local Name	LF	PU	Ethno-medicinal Uses	Accession No. (RRIHF, Tarikhet)
Family-Cuscutaceae							
79.	***Cuscuta reflexa* Roxb.**	Up to-2000	Akasbel	H	WP	Fresh whole plant paste is applied on eczema thrice a day.	Rkt 25622
Family-Cyperaceae							
80.	***Cyperus rotundus* L.**	300-2400	Motha	H	Rt	Tuber is made into paste and given in Stomachache.	Rkt 17444
Family-Dioscoreaceae							
81.	***Dioscorea bulbifera* L.**	150-2100	Gethi	H	Rh	Tubers are roasted in hot ash and given with salt to cure old cough.	Rkt 24963
82.	***Dioscorea deltoidea* Wall. ex Griseb.**	1500-3000	Tarur	H	Rh	Dry Rhizome paste is applied on cuts, boils and pimples.	Rkt 20617
Family-Dipterocarpaceae							
83.	***Shorea robusta* Gaertn.**	Upto-1500	Sal	T	Rs	Powdered resin of plant with cow milk is given twice daily during chest pain and indigestion.	Rkt 20754
Family-Ephedraceae							
84.	***Ephedra gerardiana* Wall. ex Stapf**	2500-3900	Somlata	Sh	Rt, Lf	Dried twigs are chewed to cure Asthma and hay fever. Roots and leaves with leaves of *Rhododendron anthopogon* are made into decoction and used in hydrosele, weakness and as cardio tonic.	Rkt 23993
Family-Equisetaceae							
85.	***Equisetum arvense* L.**	Upto-1800	—	H	WP, Lf	Paste of whole plant is applied as plaster on fractured bone. Juice of leaves works as diuretic.	Rkt 23870
Family-Ericaceae							
86.	***Lyonia ovalifolia* (Wall.) Drude**	1300-330	Anyar	T	Lf	The extract of leaves is rubbed on itching.	Rkt 21160
87.	***Rhododendron anthopogon* D. Don**	3000-4000	Bhotia chai	Sh	Br	Honey is mixed in decoction of bark of *Rhododendron anthopogon* and drunk to facilitate easy delivery.	Rkt 20120

(Table Contd...)

Sl. No.	Taxa	AR (m)	Local Name	LF	PU	Ethno-medicinal Uses	Accession No. (RRIHF, Tarikhet)
88.	***Rhododendron arboreum* Sm.**	1500-3300	Burash	T	Fl	Juice of calyx is dropped in eyes for treating Cataract.	Rkt 22226
89.	***Rhododendron campanulatum* D. Don**	2800-4400	Ratpa	Sh	Lf	Leaf powder is used to cure Migraine and headache.	Rkt 21894
Family-Euphorbiaceae							
90.	***Baliospermum montanum* (Willd.) Müll. Arg.**	300-1000	Jangli-jamalghota, Dantimool	Sh	Sd, Rt	Decoction of seeds is given in Ascites.Root is boiled with water and resulting water is given to cure Arthritis.	Rkt 23714
91.	***Euphorbia hirta* L.**	Upto-2000	Dudhi	H	Ltx	Latex of plant is dropped on the root of tooth during toothache.	Rkt 25783
92.	***Euphorbia ligularia* Roxb.**	Upto-1800	Syon	Sh	Ltx	Lukewarm latex is dropped in ear during earache.	Rkt 13033
93.	***Euphorbia thymifolia* L.**	700-1200	Choti-dudhi	H	WP	Whole plant is crushed with water and taken in diarrhoea and cholera.	Rkt 25745
94.	***Emblica officinalis* Gaertn.**	200-1500	Amla	T	Fr	Fruit juice is given to increase the flow of urine, acts as Diuretic, also given in diarrhoea, dysentery and to cure jaundice.	Rkt 25332
95.	***Mallotus philippensis* (Lam.) Müll. Arg.**	Upto-1800	Ruain	T	Fr	Reddish powder of ripe fruits mixed with rice water is given for expulsion of round worms.	Rkt 20786
96.	***Ricinus communis* L.**	Upto-2500	Arandi	Sh	Lf, Sd	Leaf is warmed on fire and tied over mammary gland to minimize the hardness. Oil extracted from seeds is massaged on painful joints.	Rkt 12433
Family-Fabaceae							
97.	***Abrus precatorius* L.**	300-1200	Ratti	Sh	Rt, Sd	Roots are crushed with water and used for treating gonorrhea and jaundice.Seeds are used as abortifacient.	Rkt 24910

(Table Contd...)

Sl. No.	Taxa	AR (m)	Local Name	LF	PU	Ethno-medicinal Uses	Accession No. (RRIHF, Tarikhet)
98.	*Atylosia scarabaeoides* **Benth.**	400-1200	—	H	Lf	Leaves are crushed/rubbed at painful part due to Sciatica. Leaves are chewed to cure Tonsils.	Rkt 24152
99.	*Butea monosperma* **(Lam.) Taub.**	Upto-1200	Dhak	T	Fl	Flowers mixed in water; this water is applied on soles and palms to cure insomnia.Paste made from flowers of *Butea monosperma, Syzygium aromaticum* leaves of *Urtica parviflora*, applied externally as poultice to cure hernia.	Rkt 25583
100.	*Crotalaria spectabilis* **Roth**	Upto-400	Chun-chuni	H	Lf	Juice extracted from leaves is given orally to check Dysentery.	Rkt 25344
101.	*Dalbergia sissoo* **Roxb.**	200-1400	Sisam	T	Lf, Fl	Leaf and flower extract is given in Jaundice and liver disorders.	Rkt 25664
102.	*Desmodium laburnifolium* **(Poir.) DC.**	Upto-1200	Sansarbhed	Sh	Rt	Paste of root together with fruits of *Datura metel*is applied on cyst.Root of plant ground into paste, mixed in some water is given in diarrhoea.	Rkt 25011
103.	*Dolichos lablab* **L.**	—	Chimi	H	Lf	Fresh juice is dropped in ear to get rid from earache.	Rkt 25364
104.	*Flemingia strobilifera* **(L.) R. Br.**	300-2300	Salparni	H	Rt	Powder or decoction of root is administered orally to cure asthma.	Rkt 25270
105.	*Indigofera linnaei* **Ali**	1500-2500	Latahai bel	H	WP, Lf	Juice of whole plant is given in diarrhoea.Fresh leaf juice is applied on scalp to remove dandruff.	Rkt 24771
106.	*Trifolium repens* **L.**	1500-2500	Tipatiya	H	WP	Plant paste is applied as poultice on cuts and wounds.	Rkt 24589
Family-Fagaceae							
107.	*Quercus leucotricho-phora* **A.Camus**	140-2400	Banj	T	Fr	Fruits are used as diuretic.	Rkt 22432
Family-Fumariaceae							
108.	*Corydalis govaniana* **Wall.**	3000-4800	Bhutkesi	H	Rh	Rhizome is heated with mustard oil and massaged on painful joints to cure arthritis.	Rkt 23692

(Table Contd...)

Sl. No.	Taxa	AR (m)	Local Name	LF	PU	Ethno-medicinal Uses	Accession No. (RRIHF, Tarikhet)
109.	***Fumaria indica*** **Pugsley**	Upto-1500	Pitta-papar	H	WP	The whole plant is boiled in water and used in itching, pimples and boils of skin.	Rkt 9737
Family-Gentianaceae							
110.	***Swertia angustifolia*** **Buch.-Ham. ex D. Don**	600-2600	Chirayata	H	WP, Rt	Decoction of whole plant/cold infusion is used orally to cure Fever.Root juice is taken to give relief from cold and cough.	Rkt 25110
111.	***Swertia chirayita*** **(Roxb.ex Fleming) Karsten**	1500-2500	Chirayata	H	WP, Rt	The wholeplant is dipped in water overnight and the bitter juice is taken the next morning to cure malarial fever. Decoction of the plant is used as tonicwhich influences the digestive organs and also used as anthelmintic, especially for children.Juice of the root is taken to cure liver diseases; paste of the plant is also used in common ailments like cough, cold, asthma,headache and fever.Roots crushed and paste rubbed over joints for quick relief from pain; leaves warmed and paste prepared with mustard oil applied over boils and scabies.	Rkt 25156
Family-Gesneriaceae							
112.	***Didymocarpus pedicellata*** **R. Br.**	500-2500	Ekpatta	H	Rt	Root extract is given to cure Kidney stones. Decoction of roots mixed with Bans Mishri is given in Leucorrhoea.	Rkt 25099
Family-Helminthostachyaceae							
113.	***Helminthostachys zeylanica*** **(L.) Hook.**	Upto-600	Sansari/ Kamraj	Pter	Rh	Rhizome of the plant is cleaned thoroughly with water, crushed and boiled along with cow's milk and decoction given with black pepper (*Piper nigrum*) to the patient for two months to cure leucorrhoea.The decoction of the rhizome is used for curing impotency.	Rkt 12038

(Table Contd...)

Sl. No.	Taxa	AR (m)	Local Name	LF	PU	Ethno-medicinal Uses	Accession No. (RRIHF, Tarikhet)
Family-Hippocastanaceae							
114.	*Aesculus indica* **(Wall. ex Cambess.) Hook.**	1500-2500	Pagar	T	Fr	Warm paste of fruits is applied on joints during rheumatic pain.	Rkt 22221
Family-Hypoxidaceae							
115.	*Curculigo orchioides* **Gaertn.**	Upto-1800	Kali-musli	H	Rt	Root is made into paste and applied externally as an antidote tosnake bite.Root powder/paste is administered orally for Worm infestation. Root is boiled with milk and given in general debility.	Rkt 25350
Family-Juglandaceae							
116.	*Juglans regia* **L.**	1000-3000	Akhrot	T	St	Stem bark is rubbed and paste is applied on herpes, eczema, scrofula and syphilis.	Rkt 21948
Family-Lamiaceae							
117.	*Ajuga bracteosa* **Wall. ex Benth.**	1200-5100	Neelkanth	H	Lf	The decoction of leaves is given to regulate menstrual cycle. Leaf juice is given to infants during high fever.	Rkt 25711
118.	*Colebrookea oppositifolia* **Sm.**	250-1700	Bursong	Sh	Lf	Leaf is chewed and juice is swallowed in cough.	Rkt 24944
119.	*Coleus forskohlii* **(Willd.) Briq.**	1000-2500	Pasan-bhed	H	Rt	Root decoction is used to crush the kidney stone and to increase urine flow.	Rkt 24499
120.	*Elsholtzia ciliata* **(Thunb.) Hyl.**	300-2000	—	H	Fl	Decoction/Infusion is given as diuretic.	Rkt 1891
121.	*Nepeta ciliaris* **L.**	2300-3600	—	H	Lf, WP	Decoction of dried leaves is mixed with 2-3 spoonfuls of honey to cure Tuberculosis.Whole plant decoction acts as Diuretic, given to cure painful urination.	Rkt 25178
122.	*Ocimum sanctum* **L.**	400-1000	Tulsi	H	Lf	Juice of leaves with some black pepper powder is given in chronic fever, cold and cough.	Rkt 18679

(Table Contd...)

Sl. No.	Taxa	AR (m)	Local Name	LF	PU	Ethno-medicinal Uses	Accession No. (RRIHF, Tarikhet)
123.	*Origanum vulgare* **L.**	2600-3300	Van-Tulsi	H	WP	Decoction of whole plant is given orally in urinary disorders.	Rkt 22971
124.	*Pogostemon plectranthoides* **(Burm.f.) Kuntze**	—	Masu-Peera	H	Lf	Leaf paste is heated with Ghee and applied on wounds.	Rkt 25400
125.	*Roylea cinerea* **(D. Don) Baill.**	1200-3700	Kaural	Sh	Lf, Br	Infusion of leaves is given in throat diseases. Decoction of bark is given in stomachache, dysentery.	Rkt 25517
126.	*Salvia mukherjeea* **Bennet and Raizada**	1000-1600	Ghaniya	H	Lf	Leaf poultice is applied on forehead to cure migraine.	Rkt 20517
127.	*Scutellaria repens* **Buch.-Ham. ex D. Don**	700-2400	Kurkum	H	WP	Whole plant decoction in water given with honey thrice a day to cure hyper acidity.	Rkt 20501
128.	*Thymus linearis* **Benth.**	2400-3300	Van-Ajwain	H	Fl, WP	Infusion of flowers with water is given in whooping cough, bronchitis and congested lungs, as a gargle for throat and mouth infections, and to help settle indigestion and flatulence.	Rkt 25435
Family-Lauraceae							
129.	*Cinnamomum tamala* **(Buch.-Ham.) T. Nees and Nees**	400-2000	Dalchini	T	Lf	Leaves are chewed; pills made from powdered leaves are taken for 4 days to cure cough and cold.	Rkt 25579
130.	*Litsea chinensis* **Lam.**	1000-2000	Meda-lakri	T	Fl, Lf	Paste of flowers along with juice of leaves boiled in water is taken to cure burning sensation during urination. To increase physical strength, in constipation.Leaves are boiled in water and the extracted juice is taken.	Rkt 24221
Family-Leeaceae							
131.	*Leea alata* **Edgew.**	Upto-500	—	H	Rt	Roasted roots are powdered and administered orally in constipation.Oil prepared from Roots applied locally on boils.	Rkt 10825

(Table Contd...)

Sl. No.	Taxa	AR (m)	Local Name	LF	PU	Ethno-medicinal Uses	Accession No. (RRIHF, Tarikhet)
Family-Liliaceae							
132.	***Aloe barbadensis* Mill.**	Upto-1800	Patkwar	H	Lf	Leaf is heated on low flame and tied over affected part to cure rheumatic arthritis and gout.Leaf juice is given in constipation and diarrhoea.	Rkt 15539
133.	***Chlorophytum tuberosum* (Roxb.) Baker**	800-1300	Safe-dmusali	H	Tb	Fleshy bulbs are eaten with ghee as tonic. Grounded bulbs mixed with *Piper longum* are given to cure leucorrhoea.	Rkt 24148
134.	***Drimia indica* (Roxb.) Jessop**	1200-2400	—	H	Bb	Juice of bulbs is given to induce vomiting to expel the poison.	Rkt 15562
135.	***Fritillaria roylei* Hook.**	3000-4000	Kakoli	H	Bb	Bulbs are crushed and given with honey to cure Asthma and bronchitis.	Rkt 21921
136.	***Gloriosa superba* L.**	400-2200	Langli	H	Rt	Paste of roots is applied externally on joints to cure Rheumatoid arthritis.	Rkt 20825
137.	***Lilium polyphyllum* D. Don**	1500-2200	—	H	Rt	Decoction of roots is administered orally as tonic in general debility.	Rkt 29454
138.	***Paris polyphylla* Sm.**	1500-2400	SwetVach	H	Rt	Tuberous roots in the form of paste or poultice are used externally in skin diseases, cuts and wounds and in poisonous bites. Powder or infusion of root is taken orally to treat diarrhoea and dysentery.	Rkt 25461
139.	***Polygonatum cirrhifolium* (Wall.) Royle**	1700-3500	Meda	H	Rt	Bulbs are eaten orally with milk to cure general debility.	Rkt 24319
140.	***Polygonatum verticillatum* (L.) All.**	1500-3500	Mahameda	H	Rt	Powder of bulbs is taken orally with honey in tuberculosis. Bulbs taken with milk act as tonic. Root powder is mixed with one glassful of water to leucorrhoea.	Rkt 24320

(Table Contd...)

Sl. No.	Taxa	AR (m)	Local Name	LF	PU	Ethno-medicinal Uses	Accession No. (RRIHF, Tarikhet)
Family-Linaceae							
141.	***Reinwardtia indica*** **Dumort.**	30-2300	Pyoli	H	WP	Whole plant paste is applied on wounds.	Rkt 25772
Family-Loranthaceae							
142.	***Dendrophthoe falcata*** **(L.f.) Etting**	Upto-1200	—	Sh	Lf	Leaf paste is applied on Itching.	Rkt 23852
Family-Lygodiaceae							
143.	***Lygodium flexuosum*** **(L.) Sw.**	Upto-1200	Bariyari	Pterid-ophyte	Rh	Paste of rhizome mixed with sugar is given to cure gonorrhoea.	Rkt 24344
Family-Lythraceae							
144.	***Woodfordia fruticosa*** **(L.) Kurz**	200-1800	Dhaul	Sh	Lf	Juice is good for treating dysentery.	Rkt 22997
Family-Malvaceae							
145.	***Gossypium arboreum*** **L.**	Upto-1500	Kapas	Sh	Sd	Seeds are made into paste and applied on fractured bone for bone setting.	Rkt 23234
146.	***Sida cordifolia*** **L.**	400-1200	Bala	Sh	Rt, St	Stem bark or root powder is given in general debility.	Rkt 20326
147.	***Sida rhombifolia*** **L.**	Uto-800	Atibala	Sh	Rt	Decoction of roots with ginger is given in intermittent fever. The powdered Root bark is administered with milk and sugar for urinary trouble and leucorrhoea.	Rkt 25197
148.	***Urena lobata*** **L.**	200-1400	Van Pyaz	Sh	Bb	Paste of whole plant is administered orally with milk as tonic and to cure body ache.	Rkt 24947
Family-Meliaceae							
149.	***Azadirachta indica*** **A. Juss.**	Upto-1000	Neem	T	Lf	Leaf paste with some salt is applied on abscess as dressing; it bursts within 5-6 hours thereby relieving pain.	Rkt 24117

(Table Contd...)

Sl. No.	Taxa	AR (m)	Local Name	LF	PU	Ethno-medicinal Uses	Accession No. (RRIHF, Tarikhet)
150.	*Melia azedarach* **L.**	600-1400	Meetha Neem	T	Lf	Leaf decoction is drunk, it acts as Diuretic.	Rkt 22039
151.	*Toona ciliata* **M. Roem.**	200-1700	Toon	T	Br	Bark is boiled with water and water extract is drunk to cure diabetes, fever, dysentery and gastric problems.	Rkt 20738
Family-Menispermaceae							
152.	*Cissampelos pareira* **L.**	200-2200	Patha	H	WP, Rt	Whole plant is ground and administered orally during hyper acidity. Same preparation is given in diarrhoea and dysentery. Roots are chewed during stomachache.	Rkt 12062
153.	*Tinospora cordifolia* **(Willd.) Miers**	200-1200	Gurj	H	St	Decoction of stem is given orally during Heart diseases. Juice of stems is administered orally with honey to cure the acute attacks of asthma.	Rkt 23915
Family-Mimosaceae							
154.	*Acacia catechu* **(L. f.) Willd.**	200-1400	Khair	T	Br	The bark of the tree is used in chronic diarrhoea.	Rkt 20742
155.	*Acacia nilotica* **(L.) Willd. ex Delile**	200-1100	Babool	T	St, Br, Rs	The twig of the plant is used as natural tooth brush. The extract of fresh bark is used as tonic. Gum is used as powerful tonic after delivery when given with milk.	Rkt 25352
156.	*Albizia lebbeck* **(L.) Benth.**	250-1000	Siris	T	Br	Fresh bark decoction is used three times daily in stomach troubles and dysentery.	Rkt 20579
157.	*Mimosa himalayana* **Gamble**	300-1900	Aal	Sh	Lf	Paste of leaves is applied on skin eruption.	Rkt 23010
Family-Moraceae							
158.	*Ficus benghalensis* **L.** Bargad	300-1400	Bar,	T	Rt	Root is crushed, mixed with Bans Mishri and given to cure metrorrhagia.	Rkt 18571

(Table Contd...)

Sl. No.	Taxa	AR (m)	Local Name	LF	PU	Ethno-medicinal Uses	Accession No. (RRIHF, Tarikhet)
159.	*Ficus palmata* **Forssk.**	600-2300	Beru	T	Ltx	Milky latex is applied on boils, cuts and wounds.	Rkt 2147
160.	*Ficus religiosa* **L.**	Upto-1600	Peepal	T	Br	Bark ground with turmeric powder is applied externally on cuts, wounds and skin diseases.	Rkt 12946
Family-Myrsinaceae							
161.	*Embelia ribes* **Burm. f.**	400-1500	Bividang	Sh	Sd	Seeds are used in round worms and as antidote to snake bite.	Rkt 1338
162.	*Myrsine indica***L.**	600-1400	—	Sh	Fr	Fruit powder is given to children to kill worms.	Rkt 23547
Family-Myrtaceae							
163.	*Syzygium cumini* **(L.) Skeels**	300-1500	Jamun	T	Sd	Seed powder/decoction is given in diarrhoea, dysentery and diabetes.	Rkt 15770
Family-Nyctaginaceae							
164.	*Boerhavia diffusa* **var.** *hirsuta* **Kuntze**	300-1200	Puner-nava	H	Lf	Leaf juice of plant mixed with goat's milk is dropped in eyes to cure cataract.	Rkt 25532
165.	*Mirabilis jalapa* **L.**	Upto-2000	Gulbans	H	Lf, Br	The Leaf juice mixed with water cures jaundice, dysentery, diarrhoea and dyspepsia.Bark is rubbed on burn scars.	Rkt 25039
166.	*Nyctanthes arbor-tristis L.*	—	Parijat	Sh	Lf	Young leaves of *Nyctanthes arbor-tristis*and *Zingiber officinale* are taken together in equal quantities, boiled with water and taken twice a day for three days to cure cold and cough.	Rkt 24967
Family-Orchidaceae							
167.	*Coelogyne cristata* **Lindl.**	100-1800	Harjojan	H	Bb	Bulbs are crushed and plastered on fractured bone for bone setting.	Rkt 23895

(Table Contd...)

Sl. No.	Taxa	AR (m)	Local Name	LF	PU	Ethno-medicinal Uses	Accession No. (RRIHF, Tarikhet)
168.	***Dactylorhiza hatagirea* (D. Don) Soó**	3200-3750	Salam-panja	H	Tb	Fresh roots are crushed in cold water, filtered and drunk for 15 days twice in a dayto regularize menstruation cycle.Dried and powdered tubers are mixed with 2 tablespoon mustard oil and paste rubbed externally on the affected part to check bleeding.	Rkt 25087
169.	***Habenaria intermedia* D. Don**	1500-2500	Ridhi	H	Tb	Tubers are used as general tonic.	Rkt 24504
170.	***Malaxis acuminata* D. Don**	1600-3600	Jeevak	H	Tb	Used as a tonic and to cure tuberculosis, slightly fried tubers are given to enhance sperm production.	Rkt 24597
171.	***Satyrium nepalense* D. Don**	1400-2000	Salam-misri	H	Tb	Decoction of the tubers mixed with milk and one tablespoon honey is drunk to check the excessive bleeding during child birth, also acts as a tonic.	Rkt 29084
Family-Oxalidaceae							
172.	***Oxalis corniculata* L.**	300-2900	Chalmora	H	Lf	Decoction of leaves is used as eye drop in Cataract.	Rkt 25696
Family-Paeoniaceae							
173.	***Paeonia emodi* Wall. ex Royle**	2000-2500	Chandrain	H	Lf	The leaves are eaten raw or as vegetable in dysentery and diarrhoea.	Rkt 21918
Family-Papaveraceae							
174.	***Argemone mexicana* L.**	200-1500	Satyanasi	H	WP, Lf, Sd	Whole plant paste is applied on affected part to cure leprosy.The Leaf decoction is given in ulcers and malarial fever.Seeds are useful in dropsy and jaundice. Yellow juice of plant is applied on scorpion sting.	Rkt 10742
175.	***Papaver somniferum* L.**	500-1800	Post	H	Sd	Decoction of seeds is given in Gout to reduce the frequency of pain.	Rkt 13953

(Table Contd...)

Sl. No.	Taxa	AR (m)	Local Name	LF	PU	Ethno-medicinal Uses	Accession No. (RRIHF, Tarikhet)
Family-Pittosporaceae							
176.	***Pittosporum eriocarpum*** **Royle**	1200-1500	Agnibai	T	Br	Young stem bark is made into paste and applied gently on and around boils twice a day for one week to get complete cure.	Rkt 5796
Family-Pinaceae							
177.	***Pinus roxburghii*** **Sarg.**	1100-2100	Chir	T	Rs	Used as poultice on suppurated boils.	Rkt 23528
178.	***Abies pindrow*** **Spach.**	2400-4400	Talish-patra	T	Lf	Juice of fresh leaves is administered orally to get rid of fever.	Rkt 25782
Family-Piperaceae							
179.	***Piper longum*** **L.**	200-1000	Peepli	H	Rt, Fr	Root powder of *Piper longum* mixed with honey is taken during throat infection.Powder or decoction of fruits is administered orally to cure cough.	Rkt 21113
Family-Plantaginaceae							
180.	***Plantago major*** **L.**	1200-2600	Isabgol	H	Sd	The husk of the seeds yields colloidal mucilage, used to cure gastric complaints, burning sensation in stomach and dysentery.	Rkt 25556
Family-Plumbaginaceae							
181.	***Plumbago zeylanica*** **L.**	Upto-1400	Chitrak	H	Rt	Powdered roots are given with milk in Backache. Decoction of roots if administered orally, acts as Abortifacient.	Rkt 21930
Family-Poaceae							
182.	***Cynodon dactylon*** **(L.) Pers.**	Upto-3000	Doob	H	WP	The aboveground parts are crushed with water. Two to three drops of this extract are poured in the nostril to cure nasal bleeding.	Rkt 25974

(Table Contd...)

Sl. No.	Taxa	AR (m)	Local Name	LF	PU	Ethno-medicinal Uses	Accession No. (RRIHF, Tarikhet)
183.	*Desmostachys bipinnata* **(L.) Stapf**	Upto-800	Kush	H	Rt	Its root paste is used along with milk against rheumatism. Poultice made of roots is applied on carbuncle.	Rkt 7219
184.	*Paspalum scrobiculatum* **L.**	200-2200	Paplya	H	Rt	Root extract mixed with water is diuretic, drinking this water patient gets relief from painful urination.	Rkt 23281
185.	*Saccharum spontaneum* **L.**	200-1800	Munja	H	Lf	Leaf paste is applied on cuts and wounds to cure pus formation.	Rkt 25184
186.	*Setaria italica* **(L.) P. Beauv.**	900-2300	Kauni	H	Sd	Seeds are cooked with water and given to patients suffering from chicken pox.Seeds are also used as mattresses to cure same disease.	Rkt 7389
Family-Podophyllaceae							
187.	*Podophyllum hexandrum* **Royle**	2800-4200	Bankakri	H	Rt	The root paste is applied on ulcers, cuts and wounds. It is also used as purgative, for curing skin diseases and arresting tumours growth.	Rkt 24380
Family-Polygonaceae							
188.	*Polygonum affine* **D. Don**	1600-4800	Inni	H	Rt	Roots astringent, refrigerant and their extract is used for washing ulcers. Seed purgative, emetic, and tonic and also given in colic pain.	Rkt 16480
189.	*Polygonum nepalense* **Meisn.**	1200-4100	—	H	Lf	Leaves are chewed during Indigestion.	Rkt 13690
190.	*Rheum australe* **D. Don**	3000-4000	Dolu	H	Rt	Roots heated mildly and plastered on fractured part covered with a bandage which reduces the swelling and pain.	Rkt 25094
191.	*Rheum webbianum* **Royle**	3600-4800	Tartri	H	Lf, Rt	A paste is made by the leaves and eaten to cure Anorexia. The dry roots are powdered and mixed with water; a thick paste thus obtained is applied externally on the affected part to cure swelling.	Rkt 16867

(Table Contd...)

Sl. No.	Taxa	AR (m)	Local Name	LF	PU	Ethno-medicinal Uses	Accession No. (RRIHF, Tarikhet)
192.	***Rumex hastatus*** **D. Don**	1000-2600	Bhilmora	H	Lf	Leaves are rubbed by the locals against insectstings.	Rkt 19943
193.	***Rumex nepalensis*** **Spreng.**	1200-2500 Palak	Jangli	H	Lf	Young leaves are crushed and applied on nettle stung portion for immediate relief.	Rkt 25244
Family-Ranunculaceae							
194.	***Aconitum ferox*** **Wall. ex Ser.**	3100-3600	Meeth-avish	H	Rt	The roots are chewed twice a day to control abdominal pain and vomiting. Also used in fever, body ache, and as an aphrodisiac.	Rkt 25092
195.	***Aconitum heterophyllum*** **Wall. ex Royle**	3000-3700	Ateesh	H	Rt	Paste of dried root with water and sugar, taken orally and used to treat diarrhoea, fever, body ache, and as an aphrodisiac.	Rkt 23941
196.	***Actaea spicata*** **L.**	2500-3700	Mamira	H	Rt	Roots are chewed to cure asthma, nerve disorders, rheumatism and paralysis	Rkt 20489
197.	***Anemone obtusiloba*** **D. Don**	2300-4200	Kanch-phool	H	Sd	Seeds are emetic; oil from the seeds is given in rheumatism. The decoction of the root bark is used for sores in the mouth.	Rkt 25984
198.	***Anemone rivularis*** **Buch.-Ham.**	3000-4000	Daiipha	H	Rh	Decoction/powder is prepared from rhizomes to curebronchitis.	Rkt 21654
199.	***Clematis orientalis*** **L.** ***cashmerianum*** **Royle**	1500-3300	—	Sh	Lf, WP	1-2 drops of leaf juice are dropped into ear to check migraine.Whole plant paste is used for scabies and eczema.	Rkt 14911
200.	***Delphinium***	3000-4000	Nirbishi	H	Rt, Fl	Root decoction is given for purification of blood, in heart problems, cough, typhoid, malaria and pneumonia fever, also applied on the place bitten by snake. Flower extract is used for eye redness and glaucoma and particularly for infections of eyes.	Rkt 2533
201.	***Ranunculus laetus*** **Wall. ex Royle**	1500-1800	Ainuwa	H	Lf, St	Leaf and stem paste is externally applied to cure boils.	Rkt 25648

(Table Contd...)

Sl. No.	Taxa	AR (m)	Local Name	LF	PU	Ethno-medicinal Uses	Accession No. (RRIHF, Tarikhet)
202.	***Thalictrum foliolosum* DC.**	1300-3400	Mamira	H	Rt	Roots are ground and applied on wounds, swellings. Decoction of root is taken to cure uterine tumours, paralysis and nervous disorders.	Rkt 25101
Family-Rhamnaceae							
203.	***Ziziphus mauritiana* Lam.**	200-1200	Ber	T	Fr	Fruit juice is given in Diarrhoea.	Rkt 25405
Family-Rosaceae							
204.	***Cotoneaster sp.***	2000-5400	—	Sh	Rt	Root decoction is made and drunk to treat Scrofula.	Rkt 24890
205.	***Geum elatum* Wall. ex G. Don**	3400-4200	—	H	WP	Whole plant juice is taken during diarrhoea.	Rkt 25149
206.	***Potentilla fulgens* Wall. exHook.**	1600-4800	Bajradanti	H	Rt, Lf	Decoction of roots and leaves is useful in teeth cleaning, toothache and Pyorrhoea.	Rkt 25734
207.	***Prinsepia utilis* Royle**	—	Bhekol	Sh	Rt	Root extract is taken orally as an antidote to neutralize the effect of poison intake. Root paste after heating at low temperature in an earthen pot is applied on wounds.	Rkt 23553
208.	***Prunus cerasoides* Buch.-Ham. ex D. Don**	1200-2500	Padam	T	Br	Decoction of bark is given to reduce the muscular pain and swelling.	Rkt 23524
209.	***Rosa macrophylla* Lindl.**	2100-3800	Jangli Gulab	Sh	Fl	Petals are chewed during Diarrhoea.	Rkt 20498
210.	***Rubus ellipticus* Sm.**	1100-2400	Hisalu	Sh	Rt	Roots of *R. ellipticus* with powder of *Piper nigrum* is given to cure stomachache.	Rkt 24623
211.	***Rubus paniculatus* Sm.**	1600-2900	Kala Hisalu	Sh	Rt	Root is ground with water and given to control dysentery.	Rkt 25630

(Table Contd...)

Sl. No.	Taxa	AR (m)	Local Name	LF	PU	Ethno-medicinal Uses	Accession No. (RRIHF, Tarikhet)
Family-Rubiaceae							
212.	***Galium aparine* L.**	2000-4200	Kuri	H	Lf, WP	Dried leaves are powdered and applied to remove scars. Whole plant is ground in water and this preparation is used in worm infestation.	Rkt 25514
213.	***Leptodermis lanceolata* Wall.**	1800-3500	Chirar	Sh	Lf, Fl	Leaves and flowers are boiled with water and filtered water is drunk to cure fever.	Rkt 25201
214.	***Rubia cordifolia* L.**	1200-2200	Manjith	H	WP	Whole plant pulp with honey is given to cure acne and dark spots on face.	Rkt 25428
Family-Rutaceae							
215.	***Aegle marmelos* (L.) Corrêa**	600-1100	Bel	T	Lf, Fr	Leaves of *Aegle marmelos, Azadirachta indica* and powder of *Piper nigrum* is given to the patient of Diabetes. Fruit juice is given to get rid of heat strokes and constipation.	Rkt 25402
216.	***Boenninghausenia albiflora* (Hook.)Meisn.**	600-3300	Pissumar	H	Lf, Rt	Poultice of leaves and red soil (Geru) is applied on burn scars to check the burning sensation.	Rkt 25204
217.	***Glycosmis arborea* (Roxb.) DC.**	200-1000	Ban Nimbu, Makranda	T	Br, Rt	Root bark is boiled with salt and decoction is given to the patient suffering from Pyorrhoea.Powder of roots is administered orally with sugar to cure fever.	Rkt 4445
218.	***Skimmia laureola* (DC.) Siebold and Zucc. ex Walp.**	2400-3200	Ner-Pati	Sh	Rt, Lf	Paste of roots is used as antidote to snake bite and scorpion sting.Dried leaves are burnt and inhaled to cure sinus under nasal tract.	Rkt 24999
219.	***Zanthoxylum armatum* DC.**	1100-2500	Timoor	T	St	Stem twig is used to brush the teeth to check foul smell and pyorrhoea.	Rkt 25174
Family-Sapindaceae							
220.	***Sapindus mukorossi* Gaertn.**	800-1500	Reetha	T	Fr	Fruit powder is given at intervals to regain consciousness.	Rkt 20607

(Table Contd...)

Sl. No.	Taxa	AR (m)	Local Name	LF	PU	Ethno-medicinal Uses	Accession No. (RRIHF, Tarikhet)
Family-Saxifragaceae							
221.	***Bergenia ligulata*** **Engl.**	1600-3200	Silphora	H	Rh	Rhizome powder or decoction is given orally to cure kidney stones.	Rkt 24860
222.	***Bergenia stracheyi*** **(Hook. f. and Thomson) Engl.**	3600-4200	Siilphari, Silphora	H	Rh	Fresh rhizomes are washed thoroughly, cut in to pieces and chewed like candy to cure urinary and kidney trouble.	Rkt 22861
223.	***Saxifraga diversifolia*** **Wall. ex Ser.**	3000-4000	Silyans	H	Rt	Root decoction is used as vermifuge.	Rkt 27841
Family-Scrophulariaceae							
224.	***Bacopa monnieri*** **(L.) Pennell**	600-1000	Brahmi	H	WP	Juice of whole plant is given in Mental illness. 2-3 drops are dropped in eyes to cure conjunctivitis.	Rkt 24577
225.	***Digitalis purpurea*** **L.**	1000-1800	Tilpushpi	H	Lf	Leaf juice/decoction is used as cardio tonic.	Rkt 25577
226.	***Lindenbergia indica*** **Vatke**	300-2600	Makari-Jhar	H	Rt	Root is ground and given to infants to cure throat problems.	Rkt 21380
227.	***Picrorhiza kurrooa*** **Royle ex Benth.**	3300-4800	Kutki	H	Rh	Rhizome decoction boiled mildly for 5-10min and flavoured with honey is given to cure stomach ache. Rhizome powder and black pepper mixed with honey is given orally to cure high fever.	Rkt 25001
228.	***Verbascum thapsus*** **L.**	1000-4000	Aklbeer	H	Fl, Lf	Powder of flowers mixed with mustard oil is applied on boils. Leaf juice is dropped in eyes to cure cataract.	Rkt 25167
Family-Smilacaceae							
229.	***Smilax aspera*** **L.**	1200-2600	—	Sh	Rt	Root paste is given orally with water to get rid of Diarrhoea.	Rkt 23516
Family-Solanaceae							
230.	***Datura metel*** **L.**	300-1200	Datura	H	WP	Decoction of whole plant is given to cure fever. Warm leaves are tied over affected part to cure Boils.	Rkt 25236

(Table Contd...)

Sl. No.	Taxa	AR (m)	Local Name	LF	PU	Ethno-medicinal Uses	Accession No. (RRIHF, Tarikhet)
231.	***Datura stramonium*** **L.**	200-2200	Krishna-Datura	H	Fl, Sd	Juice of flowers is dropped in ear during earache. The paste prepared from roasted seeds of drug in mustard oil is applied locally on ring worm.	Rkt 23834
232.	***Solanum anguivi*** **L.**	—	Baigan Bhatta	Sh	Rt	Root is tied as belt around back to cure hernia.	Rkt 14158
233.	***Solanum nigrum*** **L.**	800-3000	Gewain, Makoi	H	WP	Juice of whole plant is administered orally during intermittent fever and to cure jaundice.	Rkt 24283
234.	***Solanum xanthocarpum*** **Schrad. and H. Wendl.**	—	Kant-Kari	H	Sd	Fumes of seeds are inhaled to check attacks of asthma.	Rkt 25530
235.	***Withania somnifera*** **(L.) Dunal**	800-1400	Aswa-gandha	Sh	Lf, Rt	Decoction of the leaves is taken as remedy for worm infestation. The Root powder mixed with black pepper used in rheumatic swellings.	Rkt 24970
Family-Sterculiaceae							
236.	***Helicteres isora*** **L.**	Upto-1000	Bendu, Marorphali	Sh	Rt	Root of *Helicteres isora* together with Flowers of *Punicagranatum* and Black pepper is given to facilitate the Delivery.Root is crushed with water; one spoon of sugar is added and taken orally in diarrhoea.	Rkt 18292
Family-Taxaceae							
237.	***Taxus baccata*** **subsp. *wallichiana* (Zucc.) Pilg.**	1800-3400	Thuner	T	St, Lf	Decoction of stem bark is administered orally to cure cough.	Rkt 24870
Family-Thymelaeaceae							
238.	***Daphne cannabina*** **Wall. ex Steud.**	1400-2300	Satpura	Sh	Rt	Roots are boiled with mustard oil and massaged on painful joints.	Rkt 225086

(Table Contd...)

Sl. No.	Taxa	AR (m)	Local Name	LF	PU	Ethno-medicinal Uses	Accession No. (RRIHF, Tarikhet)
Family-Tiliaceae							
239.	***Grewia optiva* (Buch.-Ham. ex Roxb.) J.R. Drumm. ex Burret.**	150-1800	Bheemal	T	Fr, Br	Ground fruits are given to facilitate delivery.Bark is used as shampoo to remove Dandruff.	Rkt 25076
240.	***Grevillea robusta* Cunn. ex R.Br.**	100-1800	—	T	Lf	Leaf paste mixed with mustard oil is applied on burn scars.	Rkt 2028
241.	***Triumfetta rhomboidea* Jacq.**	500-1500	Leswa-Kura	Sh	Lf	Leaves are ground with curd and applied on cuts and wounds for healing purpose.	Rkt 25468
Family-Urticaceae							
242.	***Urtica dioica* L.**	3000-4500	Sisoon	Sh	Lf	Flogging of leaves is done during bone fracture.	Rkt 25889
243.	***Urtica parviflora* Roxb.**	600-3000	Bichhu	Sh	Lf	Flogging of leaves is done during bone fracture.	Rkt 25808
Family-Valerianaceae							
244.	***Nardostachys grandiflora* DC.**	3200-4000	Jatamasi	H	Rt	Locally roots are used as incense. The smoke is given to the patient of epilepsy at the time of fits. Roots are boiled with ghee and used to cure joint pain.	Rkt 24996
245.	***Valeriana wallichii* DC.**	1500-3300	Sameo	H	Rt	Root decoction is given in Mental disorders. Roots also act as insecticide.	Rkt 25089
Family-Verbenaceae							
246.	***Callicarpa macrophylla* Vahl**	300-1500	Daya	Sh	Lf, Fr	Leaves are heated and tied over affected painful joints and rheumatic pain. Fruits are eaten during urinary trouble.Fruit paste mixed with yoghurt is eaten to cure mouth blisters.	Rkt 2565
247.	***Clerodendrum serratum* (L.) Moon**	300-1600	Bharangi	Sh	Lf	Leaves are taken raw or are mixed with vegetable for curing diabetes, high blood pressure and asthma. Leaves are boiled and steam is inhaled to cure gonorrhoea.	Rkt 2503

(Table Contd...)

Sl. No.	Taxa	AR (m)	Local Name	LF	PU	Ethno-medicinal Uses	Accession No. (RRIHF, Tarikhet)
248.	***Vitex negundo*** **L.**	100-1300	Nirgundi	Sh	Lf	Leaf juice is dropped in eyes to cure redness. 2-3 drops are dropped in nose to cure the Migraine. Leaves are pounded with rice and water made into syrup and given to patient suffering from syphilis.	Rkt 25175
Family-Violaceae							
249.	***Viola canescens*** **Wall.**	1400-2600	Banfsa	H	WP	Decoction of whole plant is used during cold, cough and fever.	Rkt 22600
Family-Vitaceae							
250.	***Cissus quadrangularis*** **L.**	Upto-1100	Ratgal	Sh	Rt	Root mixed with *Piper nigrum*is ground and applied externally to reduce swelling and inflammation. Fresh and tuberous roots are pounded together with some salt and applied on fractured bone for 1-2 months for bone setting.	Rkt 15577
Family-Zingiberaceae							
251.	***Curcuma angustifolia*** **Roxb.**	800-1300	Jangli Haldi	H	Rh	Decoction of roots, dipped in water for overnight is taken in jaundice.	Rkt 24573
252.	***Curcuma amada*** **L.**	700-1300	Bayada	H	Rh	A gruel of rhizome with milk acts as a fantastic nutrient. Roasted rhizome taken with *syzygium aromaticum* is said to cure Leucorrhea.	Rkt 2825
253.	***Hedychium spicatum*** **Buch.-Ham. ex Sm.**	1000-2000	Sathi	H	Rh	Powder of Rhizome is used orally in neuro-muscular disorders.	Rkt 24059
254.	***Roscoea alpina*** **Royle**	2000-3500	Kakoli	H	Rh	Rhizomes ground with milk are given to the newly formed mother to get rid from weakness.	Rkt 22083
255.	***Roscoea purpurea*** **Smith**	1500-3000	Kakoli	H	Rh	Rhizomes ground with milk are given to the newly formed mother to get rid from weakness.	Rkt 22112

(Table Contd...)

Sl. No.	Taxa	AR (m)	Local Name	LF	PU	Ethno-medicinal Uses	Accession No. (RRIHF, Tarikhet)
Family-Zygophyllaceae							
256.	*Tribulus terrestris* L.	Upto-600	Gokhru	H	Sd	Seeds are fried in ghee and given to the patient suffering from Asthma	Rkt 14087

Abbreviations Used: PU=Part used; Lf=Life form; PU=Part used; H- Herb; Sh- Shrub; T- Tree; Pter- Pteridophyte; Lf- Leaf; Br- Bark; WP- Whole plant; Fl- Flower; Fr- Fruit; Sd- Seed, Inf-Inflorescence; St-Stem; Tb-Tuber; Rh-Rhizome, Bb-Bulb; Rs-Resin

In the study area, *Berberis aristata, Swertia angustifolia, Paris polyphylla, Polygonatum cirrhifolium, Polygonatum verticillatum, Habenaria intermedia, Malaxis acuminata, Zanthoxylum armatum, Bergenia ligulata, Tribulus terrestris* are the medicinal plant species which are also facing the threat of habitat degradation and over exploitation. *Acorus calamus, Baliospermum montanum, Curculigo orchioides, Gloriosa superba, Gymnema sylvestre, Cinnamomum tamala, Rauvolfia serpentinaetc.* are tropical species used by pharmaceutical companies and in traditional systems of medicines as raw material. In this region except the threat of overexploitation, grazing etc., flood is one of the main reasons of habitat destruction.

Over exploitation ofsome of high value species such as *Aconitum heterophyllum, Angelica glauca, Arnebia benthamii, Dactylorhiza hatagirea, Nardostachys grandiflora, Picrorhiza kurrooa, Podophyllum hexandrum, Berberis aristata, Swertia angustifolia, Zanthoxylum armatum, Curculigo orchioides, Cinnamomum tamalaetc.* for trade has caused severe threat to these species. Promotion of cultivation strategies of such medicinal herbs in villages may reduce the anthropogenic pressure on wild habitats. Success of such practices will provide enough time for these species to regenerate in natural conditions (Joshi *et al.*, 1999, 2001; Joshi, 2002; Maikhuri *et al.*, 1998 a and b; Samant *et al.*, 1996, 2002). Large scale cultivation of threatened species in *ex situ* and *in situ* conditions will reduce not only the pressure on wild populations but will also help in socio economic upliftment of inhabitants. However, they urgently need proper market linkage and marketing strategies for their products. Grazing, trampling and other anthropogenic activities are the major reasons for the diminishing of species and ecological imbalance of forest zones. Thus, trampling and rotational grazing may be factors that can slow down the pressure from natural habitats and wild populations.

REFERENCES

Bhatt, K.C. (1990). *Ethnobotanical Study of Some Remote Areas of Pithoragarh and Chamoli District*. Ph. D. Thesis submitted to H.N.B. University, Srinagar-Garhwal.

Datt, B. and Lal, B. (1993). *Less known Medicinal uses of some Plants Pithoragarh District of Kumaun Himalaya, U.P.* Aryavaidyan, 6: 242-246.

Dhar, U., Samant, S.S., Rawal, R.S., Sharma, S. (1997). *Studies on Biota and Resource use Pattern of the Natives within Askot Wild Life Sanctuary of Kumaun Himalaya.* Tiger Paper, 24 (4): 12-18.

Joshi, H.C., Arya, S.C. and Samant. S.S. (1999). Diversity, Distribution and Indigenous uses of Medicinal ad Edible Plants in a Part of Nanda Devi Biosphere Reserve I. Himalayan Biosphere Reserve 1 (1 and 2): 49-65.

Joshi, H.C., Arya, S.C. and Samant. S.S. (2001). Diversity, Distribution and Indigenous uses of Plant Species in Pindari Area of Nanda Devi Biosphere Reserve-II. *Indian Journal of Forestry* 24 (1): 514-536.

Joshi, H.C. (2002). Assessment of Habitat Diversity, Forest Vegetation and Human Dependence in the Buffer Zone of Nanda Devi Biosphere Reserve of West Himalaya. Ph.D. Thesis, Kumaun University, Nainital.

Kala, C.P., Rawat, G.S., Uniyal, V.K. (1998). *Ecology and Conservation of the Valley of Flowers National Park, Garhwal Himalaya Report*. Wildlife Institute of India, Dehradun.

Kala, C.P. and Rawat, G.S.(1999). Effects of Livestock Grazing on the Species Diversity and Biomass Production in the Alpine Meadows of Garhwal Himalaya, India. *Tropical Ecology* 40(1): 69-74.

Maikhuri R.K., Nautiyal S., Rao K.S. and Semwal R.L. (2000). Indigenous Knowledge of Medicinal Plants and Wild Edibles Among three Tribal Sub-communities of the Central Himalayas, India. Indigenous Knowledge and Development Monitor 8: 7-13.

Maikhuri, R.K., Nautiyal, S., Rao, K.S. and Saxena, K.G.(1998a). Medicinal Plant Cultivation and Biosphere Reserve Management: A Case Study from Nanda Devi Biosphere Reserve. *Current Science* 74(2): 157-163.

Maikhuri, R.K., Nautiyal, S., Rao, K.S. and Saxena, K.G.(1998b). Role of Medicinal Plants in Traditional Health Care System: A Case Study from Nanda Devi Biosphere Reserve. *Current Science* 75(2): 152-157.

Nautiyal S., Rao K.S., Makhuri R.K., Semwal R.L. and Saxena K.G. (2000). Traditional Knowledge Related to Medicinal and Aromatic Plants in Tribal Societies in a Part of Himalaya. Journal of Medicinal and Aromatic Plants Sciences 22/4A: 528-441.

Pande, P.C., Pokharia, D.S. and Bhatt, J.C. (1999). *Ethnobotany of Kumaun Himalaya*. Scientific Publishers, Jodhpur.

Pande, P.C. (2000). Prakriti. In: *Soldier* (Ed. C.M. Agrwal). Indian Publishers & Distributors, New Delhi. pp: 159-166.

Pande, P.C.and Joshi, G.C. 2001. Cultivated Plants of Kumaun Himalaya used for Medicinal Purpose. In: *Himalayan Medicinal Plants: Potential and Prospects* (Eds. S.S. Samant, U. Dhar and L.M.S. Palni). Gyanodaya Prakasan, Nainital. pp: 117-125.

Pant, Shreekar, Samant. S.S. and Arya, S.C. (2009). Diversity and Indigenous Household Remedies of the Inhabitants Surrounding Mornaula Reserve Forest in West Himalaya. *Indian Journal of Traditional Knowledge* Vol. 8 (4), pp. 606-610.

Pant, Shreekar, Virbala Sharma Pant (2011). Status and Conservation Management Strategies for Threatened Plants of Jammu and Kashmir. Journal of Phytology 3(7): 50-56.

Ram, J. and Singh, S.P. (1994). Ecology and Conservation of Alpine Meadows in Central Himalaya. India. In Y.P.S. Pangtey and R.S. Rawal (eds.) High Altitude of Himalaya: Biogeography, Ecology and Conservation. Gyanodaya Prakashan, Nainital. pp. 33-35.

Rawal, R.S. and Pangtey, Y.P.S.(1997). Altitudinal Zonation of High Altitude Forest in Kumaun, Central Himalaya, India. *Indian Journal of Forestry* 17(4): 332-344.

Samant, S.S., Dhar, U. and Rawal, R.S.(1996 a). Natural Resources use by some Natives within Nanda Devi Biosphere Reserve in West Himalaya. *Ethnobotany* 8: 40-50.

Samant, S.S., Joshi, H.C. and Arya, S.C. (2002 a). Studies on the Structure, Composition and Changes of Vegetation in Nanda Devi Biosphere Reserve, West Himalaya. In. J.K.Sharma, P.S.Easa, C. Mohanan, N. Saudharan and R.K.Rai (eds.). Biosphere Reserves in India and their Management. Kerala Forest Research Institute and Ministry of Environmentand Forests, New Delhi. pp. 133-139.

Sundriyal, R.C., Joshi, A.P., Gupta, S.K. (1988). Effect of Free Grazing on Population Distribution of Primary Producer Compartment in a Alpine Ecosystem. Bangladesh. *J. of Bot.*, 17: 13-18.

Tiwari, Lalit and Pande, P.C. (2010). Ethnoveterinary Medicines in Indian Perspective: Reference to Uttarakhand, Himalaya. *Indian Journal of Traditional Knowledge*, Vol. (09) 3.

Uniyal, S.K., Awasthi, A. and Rawat, G.S. (2002). Current Status and Distribution of Commercially Exploited Medicinal and Aromatic in Upper Gori Valley, Kumaun Himalaya, Uttaranchal. *Current Science*, 82 (10): 1246-1252.

Pages: 104-115

MICROBIOLOGICAL AND PHARMACOLOGICAL ASPECTS OF BIODIVERSITY
Edited by: Dr. Pankaj Sharma; Dr. Neha Gautam Sharma & Dr. Pankaj Sharma
ISBN: 978-93-5056-878-1
***Edition:* 2017**
***Published by:* Discovery Publishing House Pvt. Ltd., New Delhi (India)**

Rauwolfia serpentina: Pharmacological and Therapeutic Aspects

Showkat Ahmad Bhat*; Bilal Ahmad Mir; Muneeb U. Rahman; Insha Amin; Bilal Ahmad Sheikh; Ishraq Husain and Manzoor R. Mir

ABSTRACT

Plants as a medicine for the prevention and treatment of various metabolic and infectious disorders have been used since time immemorial. Their medicinal properties are due to their rich phytochemistry. The currently available drugs used for the disease treatment are full of side effects, ineffective and heavy costly, because of this trend is changing and blind dependence on allopatheic drugs is over and move towards plant based medicine is going on at high speed. 80% of world populations have strong belief in herbal medicine. The plants having therapeutic properties often have rich phytocompounds with strong antioxidant and anti-inflammatory properties. *Rauwolfiaserpentina* is one of the commonly known medicinal plant with rich pharmacologically active constituents used traditionally for the treatment of various diseases. Reserpine, Rescinnamine, Reserpiline, Ajmaline *etc*. are its principle phyto compound responsible for its pharmacological properties. This plant is having a full potential against infectious diseases and metabolic diseases like Hypertension, diabetes cancer and obesity. Due to all of its health promoting properties the current review is going to evaluate the various pharmacological and therapeutic properties of *Rauwolfiaserpentina*.

Keywords: Reserpine, Rauwolfia serpentine, Drug, Hypotension.

INTRODUCTION

Plants as a medicine have been used dates back from the Ebres papyrus about 1550 B.C (Kesari *et al.*, 2005). Before the introduction of pharmaceutical preparations medicinal plants had been used for the treatment of diseases.

[1] **Division of Veterinary Biochemistry, Faculty of Veterinary Sciences & Animal Husbandry, Sher-e- Kashmir University of Agricultural Science & Technology (SKUAST-K), Srinagar - 190 006 (J & K) (India)**

Uses of herbs has been practiced for centuries in all parts of the world in different systems of medicine like Ayruveda, Siddha, Unani, Naturopathy and others (Kameswara Rao and Appa Rao, 2001). Herbal remedies and plant derived compounds has gathered a lot of interest since the 1980s and the use of complementary and alternative medicine has grown in many countries around the world. 80% of world population rely on herbal based medicine. In India people use plantsto prevent and cure many diseases. Medicinal plant contain certain bioactive compounds like oxygen, carbon, hydrogen alkaloids, tannins, glycosides, resins, essential oils,fatty acidswhich are responsible for its pharmacological action. The active compounds in plants differ due to their biodiversity. Ijeh *et al.* (2004) noted the growing interest on the medicinal properties of a number of common plants. Edeoga *et al.* (2003) have explored the importance of medicinal plants and their importance in the pharmaceutical industry. *Rauvolfiaserpintina* (Family: Apocynaceae) commonly known as sarpagandha in India. It is extensively used in traditional medicine for the treatment of various commonly occurring diseases like insomnia, hypochondriasis, and irritable conditions of the central nervous system and high blood, insanity and gastrointestinal disorders.

Rauvolfia is threatened with extinction in India due to indiscriminate collection, over exploitation and limited cultivation for commercial purposes to meet the requirements of pharmaceutical industry. The Convention on International Trade in Endangered Species of Wild Fauna and Flora (CITES) and in the negative list of exportsplants by the Government of India (Notification No. 24 (RE- 98)/1977-2002 the plant has gained universal acclamation as a useful therapeutic weapon in high blood pressure states (Vakil, 1955).

	Common Name
Hindi	Chandrabhaga, Chota-chand, Sarpagandha
English	Rauvolfia/Indiansnakeroot
Latin	*Rauvolfia serpentine*
Sanskrit	Sarpaghandha
Tamil	Chevanamalpodi, Sarpagandha
Kannada	Keramaddinagaddi
Telgu	Patalaguni, Patalagandha, Sarpagandha
Malayalam	Churannavilpori, Suvapavalporiyam., Amalpori

Distribution

Sarpagndha medicinal plant is widely distributed in the foot hills of Himalyan range, and almost all over the india.it is used as a natural and traditional medicine in India, China, Africa and many other countries.it is commonly occurring in moist deciduous forests up to the elevation of 1200-1300 m high from the sea level. It grows not only in India but also in Pakistan, Sri Lanka, Burma and Thailand.

Morphological Features

Rauvolfia serpentina is anperennial evergreen erect under shrub. The height of the plant is up to 60 cm maximum. Its roots are tuberous with pale brown cork. The Leaves of the plant arelarge, darkgreen above and pale green below, simple in whorls of three, elliptic to lanceolate or obovate, reticulate venation, tapering base and slender.

Flowers: Its flowers are pantamerous and found in umbellate or corymbose cymes. A cup shaped or annular disk is found. White or pale colored flowers often have violetcoloured tinge. Calyx glabrous,l anceolate and bright red.The diameter of flower is 0.2-0.6 and the flowering time is from March to May in Indian conditions.

Fruit: Its fruits are single Drupe, or dumbbell shaped, glabrous, semi-apocarpous shining black, the average weight of single seeded fruit is 0.0192 gms inflorescence is with red pedicels and calyx and white corolla.

Seeds: its seeds are subolongoid, one side flat and other bullate,the color of seed is creamy yellow.Texture is rugose, reticulate and alveolate, its micropyle is constricted and rounded and shape of embryo is straight.

Root: Its roots are long and tuberous with pale brown cork. The root is crooked in shape and branched its diameter is usually 0.2 to 2.9 diameter goes 40 to 75 cm.

CULTIVATION

Land Preparation

Acidic to neutral soil is quite favorable for optimum growth of the plant with medium to deep drained fertile soils also soils rich in organic matter like clay–loam are suitable. It grows well in frost-free tropical to sub-tropical situations under irrigation.

Planting

Propagation of the plant can be done by various methods like seed, stem cutting and root cuttings. For commercial plantation seed propagation is ideal method. In root cutting: Nearly 5 cm long root cutting are planted during spring season closely in nursery beds containing well matured FYM, sand and saw-dust. The beds are kept moist through watering of beds. The cuttings of the plant begin to sprout within 3 weeks. These can be planted in field during rainy season after 8 to 10 cm rains are received; the seedlings are transplanted at 45 cm row to row and 30 cm plant to plant distance. In this manner, an estimated 100 kg of root cuttings are found sufficient for planting one hectare area. (ii) By stem cuttings: Hard wooded stem cutting measuring 15 to 22 cm are closely planted during June in the nursery beds where continuous moisture is maintained. After sprouting and giving.

CHEMICAL CONSTITUENTS

Chemically it containsalkaloids (1.24 to 1.48 m g/100 g), saponins (1.46 to 1.72 m g/100 g), flavonoids (1.46 to 1.86 m g/100 g), phenols (0.06 m g/100 g) and tannins (0.04 to 0.5 m g/100 g). Rauwolfia contains ascorbic acid (26.42 to 44.03 m g/100 g), riboflavin (0.20 to 0.42 m g/100 g), thiamine (0.11 to 0.18 m g/100 g) and niacin(0.02-0.09mg/100g). Among alkaloids Reserpine isa major alkaloidpresent in root, stem and leaves of plant and its concentration 1.7 to 3%. Alaloids present in *Rauwolfiaserpintina* have been divided into three major classes.Three types of alkaloids are present in *Rauwolfiaserpentina.*

1. **Weakly basic Indole Alkaloids**:

   The principal alkaloids are Reserpine, Rescinnamine.

2. **Indoline Alkaloids of intermediate basicity**:

   Reserpiline, Ajmaline, Iso- Ajmaline, rauwolfinineare tertiary Indoline alkaloids.

3. **Strong Anhydronium Bases**:

   Serpentine, serpentinine and alsotonine are strongly basic anhydronium alkaloids (Tyler *et al.*, 1988). While Ajmalinine, Ajmalicine, Chandrine, renoxidine, reserpinine, Sarpagine, Tetraphyllicine, Yohimbine, 3-epi-ayohimbineare the other alkaloids present in.

The concentration of alkaloids in plant varies with geographical positions and seaseons. Generally samples from Assam in India have higher percentage of alkaloids (2.57%) and December is the ideal month for collection of samples containing higher percentage of alkaloids.

The chemical composition of *Rauvolfiaserpentine* was evaluated by Harisaranraj *et al.* (2009) which are presented in Table 6.1 & 6.2.

Table 6.1: Phytochemical composition of *Rauwolfia serpentina* and expressed as mg/100 g dry weight

Phytochemicals	*Rauwolfia serpentina*
Alkaloids	1.48+0.02
Flavonoids	1.72+0.11
Phenols	1.86+0.11
Tannins	0.51+0.20

Results are mean of triplicate determinations on a dry weight basis ± Standard Deviation

Table 6.2: Mineral composition of *Rauwolfiaserpentina*and on m g/100 g dry weight

Minerals Macroelements	*Rauwolfia serpentine*
Magnesium	0.10+0.20
Calcium	0.32+0.10
Potassium	0.04 V 0.11
Phosphorus	0.18+0.22
Sodium	0.02+0.10
Iron and Zinc	1.85+0.20 5.38+0.11

Rauwolfiaserpentina

It contain high content of saponins it shows that its extract has potential to stop bleeding and to be used for treating woundsFlavinoids,on the other hand are potent water-soluble antioxidants and free radical scavengers, which prevent oxidative cell damage, have strong anticancer activity (Salah *et al.*, 1995). Flavonoids in intestinal tract lower the risk of heart disease. As antioxidants, flavonoids from this plant provide anti-inflammatory activity (Okowo, 2004) used for the treatment of diseases in herbal medicine. The zinc present in plant reveals that it can play an important role in management of diabetes which results from malfunction of insulin. This plant is also a significant source of ascorbic acids, thiamine, Riboflavin and niacin. Natural ascorbic acid is very significant for the vital body performance. Deficiency of ascorbic acid results impairment of the normal formation of intercellular substances throughout thebody, including collagen, bone matrixand tooth dentine. The weakening of endothelial walls of capillaries occur due to reduction in the content of intercellular matrix which in turn leads to scurvy hemorrhage of mouth and gastrointestinal tract finally manifested in the form of anemia. Tanins also play an important role in hastening the healing of wounds and inflamed mucus membranes.Thereis lower content of sodium present in this plant which in turn might be beneficial for Hypertensive patients.As a result of availability of Flavinoidis, Ascorbic acid, Zinc *in Rauwolfia serpentina* this plant is used in herbal medicine for the treatment of many diseases (Okowo, 2004).

The Pure extracted alkaloids and their synthetic derivatives have been used as basic medicinal agents due to their analgesic, antispasmodic and bactericidal effects [Stary 1998, Okowo 2004].They exhibit marked physiological activity when administered to animals.

PHARMACOLOGY

Reserpine has broad spectrum of activity. Its effects include respiratory inhibition, stimulation of peristalsis, myosis, relaxation of nictating membranes, and influence on the temperature regulating centre. It increases the gastric secretions. Reserpine also improves glycemic index and antioxidant status.Reserpine can be used as moderate hypotensive agent. It is most valuable in young patients with mild labile hypertension associated with tachycardia. The response to reserpine varies in patients and the dosage of reserpine should be adjusted to individual requirements. In severe hypertension, it might be given by intravenous or intramuscular injection when the effect begins within a few hours.

Deserpidine is almost as active as reserpine in its hypotensive and sedative activity, it is responsible for reduction of hypertension and intestinal movements. It also possesses anti-fibrillar activity. Serpentineleads to the marked inhibition of succinate dehydrogenasein brain and liver tissues. It produces hypotension both systemic and pulmonary due to its ability of causing decrease in cardiac output; Ajmaline has been revealed to stimulate respiration and intestinal movements. Ajmaline produces same action on systemic and pulmonary blood pressure as is produced by serpentine.

Reserpine Mechanism of Action

Various researchers reported that the alkaloids present in the plant produce a marked hypotensive effect which might be due to depression of central nervous system mechanisms (Chopra *et al.*, 1933). They found Reserpine injection in the systemic circulation of rabbit produce an immediate fall in systemic blood pressure which is accompanied by immediate rise in limb perfusion pressure instead of a fall and which was been expected were fall of blood pressure mediated through the nervous system. Furthermore, injection of Reserpine directly in to the artery of the perfused hind-limb causes immediate diminution in vasomotor tone. So according to this Chopra *et al.* (1933) reported that, a feature of all this reactions is their remarkably prolonged duration, suggesting binding of the drug by the musculature. They had also obtained evidence that such a direct peripheral effect may play some part in hypotensive action of Reserpine in man. Mc Queen *et al.* (1954) have been reported that, direct peripheral effect may play some part in the hypotensiveaction of Reserpine in Man.

Ajmalicine

It is derived from tryptophan which in turn is converted to tryptampine through an intermediate product of cathenamine.Cathenamine is reduced into ajmalicine by NADPH and tryptophan decraboxylaseenzyme. Decarboxylase is key enzyme involved in synthesis of ajmalicine in rauvolfia (Liu *et al.*, 2006). Ajmalicine has broad range of therapeutic applications.It provides smooth cerebral blood flow, prevents strokes, maintains normal blood flow and facilitates reduction in blood pressure (Srivastav *et al.* 2006).

Rescinnamine

Rescinnamine is chemically and pharmacologically similar to reserpine. Its potency is less as antihypertensive alkaloid as compared to reserpine and is not much effective in reducing blood pressure (Klohs, 1954). It inhibits angiotensin convetingenxyme (ACE) that converts angiotensin I to angiotensin II and in turn leads to lowering of blood pressure.

Serpentine

Ajmalicine is transformed into serpentine by the peroxidase enzyme bycatalizing bisindolalkaloid (Conner *et al.*, 2006). The beuty of serpentine is that it inhbits Topoisomerase type II enzyme and exhibits antipsychotic properties (Costa *et al.*, 2004)

Ajamaline

In 1931 Ajmaline was first isolated by Salimuzzaman Siddiqui from the roots of R. serpentine (COMSATAS, 2013). Burgada syndrome is highly diagnosed by ajmaline and helps in differentiating subtypes of this disease. Ajmaline is quite ideal for its diagnostic purpose because of its ability in inhibiting sodium ion channels when given intravenously (Rolf *et al.*, 2003). The administration of ajmaline in patients with arrhythmia is known as ajmalinetest. It has been reported to inhibit intestinal and respiratory movements.

Yohimbine

It is well characterized pharmacologically active constituent alkaloid in Rauvolfia.It is used for the treatment of erectile dysfunction due to its strong alpha adrenergic inhibiting property.It increases blood flow and maintains the firmness of penis (Morales, 2000). It dilates pupil of eye by facilitating certain chemicals.

Preparations and Dosage

Powdered root of *Rauwolfia serpentina* reduced to a fine powder to confirm to the official requirements for Reserpine-rescinnamine group alkaloids.It contains not less than 0.15% and not more than 0.20% of Reserpine rescinnamine group alkaloid calculated as Reserpine.

Dosage

The usual dose of Reserpine is initially 500 mg once a day for 1-2 weeks, maintenance 100 to 250 mg once a day. The patient should be advised to notify his physician if a change in mood occurs.

Action of Rauwolfia on different Systems of Body

*Rauwolfia serpentina*is said to have the following pharmacologic attributes (Rustom, 949)

1. It leads to generalized vasodilatation, with a lowering of blood Pressure by the action on vasomotor tone.
2. Itsoothes the general nervous systemby its depressant action on the cerebral centers (Werner 1953).
3. It stimulates the bronchial musculature.

Siddiqui and Siddiqui reveled in 1931 that Ajmaline group acts as a general depressant to the heart while serpentine group causes paralysis of respiration, depression of the nerves and stimulation of the heart on the experiment on frog (Siddiqi S.S and Siddiqi R.H 1931). Ajmaline has been reported to stimulate respiration and intestinal movements. The action of Ajmaline on systemic and pulmonary blood pressure is similar to that of Serpentine; Rauwolfinine has hypotensive properties on the autolysis of rat brain and liver tissue, but to a lesser extent than Reserpine (Herbal monograph)

Medicinal Uses

Rauwalfia roots are commonly used in medicine for the treatment of various nervous disorders including schizophrenia, psychosis, insanity and epilepsy, intestinal disorders including diarrohea, dysentery can be treated by the extract of the roots of *Rauvolfia*. The roots of Rauwalfia also leads to the contaction of uterine muscles and recommended for the use in parturition in dystocia cases.the juice of its leaves can be used for the treatment of opacity of cornea.

Anidiabetic Activity

It has been revealed that extract of Rauwalfia improves glycemic index in alloxan induced diabetic mice by significantly upgrading the antioxidant status in diabetes. It scavenges the Reactive oxyen species (ROS) which are responsible for the major complications in diabetes (Bilal Azmi and A. Qureshi, 2013)

Lipolytic activity therapeutic uses of commercially available lipid lowering drugs are associated with side effects. The root powder of *R. serpentina*is a potent hypolipidaemic agent especially having hypotriglyceridemic and hypocholesterolemic effects with undetectable side effects on liver and cardiac functions. And can be used as potent lipolyticagent (shami *et.al* 2009)

Hypotensive activity: Rauwalfia exhibits potent hypotensive activity in patients suffering from hypertension. It reduces both systemic and pulmonary bllod pressure by decreasing crdiacout put. Half a teaspoon of its powder taken thrice a day is effective in relieving hypertension.

Sedatitve activity: Rauwalfia is used for the treatment of insominia and insanity because of its highly sedative properties. The very first dose of *Rauwolfia* enables the patient of a phlegmatic and gouty nature to go to sleep. About 0.6 to 1.25 grams of the powder of its root is mixed with some scented vehicle and taken. It is non-stimulating and should be given in doses of 0.25 grams to the patient at bedtime for sound sleep.

Antidiarroheal activity: Rauwalfia extracts has been reported to have antidiarroheal action, which may be due to inhibition of prostaglandin biosynthesis with resultant decrease in secretion of fluid into the lumen or may be due to promotion of absorption of water and electrolytes in the gut. Suppression of intestinal fluid accumulation by extracts (Ezijibo *et al.*, 2012)

Antibiotic Activity

The extract of Rauwolfia is highly effective against *staphylococcus aureus bacteria* so it can be used as antibiotic against the infectious diseases like respiratory tract infections, urinary tract infections etc caused by staphylococcus aureus (Vishal and kavita, 2012)

Anticancer Activity

Cancer is a lethal disease and causing tremendous mortality in allover the world. The transformation of normal dividing cell to uncontrolled cancerous cell is caused by so manyfactors including genetic, environmental and lifestyle changes. Prostate cancer is leading cause of death among males. Modern therapeutic techniques including chemotherapy and radiotherapy have not proven to be effective against prostate cancer (American C.A.S 2006). Plant phytocompounds with anticancer propery is need of hour because of their effectiveness, minimum side effects and economical. ß-carboline alkaloid present in Rauvolfia have been reported to tumor cell growth in mice (Beljanski, 1986). This plant exhibits its anticancer activity against prostate cancer both invitro and invivo models by its cell control signaling pathway. (*Bemis et al.*, 2006). It also shows strong anticancer activity against breast cancer (Stanford *et al.*, 1986).

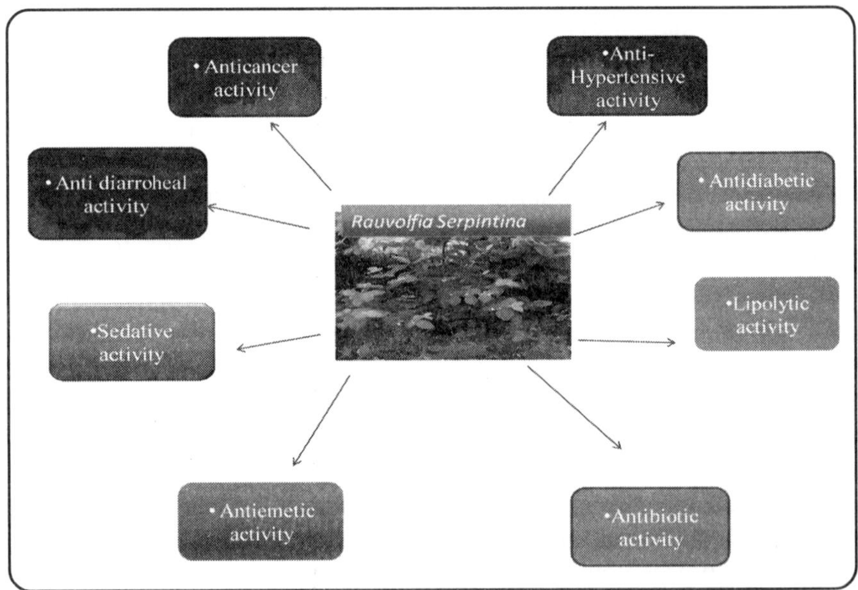

Summary of Pharmacological Properties of *Rauvolfiaserpintina*

Side Effects

Although there are very less side effects of the plant as a medicine but the overdose of it produces few side effects but none of serious consequence like over dose of Rauwolfia leads to bradycardia, hypotension, drowsiness.

CONCLUSION

The currently used Allopatheic drugs are full of side effects. Plants used in tradional medicine represent valuable alternative for the treatment of various diseases. Among these plants Rauwolfia serpintina is quite superior in its effect on high blood pressure, besides it has been proved to be used a antilipolytic, antidiabetic, antidiarroheal and antibiotic. The drug is useful in releving various nervous symptoms such as headache, insomnia, vertigo etc. The effect of drug is long lasting and is effective in small doses. Due to its abundance avilability, low cost and safety in consumption, Rauwolfia has been the subject of intensive scientific research over the past two decades. Due to antioxidant properties of this herbal plant, it can be widely used in the treatment of many diseases like in diabetes. Besides, this plant also has anti lipolytic properties. It also has immense role against hypertension and helps in reduction of blood pressure. There are ill effects of this plant as well if ever taken in excess. Sedation is the main ill effect of this plant. Bradycardia may occur which may lead to shock.In my opinion it is safe and beneficial in small doses in hypertensive cases.

REFERENCES

American Cancer Society, Cancer Facts and Figures 2006, Atlanta: American Cancer Society, 2006

Beljanski, M. and Beljanski, M.S. 1986. Three Alkaloids as Selective Destroyers of Cancer Cells in Mice, Synergy with Classic Anticancer Drugs, *Oncology*, 43: 198-203.

Bemis, D.L., Capodice, J.L., Gorroochurn, P., Katz, A.E., Buttyan, R. 2006. Antiprostate Cancer Activity of a beta-carboline Alkaloid Enriched Extract from *Rauvolfiavomitoria. International Journal of Oncology*, 29(5):1065-1073.

Bhatia, B.B., M.D., M.R.C.P. (Lond.), 2004. Head of the Department of Pharmacology, K.E.M. Medical College, Lucknow, India. 10. Okwu, D.E., Phytochemicals and VITAMIN Content of Indigenous spices of Southeastern Nsigeria. *J. Sustain. Agric. Environ* 6(1): 30-37.

C OMSATS Newsletter: Biographies of Eminent Scientists. 2013. Dr. Salimuzzamman Siddiqui, COMSATS Secretariat, Islamabad – Pakistan 5(3)

Chopra, R.N., Gupta, J.C. and Mukherjee, B. 1933. The Pharmacological Action of an Alkaloid Obtained from Rauvolfiaserpentina. A Preliminary Note, *Ind., J.Med. Res* 21: 261-71.

Connor, S.E., Maresh, J. 2006. Chemistry and Biology of Monoterpene indole alkaloid Biosynthesis, *Natural Product Reports*, 23: 532-547.

Costa-Campos, L., Dassoler, S.C., Rigo, A.P., Iwu, M., Elisabetsky, E. 2004. Anxiolytic Properties of the Antipsychotic Alkaloid Alstonine, *Pharmacology Biochemistry & Behaviour*, 77: 481-489.

Del-Rio, A., Obdululio, B.G., Casfillo, J., Marin, F.G. and Ortuno, A. 1997. Uses an Properties of Citrus Flavonoids. *J. Agric Food Chem* 45: 4505-4515.

Edeoga, H.O., Okwu , D.E. and Mbaebie, B.O. 2003. Minerals and Nutritive Values of some Nigerian Medical Plants. *J. Med. Aromatic Plants Sc* 25: 1010-1015.

Edeoga, H.O., Okwu, D.E. and Mbaebre, B.O. 2005. Phytochemical Constituent of some Nigerian Medicinal Plants. *Afr. J. Biotechnol* 4(7): 685-688.

Ezeigbo II., Ezeja, M.I., Madubuike, K.G., Ifenkwe, D.C., Ukweni, I.A., Udeh, N.E., Akomas S.C. 2012. Antidiarrhoeal Activity of Leaf Methanolic Extract of Rauwolfia Serpentine. *Asian Pac J Trop Biomed* 2(6): 430-432.

Harisaranraj, R., Suresh, K and Saravanababu, S. 2009. Evaluation of the Chemical Composition Rauwolfia serpentina and Ephedra vulgeris. Advances in Biological Research 3(5-6): 174-178.

Herbal Monograph, The Himalaya Drug Company, http://www. himalayahealthcare. com/herbfinder/h_ber ber.htm

Ijeh, I.I., O.U. Njoku and E.C. Ekenze, 2004. Medicinal Evaluation of Extracts of *Xylopiaaethiopica* and *Ocimumgratissimum. J. Med. Aromatic Plant Sci* 26: 44-47.

Kesari, A.N., Gupta, R.K., and Watal, G. (2005). Hypoglycemic Effect of *Murray koenigii* on Normal and Alloxan Diabetic Rabbits. *Journal of ethnopharmacology* 97: 247-255.

Klohs, M.W., Draper, M.D., Keller, F. 1954. Alkaloids of *Rauvolfia serpentine* Benth III. Rescinnamine, A New Hypotensive and Sedative Principle, *Journal of American Chemical Society*, 76(10): 28-43.

Liu, W., Chen, R., Chen, M., Zhang, H., Peng, M., Yang, C., Ming, X., Lan, X., Liao, Z. 2012. Tryptophan Decarboxylase Plays an Important Role in Ajmalicine Biosynthesis in *Rauvolfiaverticillata, Planta* 236(1): 239-250.

Mc Queen, E.G., Doyle, A.E., *et al*, 1954: "Mechanism of Hypotensive Action of Reserpine, an Alkaloid of *Rauwolfiaserpentina*", *Nature*, 174: 1015-1021.

Ministry of Health & Family Welfare Regional Research Laboratory Journal of Indian Medical Association (1942): (XI), 9, 262] Available at www.ecoplanet.in/herbs and plants/Rauwolfiaserpentina.htm

Morales, A., Yohimbine in Erectile Dysfunction: The Facts, *International Journal of Impotence Research*,12(1): 70-74.

Muhammad Bilal, Azmi and Shamim Qureshi, A. 2013. *Rauwolfia Serpentina* Ameliorates Hyperglycemic, Haematinic and Antioxidant Status in Alloxan-Induced Diabetic Mice. *Journal of Applied Pharmaceutical Science*, 3: 136-141.

Okwu, D.E. and Okwu, M.E. 2004. Chemical Composition of *Spondiasmombin*linn Plant Parts. *J. Sustain Agric. Environ*6(2): 140-147.

Ray, G.K., Roy, P.K., Dasgupta, S.R., *et al*. 1953. Action of Rauwolfia serpentina on Vasomotor Reflexes, *Arch. Exp. Path. U. Pharmakol* 219: 310-14.

Rolf, S., Bruns, H.J., Wichter, T., Kirchhof, P., Ribbing, M., Wasme, R K., Pau, l M., Breithardt, G., Haverkamp, W., Eckardt, L. 2003. The Ajmaline Challenge in Brugada Syndrome: Diagnostic Impact, Safety, and Recommended Protocol, *European Heart Journal*, 24(12): 1104-1112.

Rustom Jal, Vakil. 1949. "A Clinical Trial of *Rauwolfia serpentina* in Essential Hypertension", *British Heart Journal*, 11(4): 350-355.

Salah, N., Miller, N.J., Pagangeg, G., Tijburg, L., Bolwellg, P., Rice, E. and Evans, C. 1995. Polyphenolic Flavonoils as Seavenger of Aqueous Phase Radicals as Chain Breaking Antioxidant. *Arch Biochem. Broph* 2: 339-346.

Sen, G., Bose, K.C. 1931. Rauwolfia Serpentina, a New Indian Drug for Insanity and High Blood Pressure, – *Indian Med. World* 2: 194-201.

Shamim, A., Qureshi and Shamsa, K. 2009. Udani Hypolipidaemic Activity of *Rauwolfiaserpentina Pakistan Journal of Nutrition* 8 (7): 1103-1106.

Siddiqui, S.S. and Siddiqui, R.H. 1931. "The Alkaloid of *Rauwolfia serpentina*, Benth", *J. Indian Chem. Soc*, 8: 667-674.

Sihag, R.C and Nidhi, Wadhwa. 2011. Floral and Reproductive Biology of Sarpagandha Rauvolfia Serpentina (Gentianales: Apocynaceae) in Semi-arid Environment of India. *J. Threatened Taxa (JoTT) Short Commun*. 3(1): 1432-1436.

Srivastava, A., Tripathi, A.K, Pandey, R., Verma, R.K, Gupta, M. 2006. Quantitative Determination of Reserpine, Ajmaline and Ajmalicine in *Rauvolfia serpentina* by Reversed-phase High-performance Liquid Chromatography. *Journal of Chromatographic Science*, 44: 557-560.

Stanford, J.L., Martin, E.J., Brintin, L.A., Hoover, R.N. 1986. Rauvolfia use and Breast Cancer: A Case-control Study, Journal of the National Cancer Institute, 76: 817-822.

Stary, F., 1998. The Natural Guide to Medicinal Herbs Sand Plants. Tiger Books International, London,. pp: 12-16.

Tyler, V.E., Brady, L.R., Robbers, J.E. 1988. Pharmacognosy, 9th Edition, Lea and Febiger, Philiadelphia 222-224.

Vakil, R.J. 1955. Rauwolfia Serpentina in the Treatment of High Blood Pressure. American Heart Association , Inc Available at circ.ahajournals.org/content/12/2/220.abstract

Vishal kumar, Deshwal* and Kavita. 2012. Study on the Antibacterial Effect of *rauwolfia serpentina* on *staphylococcus aureus* International Journal of Pharmaceutical Invention August, Volume 2(7): 4265-4268.

Pages: 116-128

MICROBIOLOGICAL AND PHARMACOLOGICAL ASPECTS OF BIODIVERSITY
Edited by: Dr. Pankaj Sharma; Dr. Neha Gautam Sharma & Dr. Pankaj Sharma
ISBN: 978-93-5056-878-1
Edition: 2017
Published by: Discovery Publishing House Pvt. Ltd., New Delhi (India)

Ecological Assessment of Alien Invasive Plants in Uttarakhand Himalaya
Implications for Biodiversity Conservation

Ajay Maletha and Prakash C. Phondani*

ABSTRACT

Invasive plants are commonly recognized to have severe ecological impacts in a wide range of ecosystems throughout the world. They can alter ecosystem structure and function, tropic structure, resource availability and alter biodiversity of natural landscape. The present study highlights the current scenarios' of invasive alien plant species in Alaknanda Valley of Uttarakhand Himalaya, India. Data were collected using quadrates along an altitudinal gradient (460-2000m asl). A total of 5 invasive plant species i.e. *Lantana camara, Parthenium hysterophorus, Eupatorium adenophorum, Ageratum conyzoides,* and *Xanthium strumarium* were documented. Results revealed that invasion of *Eupatorium adnophorum* was maximum in higher altitude, however, the most frequent invasive species at low altitude were *Lantana camara, Parthenium hysterophorus, Eupatorium adnophorum* and *Ageratum conyzoids.* The most frequent and dominating invasive species was *Eupatorium adnophorum* with average density of 40.36 and least dominate species was *Xanthium strumarium..* The R square values for *Eupatorium adnophorum* and *Lantana camara* were found below 0.0002, which also confirmed that there was no trend of species distribution with variation of soil.

Keywords: Invasive plants, Biodiversity conservation, Alaknanada valley, Central Himalaya.

INTRODUCTION

Invasive plant species are colonizing aggressively and threatening the native biodiversity of Himalayan landscape. Invasive species can have a

G.B. Pant National Institute of Himalayan Environment and Sustainable Development, Garhwal Unit, Srinagar - 246 174 (Uttarakhand) (India)

significant impact on development, affecting sustainability of livelihood, food security and essential ecosystem services and dynamics. Invasive plants are now recognized as a serious threat to most extensive management systems, such as forest, meadows, desert and riparian areas (Vitousek *et al.*, 1996; Enserink, 1999; Ewel *et al.*, 1999). Invasive plant species has potential to damage our crops, our industries, the environmental and public health. Scientist, academics, leaders of industry and land managers are realizing that invasive species are serious environmental threats for the 21st century (Mooney and Hobbs, 2000; Yaduraju *et al.*, 2000). Invasive species has a significant effect on the biological and human communities in which they appear. These effects include economic, environmental, aesthetic, and biological harm to biodiversity, ecosystem function and human welfare (Dekker and Comstock, 1992). The invasion of terrestrial community by exotic plant species is a major concern for ecologists and natural resources managers. With the greater rate of disturbance exotics plants are becoming a large components of regional floras (Mooney *et al.*, 1986; Robinson *et al.*, 1994; Knops *et al.*, 1995). There has been an increase in awareness of the problem associated with exotic invasive plant species, there community level impacts remain relatively unknown (Woods, 1997; Alvarez and Cushman, 2002; Byers *et al.*, 2002).

Many invasive plants continue to be admired by people who may not be aware of their weedy nature. Alien plants can spread rapidly because of our mobile society and the intentional transportation of ornamental and forage plants (Randall and Marinelli, 1997). The loss due to invasive species in United States estimated to be approximate $125-150 billion each year and 25% of US agriculture gross national product lost due to foreign pests and weeds (McNeely, 2001). Spread of *Lantana camara*, an invasive plant species has been found in diverse geophysical environments causing a threat to the native flora. Various eradication programmes have been attempted such as burning, chemical sprays, bio-control agents and physical plugging mechanism for removing such invasive species in India. The efforts and success of these programmes need to be augmented with a correct, quick and cost effective technique of mapping in order to locate them, understand their spatial extent and hence make the process comprehensive (Love *et al.*, 2009). Invasive species are a current focus of interest for ecologists, biological conservationists and natural resource managers, the reason being their rapid spread, their threat to biodiversity and damage to ecosystems (Joshi *et al.*, 2004). The global extent and rapid increase in floral invasive species is recognized as natural cause of global biodiversity loss (Wilcove and Chen, 1998).

Alien invasive plant species often used as a hedge plant is found abundantly in India and hinders proper vegetation cover mapping (Sharma *et al.*, 2005). The study of biological invasions has become one of the most dynamic and developing fields of ecology in recent decades because invasive species represent a threat to native biota and contribute to the decrease of native biological diversity (McNeely, 2001). Species introduced to the region where they have not been present before provide a unique opportunity for the study of ecological process (Williamson, 1996), such as competition with native taxa unbiased by common evolutionary history relationship with biota on other tropic levels (Keane and Crawley, 2002) and patterns of colonization's of new sites that occur with unprecedented dynamics (Williamson, 1996). It may be noted that all the alien/exotics species that enter a new area may not be invasive. It has been reported by a number of researchers that the invasion of plant species in the new environments is triggered by human induced habitat fragmentation, land degradation, forest degradation, land use and land cover changes, fire regimes and other kinds of anthropogenic stresses that impact natural ecosystems. The effect of invasive alien species on the distribution, abundance and population dynamics of native plant species in natural ecosystems, hydrology, and soil biology of plant invasion have been only scanty. Researches on weed biology have been conducted at some other universities and research organization in India, but the plant invasion perspective has been missing in most of these studies (Tripathi 2009). Therefore, the present study is an attempt to (i) ecological assessment of invasive species and (ii) study on physical and chemical properties of soil.

MATERIAL AND METHODS

The present study was carried out in Alaknanda valley, covering four districts of Uttarakhand, i.e. Chamoli, Rudraprayag, Tehri, and Pauri in Uttarakhand state of India (Figure 7.1). The study area was located between 30°33.812′ to 30°8′45.68″N latitude and 79°34.408′ to 78°35′15.22″E longitude with 460 to 2000m elevation range. The climate of the study area is of monsoon type and can be divisible in three different seasons i.e., summer, winter and rainy.

The phyto-sociological study was carried in five invasive species by using 2 × 2m Quadrate. Total 25 sites were selected and at each site four randomly placed quadrates were used. The vegetation data were quantitatively analyzed for frequency, density, abundance and A/F ratio by using the following standard formula. To investigate the pattern of species invasiveness along the altitudinal gradients, species density was regressed with altitude soil temperature, soil pH, water holding capacity and light intensity of habitat and trend lines were drawn. Soil sample collection of the habitat i.e. *Lantana camara, Parthinium hysterophorus, Eupatorium adenophorum, Ageratum conyzoides,* and *Xanthium strumarium* species were collected from each study site. A total of four samples were collected randomly from each site, thus a total of 100 samples were collected from all the 25 sites. The samples were placed in clean air tight polythene bags and were marked site-wise properly. The soil characteristics of each site were analyzed for physical and chemical properties. In water holding capacity (%), weight of empty crucibles (without soil) were recorded and then 20 gm of air dry soil samples were placed in Crucibles, thereafter samples were placed in a water tray for 24 hours to absorb the water. The samples were again weighed and the water holding capacity was calculated as:

For soil pH twenty gm soil was placed in the beaker with 50 ml. distilled water (1:2:5 ratio) and stirred for 5 minutes then allowed to stand for 2-3 hours. Thereafter, the pH of soil was determined directly with the help of control dynamics digital pH meter. Describe the geographical status of invasive species in Uttarakhand Himalaya, geographical parameters like latitude and altitude were recorded. In environmental status light intensity of both over story and understory cover were measured by lux meter at 10× and 100× for each quadrate. Soil temperature of each quadrate was also measured using digital soil meter.

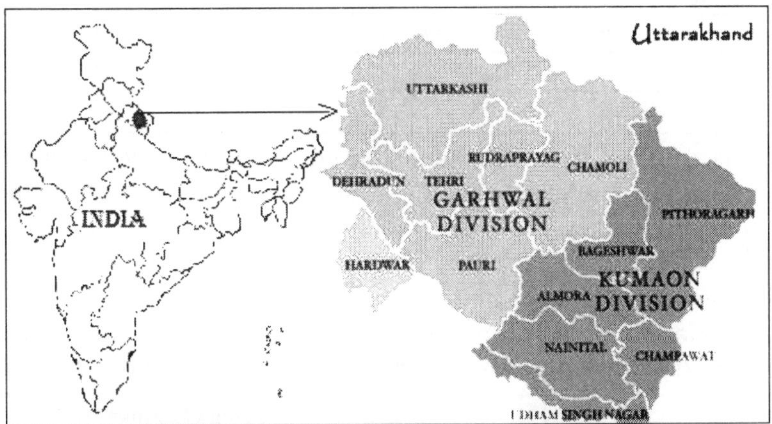

Fig. 7.1: Location Map of the Study Area in Alaknanda Valley, Uttarakhand, India

RESULTS

In Alaknanda valley, the five most common and abundant invasive species were found, i.e. *Lantana camara, Parthinium hysterophorus, Eupatorium adenophorum, Ageratum conyzoides,* and *Xanthium strumarium*. The most frequent and dominating invasive species was *Eupatorium adnophorum* with average density of 40.36 and least dominate species was *Xanthium strumarium* (Table 7.1).

Table 7.1: Average density, frequency, abundance and A/F ratio of invasive species in Alaknanda Valley, Uttarakhand, India (n = 100)

Species	Phytosociological Parameters			
	Density	Frequency	Abundance	A/F Ratio
Lantana camara	35.64	82	37	0.42
Parthenium hysterophorus	32.14	85	33	0.39
Eupatorium adnophorum	40.36	95	41	0.45
Ageratum conyzoids	30.29	87	31	0.34
Xanthium strumarium	1.35	12	3.4	0.10

Results revealed that invasion of *Eupatorium adnophorum* was more in higher and inner Himalayan region (Joshimath to Karnprayag) as compare to other invasive species. The most frequent invasive species in lower valley region (Karnprayag to Devprayag) were *Lantana camara, Parthenium hysterophorus, Eupatorium adnophorum* and *Ageratum conyzoids* (Table 7.2).

Table 7.2: Variation in average frequency of invasive species along the geographical location in Alaknanda Valley, Uttarakhand, India

Species	Variation in Average Frequency		
	Joshimath to Karnprayag	Karnprayag to Kirtinagar	Kirtinagar to Devprayag
Lantana camara	35.7	100	100
Parthenium hysterophorus	50	100	96.4
Eupatorium adnophorum	92.9	100	89.3
Ageratum conyzoids	57.1	97.7	100
Xanthium strumarium	0	15.9	17.9

The density of *Lantana camara, Parthenium hysterophorus, Ageratum conyzoids* and *Xanthium strumarium* shown a negative trends while the *Eupatorium adnophorum* shown a positive trends with increase in altitude (Figure 7.2).

Similar reverse pattern of trends were observed with variations in soil temperature of the habitat. *Eupatorium adnophorum* density decreased as soil temperature increases, while the density of *Lantana camara, Parthenium hysterophorus, Ageratum conyzoids* and *Xanthium strumarium* increased with high soil temperature (Figure 7.3).

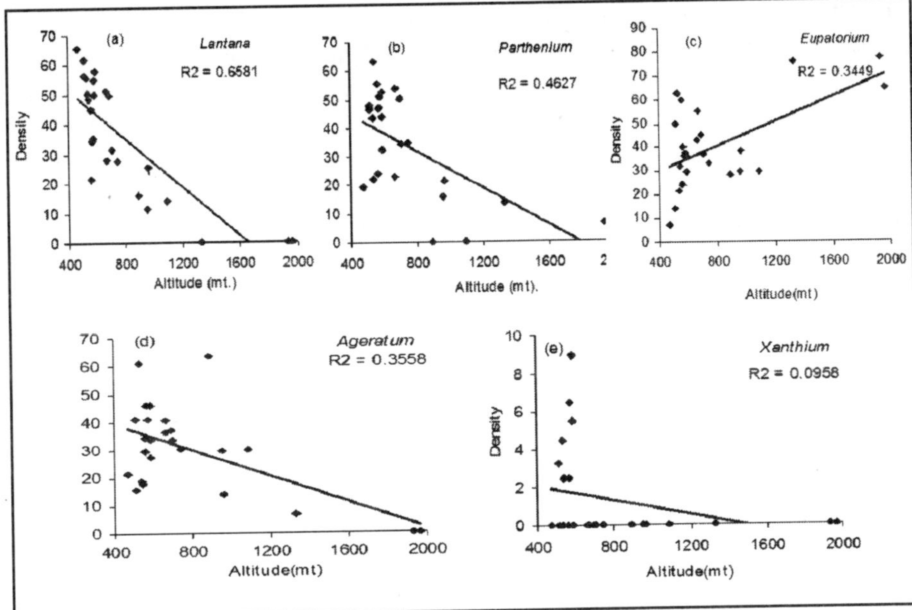

Fig. 7.2: Trends of Plant Density with Altitudinal Variation for (a) *Lantana camara, (b) Parthinium hysterophorus,(c) Eupatorium adenophorum,(d) Ageratum conyzoides,* (e) *strumarium strumarium*

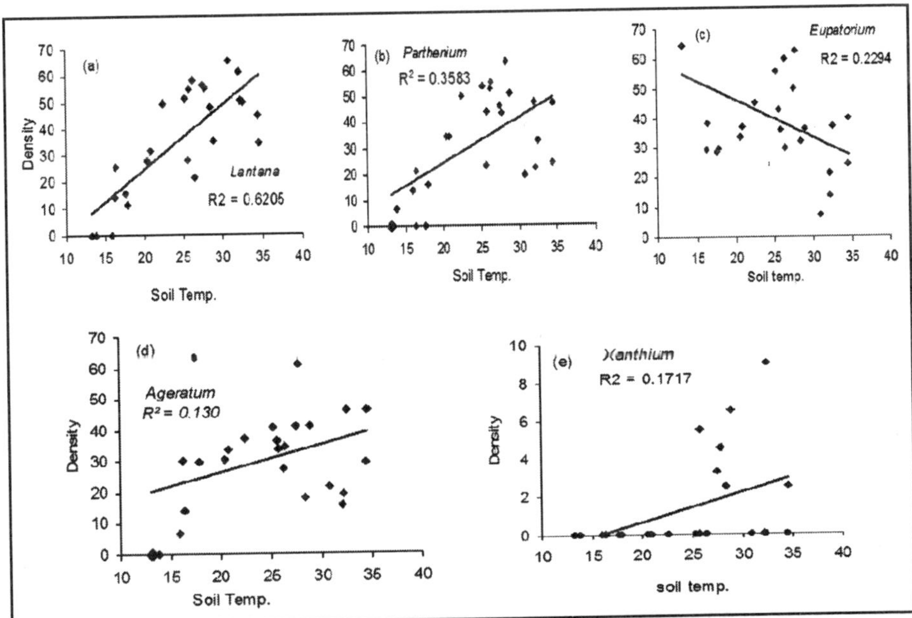

Fig. 7.3: Trends of Plant Density with Variation in Soil Temperature for (a) *Lantana camara,(b) Parthinium hysterophorus,(c) Eupatorium adenophorum,(d) Ageratum conyzoides,* (e) *Xanthium strumarium*

Thus, these four species were showing positive trend with soil temperature. Figure 7.4 revealed that soil pH had no considerable effect on distribution of *Eupatorium adnophorum* and *Lantana camara*. The R square values for these two species were found below 0.0002, which also confirmed that there was no trend of species distribution with variation of soil pH. *Parthenium hysterophorus, Ageratum conyzoids* and *Xanthium strumarium* were showing positive correlation with soil pH. As the soil pH increased their density was also increased (Figure 7.4).

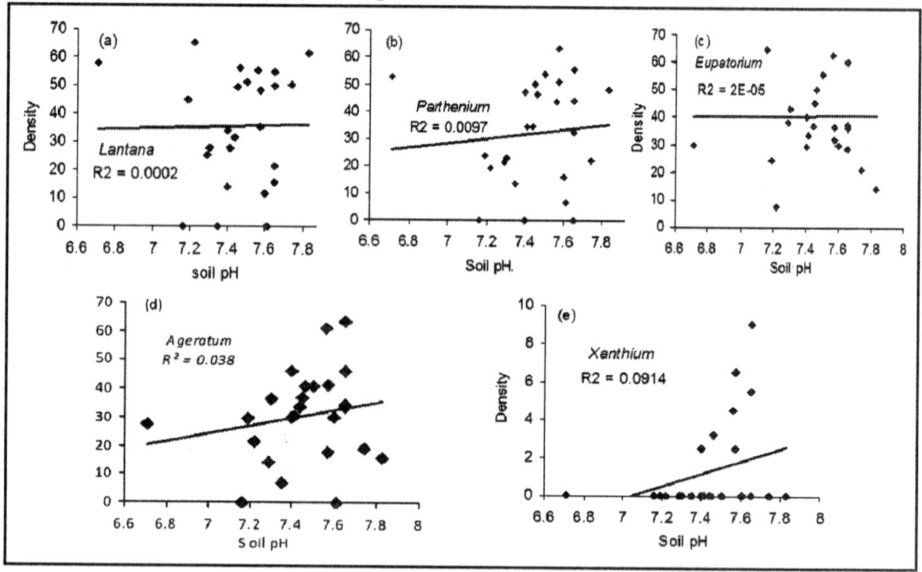

Fig. 7.4: Trends of Plant Density with Variation in Soil pH for (a) *Lantana camara,* (b) *Parthinium hysterophorus,* (c) *Eupatorium adenophorum,* (d) *Ageratum conyzoides,* (e) *Xanthium strumarium*

The variation in soil water holding capacity revealed that density of *Parthenium hysterophorus, Eupatorium adnophorum, Ageratum conyzoids, Xanthium strumarium* had increased with higher water holding capacity of soil. The density of *Lantana camara* was decreased as water holding capacity increased (Figure 7.5).

Lantana camara increased was showing a positive trend with increase in light intensity both at over and under story cover. No trends of light intensity on density of *Ageratum conyzoids* and *Eupatorium adnophorum* were seen of *Parthenium hysterophorus* and *Xanthium strumarium were* showing a contradictory trend with light intensity over and under story cover (Figure 7.6).

DISCUSSION

During the present studies, we tried to evaluate the status of invasive plant species in Alaknanda Valley and recorded phyto-sociological, geographical and edaphical characters of invasive species inhibited the valley.

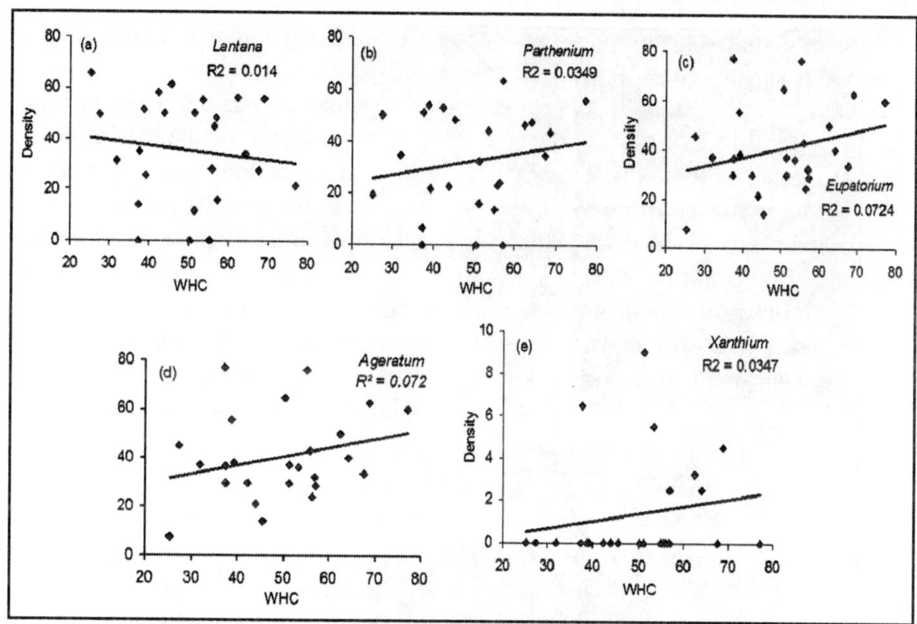

Fig. 7.5: Trends of Plant Density with Variation in Soil Water holding Capacity for (a) *Lantana camara,* (b) *Parthinium hysterophorus,* (c) *Eupatorium adenophorum,* (d) *Ageratum conyzoides,* (e) *Xanthium strumarium*

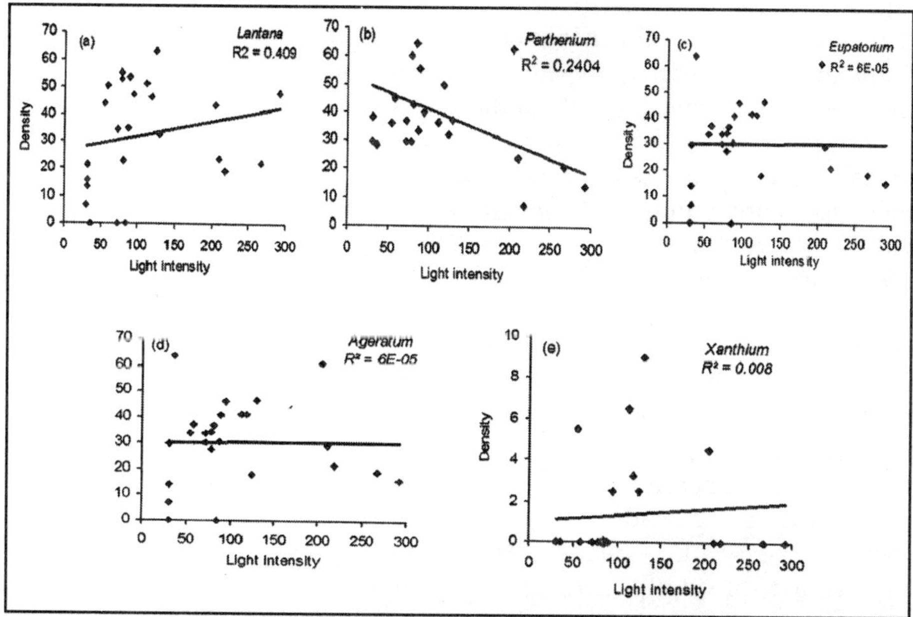

Fig. 7.6: Trends of Plant Density with Variation in Light Intensity at 100 x over Story Cover for (a) *Lantana camara,* (b) *Parthinium hysterophorus,* (c) *Eupatorium adenophorum,* (d) *Ageratum conyzoides,* (e) *Xanthium strumarium*

Fig. 7.7: Reported Invasive Plant Species in the Study Area, Uttarakhand, India

It was noticed that the Alaknanda Valley invaded by *Lantana camara, Parthinium hysterophorus, Eupatorium adenophorum, Ageratum conyzoides,* and *Xanthium strumarium.* Majority of these species are now naturalized in newly exposed or disturbed areas. Considering the overall distribution pattern of invasive species in whole Alaknanda valley. *Eupatorium adnophorum* found most dominating and *Xanthium strumarium* least dominant species in whole valley. However, *Lantana camara, Parthinium hysterophorus, Eupatorium adenophorum,* and *Ageratum conyzoides* were dominated the warmer place of the valley. The relation between edaphic and geographical parameters with species dominance has been discussed in this report.

An invasive species is a non-native species whose introduction does or is likely to cause economic or environmental harm or harm to human, animal, or plant health. The US National Invasive Species Management Plan indicates that non-native species known to cause or likely to cause negative impacts and that do not provide an equivalent or greater benefit to society. In the technical sense, the term 'invasion' simply denotes the uncontrolled or unintended spread of an organism outside its native range with no specific reference about the environmental or economic consequences of such spread or their relationships to possible societal benefits. However, the policy context and subsequent management decisions necessitate narrowing what is meant and what is not meant by the term invasive species. Essentially, we are clarifying what is meant and not meant by comparing negative effects caused by a non-native organism to its potential societal benefits (ISAC, 2006).

Uttarakhand state is located in mountain region of Himalayas, known for its sensitivity towards the earthquake and other natural disaster. This region is also fall under very high anthropogenic pressure due to religious pilgrimage and other touristic activities, which facilitate transportation and dispersal of alien invasive species in this region. The landslides, road and dam-construction activities are exposing the natural sites and disturbing to the local vegetation. These natural and manmade disturbances are ultimately facilitating the establishment of alien invasive species in remote areas. During the present studies, it was noticed that the entire Alaknanda Valley has been invaded by *Lantana camara, Parthinium hysterophorus, Eupatorium adenophorum, Ageratum conyzoides,* and *Xanthium strumarium.* Majority of these species are now naturalized in newly exposed or disturbed areas of Alaknanda Valley. Evaluating the whole Alaknanda Valley for the status of invasive species, it is found that *Eupatorium adnophorum* dominates with average density of 40.36 and A/F rate of 0.4. The least dominating species in this valley is *Xanthium.* The possible reason of the dominance of *Eupatorium adnophorum* in Alaknanda Valley may be its perennial weedy nature, which reproduces by both seeds and vegetative means (Liu *et al.,* 1995) and its ability to persist in soil to make a soil seed bank (Phartyal *et al.,* 2009). The results also indicates that invasion of *Eupatorium adnophorum* is more noticed in higher and inner Himalayan region (Joshimath to Karnprayag) as compare to other four invasive species included in the study. The possible explanation for this is the ability of *Eupatorium adnophorum* to tolerate low temperature. The most frequent invasive species in lower valley region (Karnprayag to Devprayag) are *Lantana camara, Parthenium hysterophorus, Eupatorium adnophorum* and *Ageratum conyzoids,* which shows a positive trends with increase in soil temperature. It has been reported that *Lantana camara* doesn't grow at ambient temperatures below 5°C (Sankaran, 2010). Similar trend is also noticed in present study. The population of *Lantana camara* deceases as altitude increase in Alaknanda Valley. For the seeds of *Ageratum* the optimum germination temperature ranges from 20 to 25°C (Sauerborn and Koch, 1988), which is another reason for low abundance of *Ageratum* in inner and higher Himalayan region of Alaknanda Valley.

The soil pH did not show any distribution trend of *Eupatorium adnophorum* and *Lantana camara,* which indicates that these species may survive both in acidic and basic soil. *Parthenium hysterophorus, Ageratum conyzoids* and *Xanthium strumarium* were showing positive correlation with soil pH. As the soil pH increased their density was also increased. It reflects that these species prefer more basic soil then acidic soil. The variation in soil water holding capacity revealed that density of *Parthenium hysterophorus, Ageratum conyzoids,*

Xanthium strumarium and *Eupatorium adnophorum* had increased with higher water holding capacity of soil. The density of *Lantana camara* was decreased as water holding capacity decreased. The decrease in density of *Lantana camara* with decease in water holding capacity may be attributing by its perennial nature and ability to grow and survive in forest gap with high light intensity. *Lantana camara* was showing a positive trend with increase in light intensity both at over and under canopy. Sankaran (2010) also reported that *Lantana camara* generally grows best in open, un-shaded conditions such as wastelands, in agricultural areas, grasslands, riparian zones, scrub/shrub lands, urban areas, wetlands and forests recovering from fire or logging. *Lantana camara* cannot survive under dense, intact canopies of taller native forest species. The plant is susceptible to frosts and low temperatures, saline soils, boggy or hydromorphic soils, low rainfall, coralline soils with poor water-holding capacities and high incidence of tropical hurricanes (Sankaran, 2010). No trends of light intensity on density of *Ageratum conyzoids* and *Eupatorium adnophorum* were seen. *Parthenium hysterophorus, Xanthium strumarium* showing contradictery trends with light intensity at over and under story cover. Elsewhere, a differential response of light intensity has also been reported in *Prunus serotina* (a highly invasive species), which needs light at the seedling stage and become shade plant at sapling stage (Godefroid *et al.*, 2005). This differential response may facilitate the invasion strategy of these species.

CONCLUSION

The overall analysis indicates that invasive species rich communities are not only being reduced in area but they are also becoming species poor and less diverse due to rapid deforestation and forest fragmentation. The community organization is also changing in response to increased anthropogenic disturbance. Serious measures are needed to preserve and conserve whatever intact forest is left in the study area so that this alarming trend of disappearance of species rich communities is halted.

REFERENCES

Alvarez ME and Cushman JH (2002). Community Level Consequences of a Plant Invasion. Effects on Three Habitats in California. Ecol App 12: 1434-1444.

Byers JE, Reichard S, Randall JM, Parker IM, Smith CS, Londale WM, Atkinson IAE, Seastedt TR, Williomson MB and Chornesky E (2002). Directing Research to Reduce the Impact of Non-indigenous Species. Cons Biol 116: 630-640.

Dekker J and Comstock G (1992). Ethical, Environmental and Ecological Consideration in the Release of Herbicide Resistant Crops. Agric Human Values 9: 31-44.

Enserink M (1999). Biological Invaders Sweep in ESA B. 285: 1834-1836.

Ewel J, Odowd DJ, Bergeson J, Daehlar CC, Antonio CM, Diego-Gomez L, Gordon DR, Hoobs RJ, Holt A and Hoper KR (1999). Deliberate Introduction of Species: Research Needs. Bio Science 49, 619-630.

Godefroid S, Phartyal SS, Weyembergh G and Koedam N (2005). Ecological Factors Controlling the Abundance of Non-native Invasive Black Cherry (*Prunus serotina*) in Deciduous Forest Understory in Belgium. Forest Ecology and Management 210: 91-105.

ISAC-NISC (2006). Invasive Definition Clarification and Guidance White Paper. Submitted by the Definitions Subcommittee of the Invasive Species Advisory Committee (ISAC) of the National Invasive Species Council (NISC).

Joshi C, Lieu JD and Dursen ICV (2004). Remote Sensing and GIS Applications for Mapping and Spatial Modeling of Invasive Species. In: ISPRS 2004: Proceedings of the XXth ISPRS Congress: Geoimagery Bridging Continents, held at Istanbul, Turkey. Comm. VII, 669-677.

Sankaran KV (2010). *Lantana camara.* Invasive Pest Fact Sheet. Asia-Pacific Forest Invasive Species Network. http://www.fao.org/forestry/13375-1-0.pdf (visited August 3, 2010).

Keane RM and Crawley MJ (2002). Exotic Plant Invasions of and the Enemy Release Hypothesis. Trends Ecol 17: 164-170.

Knops JMH, Griffin JR and Royalty AC (1995). Introduction and Native Plants of the Hasting Reservation, Central Costal California, a Compression. Biol Conserve 71: 115-123.

Liu LH, Xie SC and Zhang JH (1985). Distribution, Harmfulness of Pamakani (*Eupatorium adenophorium*) and Discussion on the Prevention Strategies. Acta Ecological Sciences 5, 1-6 (in Chinese with English abstract).

Love A, Babu S and Babu CR (2009). Management of Lantana, an Invasive Alien Weed, in Forest Ecosystems of India. Current Science 97: 3.

McNeely JA (2001). An Introduction to Human Dimensions of Invasive Alien Species, ISSG; www.issg.org. (Accessed April 2010).

Mooney HA, Hamurg SP and Drake JA (1986). The Invasion of Plant and Animals into California In: H.A. Mooney (ed): Ecology of Biological Invasion of North America and Hawaii. Springerverlag. New York, 250-272.

Mooney HA and Hobbs RJ (2000). Invasive Species in a Changing World. Island Press Washings tans DC.

Phartyal SS, Godefroid S and Koedam N. (2009). Seed Development and Germination Ecophysiology of the Invasive Tree Prunus Serotina (Rosaceae) in a Temperate Forest in Western Europe. Plant Ecol. 204: 285-294.

Randall JM and Jane M (1997). Invasive Plants: Weeds of the Global Garden. Brooklyn Botanic Garden, Brooklyn, New York.

Robinson GR, Yurlina ME and Handel SN (1994). A Sanctuary Change in Staten Island Ecological Correlates of Species Losses and Invasion. Bull Torrey Bot Club 121: 119-129.

Sauerborn J and Kock W (1988). Untersuchungen zur Keimungsbiologie von sechs tropischen Segetalaten. Weed Res. 28(1): 47-52.

Sharma GP and Singh JS (2005). Lantana Invension: An Overview. Weed Biology Manage 5: 157-165.

Tripathi RS (2009). Alien Plant Invasion: A Hot Ecological Issue. Environews-news Letter of ISEB India 15:3.

Vitousek PMD, Antonio CM, Loope LL and Westbrooks R (1996). Biological Invasion as a Global Environment Change. Am. Sci. 84; 468-478.

Wilcove DS and Chen LY (1998). Management Costs for Endangered Species. Conservation Biology 12: 1405-1407.

Williamson M (1996). Biological Invasion. London, Chapman and Hall.

Woods KD (1997). Community Response to Plant Invasion, Luken, J.O. (ed): Assessment and Management of Plant Invasion. Ecol, App 112: 1434-1444.

Yaduraju NT, Bhowmik PC and Kushwaha S (2000). The Potential Threat of Alien Weeds to Agriculture and Environment In: Jha, P.K. and Karmacharya, S.B., (Ed): Environment and Agriculture: At the Crossroad of the New Millennium, 2000 Ecology Society, (ECOS) Katmandu, Nepal, 229-234.

Pages: 129-155

MICROBIOLOGICAL AND PHARMACOLOGICAL ASPECTS OF BIODIVERSITY

Edited by: Dr. Pankaj Sharma; Dr. Neha Gautam Sharma & Dr. Pankaj Sharma

ISBN: 978-93-5056-878-1

Edition: 2017

Published by: Discovery Publishing House Pvt. Ltd., New Delhi (India)

Anti-nutritional Factors and their Remedial Measures in Plant based Foods
A Review

Nivedita Sharma* and Shweta Handa

ABSTRACT

Dietary quality is an important limiting factor to adequate nutrition in many resource-poor settings. Anti nutrients and toxins are the main obstacles in the intake of major nutrients from food. The amount of secondary plant factors that they contain vary widely in quantity and structure and their effects after consumption on living beings. Considering the varied harmful effects exerted by ANF, target upon elimination ofphytate, tannins, polyphenols, protease inhibitors and mycotoxins etc. Simple methods based on post harvest technology, treatment with low-cost chemical, biological treatments utility of management and biodegradation of secondary plant factors are presented as means of alleviating detrimental effects of these secondary plant factors. These include thermal processing, mechanical processing, soaking, fermentation, and germination/malting. Genetic modifications are also gaining importance in removing antinutrients from food and feed stocks.

Keywords: Antinutrients, Toxins, Biological treatments, Genetic modifications

INTRODUCTION

Food is an elixir of life. It is usually of plant or animal origin, and contains essential nutrients, such as carbohydrates, fats, proteins, vitamins and minerals. The substance is ingested by the organism and assimilated by the organism's cells in an effort to produce energy, maintain life, or stimulate growth. Most food has its origin in plants. There are around 2,000 plant

*Microbiology Research Laboratory, Department of Basic Sciences, Dr. Y.S. Parmar University of Horticulture and Forestry, Nauni, Solan - 173 230 (H.P.) (India)

species which are cultivated for food, and many have several distinct cultivars. There is a wide distribution of biologically-active constituents throughout the plant kingdom, particularly in plants used as in human nutrition and animal feeding stuff (Igile, 1996). The knowledge that these compounds elicit both toxic and advantageous biological responses has given rise to several investigations in recent times as to their possible physiological implications in various biological systems (Igile, 1996). It is well known that plants generally contain antinutrients acquired from fertilizer and pesticides as well as several naturally-occurring chemicals (Igile, 1996). The anti nutritional factors (ANFs) may be defined as those substances generated in natural food by the normal metabolism of species and by different mechanisms (e.g., inactivation of some nutrients, diminution of the digestive process or metabolic utilization of the feed) which exert effects contrary to optimum nutrition.

Anti nutritional factors may occur naturally, such as glucosinolates in mustard and rapeseed protein products, trypsin inhibitors and hemagglutinins in legumes, tannins in legumes and cereals, phytates in cereals and oilseeds, and gossypol in cottonseed protein products. Some of these chemicals are known as "secondary metabolites" and they have been shown to be highly biologically active (Zenk, 1991). They include saponins, tannins, flavonoids, alkaloids, trypsin (protease) inhibitors, oxalates, phytates, haemagluttinins (lectins), cyanogenic glycosides, cardiac glycosides, coumarins and gossypol. The list is inexhaustible. Some of these plant chemicals have been shown to be deleterious to health or evidently advantageous to human and animal health if consumed at appropriate amounts (Kersten *et al.*, 1991; Sugano *et al.*, 1993). Most of these secondary metabolites elicit harmful biological responses, while on the other hand some are widely applied in nutrition and also as pharmacologically-active agents (Oakenfulland Sidhu, 1989; Soetan, 2008). The pharmacological and other beneficial effects of these anti-nutritional factors in plants have been reviewed by Soetan (2008). ANF presents in various foods, their possible harmful effects on health of consumers and different methods to combat their toxicity have been discussed in the present study.

PROPERTIES AND GENERAL CHARACTERISTICS OF SOME ANTI-NUTRITIONAL FACTORS AND TOXINS

Plant, fungi and bacteria produces secondary metabolites in their defence which generally act as antinutrients in food and feed. The structures of the antinutrients and their chemical properties, especially their heat labiality, dictate which physical processes will be most effective in their reduction or removal, thereby minimizing adverse biological effects. So it is important to study the general characteristics of these anti-nutrients so that it become easy to reduce these factors and make food and feed more nutritious. Some of the antinutrients of plant, fungul and bacterial origin on the bases of their molecular weight are listed in table 8.1.

Table 8.1: Some of the major anti nutritional factors and toxins

Low Molecular Weight ANF	Protein ANF and Toxins
β-ODAP (nonprotein amino acids), Lathyrogens	Allergens
Glucosinolates	α-Amylase inhibitors
Cyanogens	Lectins
Mycotoxins	Lipase inhibitors
Phytic acids	Protease inhibitors
Saponins	Viruses
Flatulence factors (α-galactosides, oligosaccharides, e.g., raffinose)	
Polyphenols & Tannins	Transmissible spongiform encelopethies (TSE)
Other: alkaloids, gossypol, oestrogenic factors, sinapins	

Phytic Acid

Phytic acid is widely distributed in commonly consumed foods. Phytate are the principal storage form of phosphorus and are particularly abundant in cereals and legumes (Reddy *et al.*, 1989). It is found in high concentrations in the seeds of grains, pulses and legumes, tubers and garden produce (Alabaster *et al.*, 1996). In cereals, approximately 1-2% weight of the seed is phytic acid, and it can even reach 3-6%.Referring to its location, 90% is found in maize germ, while in wheat and rice it isdistributed in larger proportions in the external covers inthe pericarp and in the aleurone layer (Alabaster *et al.*, 1996).

Phytic acid is myoinositol 1, 2, 3, 4, 5, 6-hexakisdihydrogen phosphate. It is a primary phosphate reserve in most seeds accounting for 60% to 90% of total phosphorous (Figure 8.2). Inositols with 4, 5 or 6 phosphate groups are common in the seeds of many of our grain legumes and can reachconcentrations higher than 10% of dry matter (Cheryan, 1989). Antinutrientphytic acid reduces the minerals and also act as powerful chelating agent reduces the bioavailability of divalent cations by the formation of insoluble complexes such as calcium, magnesium, zinc and iron (Lestienne *et al.*, 2005; Weaver and Khanna, 2002; Sandberg, 2002). These are the mobilizing secondary metabolic compounds which are thought to function as reserve nutrients (Reddy *et al.*, 1978).

Saponins

These are a diverse class of glycosides comprise a steroidal or triterpene aglycone linked to one, two or three saccharide chains of varying size complexity via ester and/or ether linkages (Figure 8.2). The most common sugar linked to an aglycone (or sapgenin) are galactose, arabinose, xylose and glucose. Saponin occurs in broad range of plants consumed in human diet. Legumes (soya, peas and beans), root crops (potato, yams, asparagus and alliums) as well as oats, sugar beet, tea and many medicinal herbs are the source of saponins.

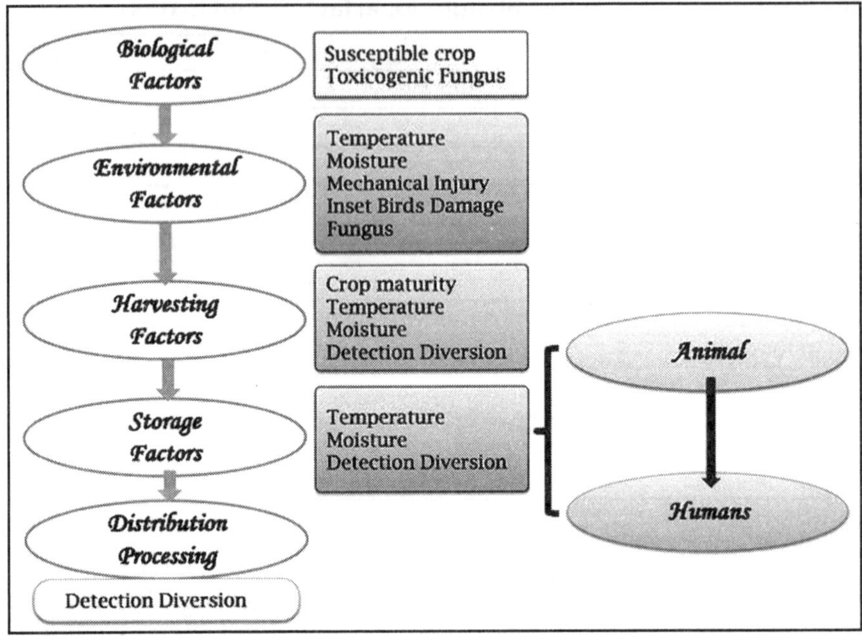

Fig. 8.1: Factors Affecting Mycotoxin Occurrence in the Food and Animal Feed Chains

Table 8.2 showing some major plant crops containing saponins. Saponins are characterized by bitter taste and foaming properties. Erythrocytes lyse in saponins solution and so these compounds are toxic when ingested intravenously.

Table 8.2: Saponin levels in some plant sources

Source	Saponins (% dry weight)
Soybeans (*Glycine max*)	5.6
Chickpea (*Cicerarientinum* L.)	3.6
Lucerne (*Medicagosativa*)	2.5
Lupine (*Lupinousangustifolius*)	1.5
Quinoa (*Chenopodium quinoa*)	0.02-0.04
Ginseng	0.5-3.0

Protease Inhibitors

Protease inhibitors are proteins of low molecular weight with generally inhibit protein forming stable complexes with digestive enzyme, irreversibly inhibiting their activity. The presence of protease inhibitors in food decreases the apparent nutritional quality of proteins in the diet by affecting the ability of body digestive enzymes to degrade dietary protein, and thus limiting the intake of amino acids needed to construct new proteins (Krupa, 2008). These protease inhibitors are characterised in various food crops, legumes, beans, cereal etc. The major protease inhibitors of plant origin are trypsin inhibitors.

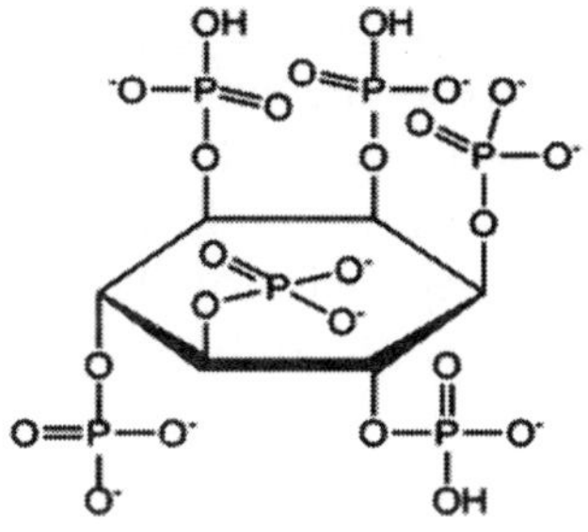

Phytic Acid

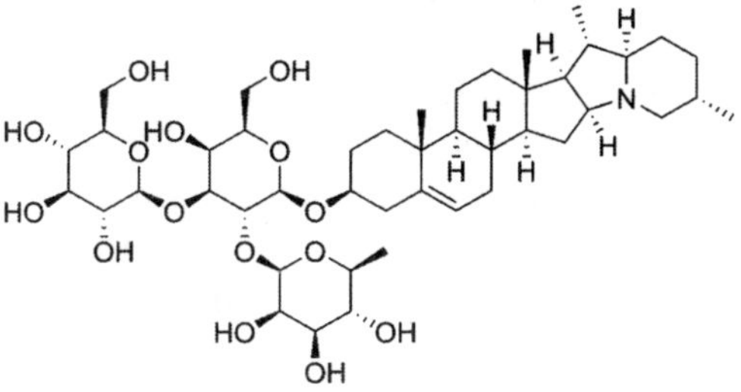

Saponin

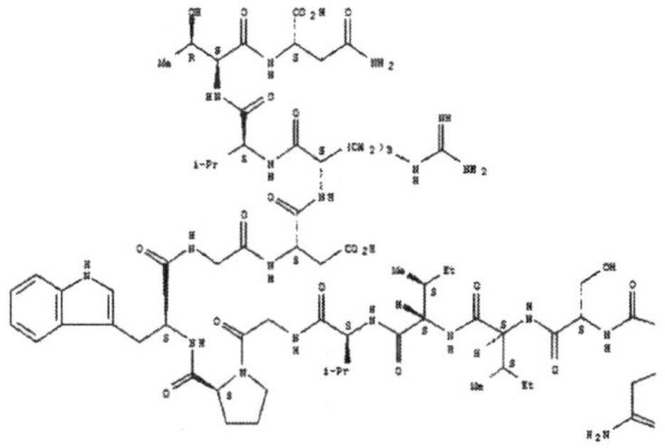

Lathyrogens

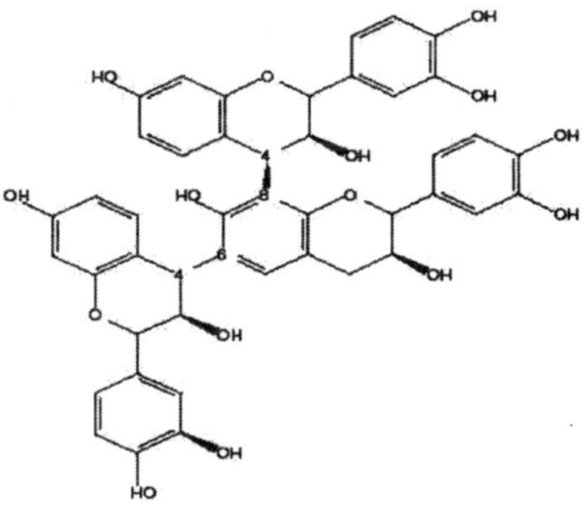

Tannins

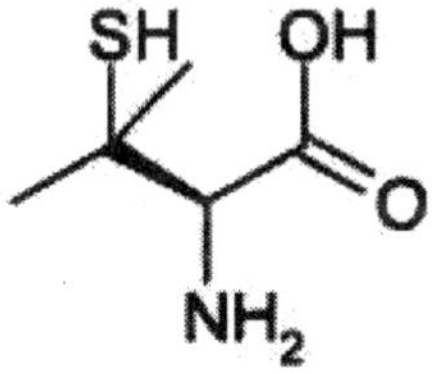

Polyphenols

Fig. 8.2: Chemical Structure of Different Major Food Anti-nutrients

Other than protease inhibitors, lipase and α-amylase inhibitors are also present. They inhibit lipid formation and amylase activity respectively. Lipase inhibitors interfere with enzymes, such as human pancreatic lipase, that catalyze the hydrolysis of some lipids, including fats.

Amylase inhibitors prevent the action of enzymes that break the glycosidic bonds of starches and other complex carbohydrates, preventing the release of simple sugars and absorption by the body. Amylase inhibitors, like lipase inhibitors, have been used as a diet aide and obesity treatment. Amylase inhibitors are present in many types of beans; commercially available amylase inhibitors are extracted from white kidney beans (Preuss, 2009).

Polyphenols and Tannins

These are secondary plant metabolites distributed ubiquitously within plant foods (Vegetables, cereals, legumes, fruits, and nuts) and beverages (tea, wine, cocoa) (Figure 8.1 and Table 8.3). Oxidation products of phenolic compounds are known to be involved in plant defence against insects, pests, and invading pathogens including bacteria, fungi and viruses. Polyphenols also resulted in deterioration of flavour, color and nutritional quality of food by undergoing enzyme catalyzing browning reaction.Thehigh polyphenole content in plant food grains (Saharan *et al.*, 2001) may also adversely affect the mineralavailability.

Tannin is a polyphenolic compound that binds to and precipitates proteins and various other organic compounds including amino acids and alkaloids. They are widely distributed in many species of plants, where they play a role in protection from predation, perhaps also as pesticides, and plant growth regulation (Figure 8.1). Sorghum, cereal grains and pulsesare rich in minerals content but their nutritional quality is dictated by chemical composition and presence of considerable amount of anti-nutritional factors such as polyphenols, tannins, phyticacid and trypsin inhibiters (Elsheikh *et al.*, 2000). Although phenolic and polyphenolic compounds constitute an important class of secondary metabolites that act as free radical scavengers and inhibitors of LDL (low density lipoprotein), cholesterol oxidation and DNA breakage (Shahidi, 2004) but complex is formed with minerals which reduce the bioavailability of minerals. Polyphenols render iron and zincin cereal based foods poorly bioavailable that reduce their intestinal absorption, resulting inhigh rates of iron and zinc deficiency especially in infant, children and women of child bearing age (Sandsteed, 2000). Phenolic compounds such as lignans, alk(en)ylresorcinols and phenolic acids are potential bioactive compounds due to their antimicrobial, antioxidative and anticarcinogenic effects (Pratt, 1992). Folates are cofactors in many enzymatic reactions and deficiency increases the risk of mutations and DNA breakdown (which may lead to cancers). Furthermore, sufficient intake of folate lowers elevated level of serumhomocysteine, which is a risk factor for coronary heart disease (Brouwer *et al.*, 1999).

Table 8.3: Polyphenolic content of different plant foods and beverages

	Mg/100g dry matter	
Food	Cereals	22-102.60
	Legumes	34-1710
	Nuts	0.04-38
	Vegetables	6-2025 (mg/fresh matter)
	Fruits	2-1200 (mg/fresh matter)
Beverages	Tea	150-210 (mg/200ml)
	Red wine	1000-4000 (mg/L)
	White wine	200-300 (mg/L)

Mycotoxins

Mycotoxins are chemically and biologically active secondary metabolites produce by fungal (mold) growth in cereals, nuts, fruits and vegetables (Sinha and Sinha, 1991). The Food and Agriculture Organization has estimated that at least 25% of the world's food crops are affected by mycotoxins annually. They consist of Aflatoxin, produced by fungus *Aspergillus flavus*and *Aspergillus parasiticus*, Ochratoxins produced by *Aspergillus ochraceous* and *Penicilliumverrucosum* fungi (Khoury and Atoui, 2010, Rai and Ajit, 2010; Husain and Brasel, 2001) and several others (Zearalenone, Trichothecenes, Fumonisins, and the Ergot Alkaloids) (Table 8.4). Four different aflatoxins, B1, B2, G1 and G2 have been identified, with B1 being the most toxic, carcinogenic and prevalent. Aflatoxins taken in the diet are further converted to the still harmful aflatoxins M1 and M2 that are secreted in dairy products. The complex process of enzymology and molecular biology of aflatoxin biosynthesis has been well documented (Husain and Brasel, 2001; Delage *et al.*, 2003; Jayaramachandran *et al.*, 2013). Ochratoxin is a mycotoxin often referred to as Ochratoxin A – OTA (Makun *et al.*, 2007). Aflatoxin contamination of food results in some toxic effects such as liver cancer and immuno suppression in various animals and humans (Reddy *et al.*, 2009).The major food crops i.e., wheat, coffee, cotton, soybeans, barley, sunflower, groundnuts, cocoa and dairy products are highly susceptible to fungal contamination and mycotoxin production. Therefore, food organisation has constituted some regulatory bodies to decide mycotoxins levels for the safe consumption of these crops. The threshold levels of different mycotoxins for food safety have been devised beyond which food may not be allowed to be sold or consumed (Table 8.4).

Table 8.4: Worldwide permissible limits of different mycotoxins in food

Mycotoxins	Permissible Limits in Foods
Aflatoxins (Food)	4.00 μg/kg
Aflatoxins (Milk)	0.05 μg/kg
Aflatoxins (Feed for dairy)	20.0 μg/kg
Aflatoxins B1 (Food)	2.00 μg/kg
Patulin	50.0 μg/kg
Ochratoxin A	5.00 μg/kg
Zearalenone	1000 μg/kg
Deoxynivelenol	750 μg/kg
Fumonisins	1000 μg/kg

Major factors affecting mycotoxins occurrence in food are shown in figure 8.1. The diverse climatic conditions with respect to altitude, moisture, temperature and relative humidity provide variation in their infestation with molds. Apart from these, frequent and heavy rainfall and floods, particularly near harvest, in coastal areas in eastern,southern, and western regions of the country wet the crop and make panicles more prone to invasion by filamentous fungi and bacteria leading to the secretion of many mycotoxins. (Makun *et al.*, 2007; Reddy *et al.*, 2005, 2009).

Preharvest prevention of aflatoxin formation is difficult; therefore, aflatoxinsin foods and feeds are considered a continuous risk. There is a need to manage the risks associated with aflatoxin contamination before using these products as animal feed or human food. Thus, several methods for decontamination and post harvest control have been reported (Lopez-Garciaand Park, 1998).

Aflatoxins have become generally accepted to be poisonous and deleterious, and are now widely regulated in foods. In the U.S., the Food and Drug Administration (FDA) regulates feed and food containing aflatoxins at regulatory levels of 20 ppb of AFB1 for human foods and selected animal feed. Zearalenone (ZEN) is produced by *Fusarium graminearum* and *F. sprotrichoides* in the field and during storage of commodities such as corn, barley, pig feeds, silage, sorghum, and hay. Chemically, zearalenone is (R,S)-2, 4-dihydroxy-6-(62 -(62 -oxo-102 -hydroxy-1-undecenyl) -benzoic acid unlactone (Cordier *et al.*, 1990).

Table 8.5: Mycotoxigenicmolds of significance in foods and their mycotoxins (Moss, 1999; Kawashima *et al.*, 2002)

Mold	Mycotoxins
Aspergillus spp.	Aflatoxins (B1, B2, G1, G2, M1)
A. flavus, A.parasiticus, and *A. nomius*	Cyclopiazonic acid
A. flavus, A. parasiticus, and *A. nidulans*	Sterigmatocystin
A. versicolor	Tricothecenes: T2, HT-2
Fusarium sp.	Nivalenol (NIV)
F. graminearum, F. culmorum, and F. cerealis	Deoxynivalenol (DON)
F. poae, F. moliniforme and F. proliferatum	Fumanosins
*Penicillium*and *Aspergillus spp.*	Patulin
P. expansum and *P. crustosum*	Penitrem A
P. ochraceus, P. verrucosum, A. carbonarius, and *A. ochraceus*	Ochratoxin A
P. roqueforti and *P. citranum*	Citrinin and roquefortine

Lathyrogens

Lathyrogens are β-N-oxalyl-L-α, β-diaminopropionic acid, a naturally occurring amino acid, possesses potent neurotoxic activity and has been shown to be responsible for outbreaks of neurolathyrism. This antinutrient is mainly present in chickling vetch or grass pea (*Lathyrussativus*) a type of legume commonly grown for human consumption. This occurs naturally as two isomeric forms with the α-form being approximately 5% of the total. Level of this neurotoxin varied between 1.25 g/kg with a narrower range of 5 g/kg to 8 g/kg in seed. β-ODAP is biosynthesized during the ripening of the seed and is further increased during germination.

Positive Effects of Anti-nutritional Factors in Humannutrition

The anti-nutritional factors found to have effect on gastrointestinal tract and affect the microflora count of the intestine by promoting the growth of beneficial bacterias. *Lupinuscampestris* seed found to have anti-mutagenic activity and prevents the mutagenic process involved in development of cancer. Anti-nutritional factors decreases levels of heat shock protein 70 and 90 in gut epithelial cells after exposure to plant lectins. Lectins present in legumes assessed to act as a mucosal adjuvant. Beneficial outcome in hypercholesterolemia after intake of heat treated chickpea in rats have been observed (Price *et al.*, 1987; Jansman *et al.* 1998; Friedman, 2001; Young, 2011).

Negative Effects of Anti-nutritional Factors in Human Nutrition

Low toxic substances in legumes produce serious pathological conditions. They are the factors in kesari dhal which cause lathyrism and haemolytic factor in *Viciafaba* associated with disease favism.

Lathyrism: Lathyrism is a paralytic disease affecting the lower limbs. The incidence of the disease is higher in males than females and recovery from the condition does not usually occur. The disease has been known since early times and there is reference to it in early Indian medical writing. Serious outbreak of lathyrism has occurred in this country quite a few times. The disease has been associated with consumption of kesari dhal and is commonly noticed in poor families who regularly eat considerable quantity of the dhal. However, lathyrism develops only when the consumption of dhal is high (300 g daily) and the diet does not contain adequate quantities of cereals and is used for long time (six months or more). In lathyrism, the toxic substance interfaces with the formation of normal collagen fibre in the connective tissue. The disease can be prevented by ensuring reasonable balance between kesari dhal and other material and its replacement by other pulses where practicable. Lathyrogens i.e. Beta N oxayl, Beta diamino propionic acid (BOAA), a naturally occurring amino acids, possess potent neurotoxic activity and has been shown to be responsible for outbreaks of neurolathyrism following consumption of *Lathyrussativus*. BOAA occurs naturally as two isomeric forms with the Beta N oxayl L form being approximately 5% of the total. The level of BOAA in dry seeds varies considerably according to genetic factors and environmental conditions. *Lathyrussativus* grown in nutrient solution that are zinc deficient or rich in ferrous iron, produced seeds with elevated levels of BOAA (Burbano,1999).

Favism: Favism is a disease characterized by haemolytic anaemia which affects certain individuals following the ingestion of fresh or cooked broad beans. The victims suffer from an inherited biochemical abnormality which affects the metabolism of glutathione in red blood cellsand is the result of decreased activity of the enzymesglucose-6-phospate dehydrogenase. In person with his abnormality, the red cells are more prone to injury and destruction by certain drugs, such as sulphonamide and this raises complications in the treatment of infectious disease (Dmello *et al.*, 1991).

ANALYTICAL TECHNIQUES FOR THE DETECTION OF ANTI-NUTRIENTS AND TOXINS

Several methods are used for the quantitative determination of anti-nutritional factors in foods based on reports by different authors examples trypsin inhibitor activities are determined according to Liener (1979); haemagglutinatin-Jaffe (1979); cyanogenic glucosides (HCN)-Bradbury *et al* (1999); oxalates-Fasset, (1996); phytates-Maga (1983); tannin-Dawra *et al.* (1988); saponins-Brunner (1984); and alkaloids-Henry (1973). There are other new methods for quantification of antinutritional factors due to recent advances in the nutritional sciences. Some common analytical methods to detect toxins in foods are enlisted in Table 8.6.

Table 8.6: Annalytical methods to detect mycotoxins

Organism	Toxin	Assay Method	References
Aspergillus spp.	Aflatoxins	HPLC	
		ELISA	
		Tandem mass spectrometry (MS/MS)	Kotretsou and Koutsodimou, 2006
		Real time PCR	
		Electrochemical biosensors	
Penicillium and *Aspergillus spp.*	Patulin	Liquid chromatography	Arranz *et al.*, 2005; Ware *et al*, 1974
		Tandem mass spectrometry (MS/MS)	Kotretsou and Koutsodimou, 2006
		Real time PCR	
		Electrochemical biosensors	
P. ochraceus, P. verrucosum, A. carbonarius, and *A. ochraceus*	Ochratoxin A	LC-MS/MS with electrospray ionization	Cigic *et al.*, 2006
		Tandem mass spectrometry (MS/MS)	Kotretsou and Koutsodimou, 2006
		Real time PCR	
		Electrochemical biosensors	

Chromatography and Elecrtophoresis Techniques

Extraction, by ion exchange chromatography determination of phosphorous is the most commonly used method for analysis. This method is also efficient for the detection of other antinutrients like saponins, tannins, polyphenols, mycotoxins etc. Now days, HPLC is mainly used for the detection purpose as it is found to be an efficient technique. HPLC employs gradient or isocratic techniques, which is generally efficient for detection. Liquid chromatography is used to determine patulin in apple juice, apple juice concentrate, and also apple-based products for infants (Arranz *et al.*, 2005; Ware *et al*, 1974). Tandem mass spectrometry (MS/MS) coupled with chromatographic techniques improves identification and confirmation of food contaminants such as mycotoxins(Kotretsou and Koutsodimou, 2006). HPLC with fluorometric detection and LC-MS/MS with electrospray ionization methods were used to determine ochratoxin A and its photostability in wine (Cigic *et al.*, 2006).

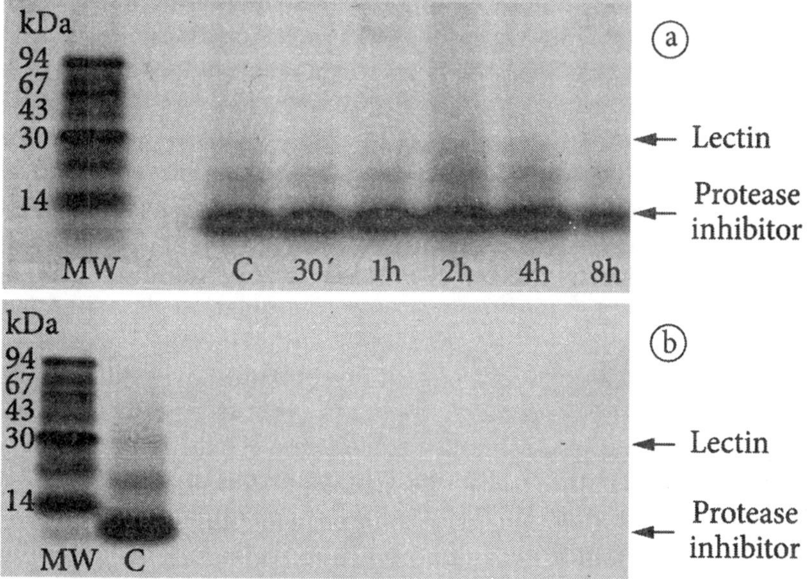

Fig. 8.3: Tricine SDS-PAGE Electrophoresis of Samples of Fraction 4 Digested with Pepsin. (MW) Molecular Weight markers; Times of Incubation: 30min to 8h; (C) Control without Enzyme. Gel (a), Native Samples and (b), Heat Treatment. Arrows Indicate Storage Proteins (*Source*: Silva *et al.*, 2015)

ELISA

Immunological methods vizEnzyme linked immunosorbent assay (ELISA) have been used to estimate mold counts or mold biomass and presence of molds or aflatoxins. DIPSTICK immunoassay method is used to detect postharvest contamination of rice by Humicola lanuginose. Latex agglutination test has been used to detect molds in spices and nuts. Antibodies raised against *P. digitatum* detect both Aspergillius and Penicillium sp. in nuts and spices. One of the problems with immunological methods includes cross reactivation of antibodies raised (Samarajeewa and Vasavada, 1995).

Biosensors

The development of biosensors for the rapid, reliable and low-cost determination of mycotoxins in foodstuffs has received considerable attention in recent years, and various types of assays have already been devised for several of the major groups of mycotoxins (Logrieco *et al.*, 2005). One format uses the phenomenon of *surface plasmon resonance* (SPR) to detect the change in mass that occurs when mycotoxin-specific antibodies attach to a mycotoxin that has been covalently bonded to the surface of a sensor chip (Schnerr *et al.*, 2002; Van der Gaag *et al.*, 2003; Tüdös *et al.*, 2003). A recent application developed and optimized for measuring deoxynivalenolin wheat extracts gave results that were in good agreement with LC/MS data (Maragos and Thomson, 1999). Moreover, SPR sensor chips with immobilized deoxynivalenol could be re-usedmore than 500 times without significant loss of activity (Maragos and Thomson, 1999). Because the instrumentation is now commercially available, this format could find widespread application to future mycotoxin analysis. A second format using *fiber-optic probes* can be adapted for continuous monitoring of mycotoxin levels. This sensor uses the evanescent wave of light that can form around the surface of an optical fiber. Antibodies attached to the surface of the fiber trap fluorescent mycotoxins (e.g. aflatoxins) orfluorescent analogs of mycotoxins (e.g. derivatizedfumonisins) with the evanescentzone, permitting their detection. Two different benchtop devices have been designed for the fumonisins and aflatoxins (Maragos and Thomson, 1999). Unfortunately, most of the SPR and fiberoptic biosensor procedures for mycotoxin analysis still require some form of samplecleanup/preconcentration in order to be truly effective in the analysis of real samples and to achieve adequate sensitivity. Moreover, the majority of these devices lack theability to perform simultaneous analyses of multiple samples.

REMEDIAL MEASURES

Today several strategies are available to minimise the impact of ANFs in food in order to improvetheir utilisation

Cooking

Cooking is one the oldest method of reducing antinutrients in food and feed (Fig. 8.4). Cooking includes various processes like, autoclaving, pressure cooking and steaming. It was found that the effect of cooking generally depends upon temperature, moisture and pressure. Cooking treatments caused significant decreases in fat, total ash, carbohydrate fractions (reducing sugars, sucrose, raffinose and stachyose, while verbascose was completely eliminated after cooking treatments), antinutritional factors (tryps in inhibitor, haemagglutinin activity, tannins, saponins and phyticacid), minerals and B-vitamins. Cooking treatments decreased the concentrations of lysine, tryptophan, total aromatic and sulphur containingamino acids. Trypsin inhibitor activity in chickpea (Cicer arietinum L.) was found to be decreased by cooking treatments. El-Adawy, (2002) noticed a highest reduction after autoclaving (83.87%), followed by boiling (82.27%) and microwave cooking (80.50%). However, Hernandez-Infante *et al.* (1998) reported that microwave cooking destroyed trypsin inhibitors to a degree similar to that observed in six legumes cooked using the conventional method. Trypsin inhibitor activity in faba bean was significantly reduced by heat treatments and germination. Khalil and Mansour, (1995) reported autoclaving as more effectiveprocess inreducing trypsin inhibitor activity than cooking.

Fig. 8.4: Cooking of Kidney Beans

Soaking

Soaking cereal and most legume flours (but not whole grains orseeds) in water can result in passive diffusion of water-solubleNa, K, or Mg phytate, which can then be removed by decanting the water (Perlasamd Gibson, 2002; Hotz and Gibson, 2001) (Fig. 8.5). The extent of the phytate reduction dependson the species, pH, and length and conditions of soaking. A simple soaking procedure appropriate for rural subsistence households has been developed that can reportedly reduce the phytate content of unrefined maize flour by; 50% (Hotz and Gibson, 2001). This is important because several recent in vivo isotope studies in adults (Mendoza *et al.*, 1998; Egli *et al.*, 2004; Hambidge *et al.*, 2004; Hambidge *et al.*, 2005) and infants (Davidsson *et al.*, 2004) have reported improvements inabsorption of iron, zinc, and calcium in cereal-based foods prepared with a reduced phytate content. Some polyphenols and oxalates that inhibit iron and calcium absorption, respectively, may also be lost by soaking (Erdman and Pneros-Schneier, 1994).

Fig. 8.5: Soaking of Wheat

Blanching

It is process in which mild boiling at 75°C - 95°C was done to inactivate endogenous enzymes (Fig. 8.6). Mosha *et al.* (1995) reported the effect of blanching onthe content of anti-nutritional factors in selected vegetables. Levels of both tannic acid and phytic acid were significantly reduced by conventional and microwave blanching methods while oxalic acid levels were not significantly reduced in most of the treatments by either of the blanching methods. In general, they recommended blanching as an effective method for reducing the anti-nutritional factors in green vegetables; however, further investigation on the heating times for both conventional and microwave blanching methods has been suggested.

Fig. 8.6: Blanching of French Beans

Extrusion

A form of high temperature short time (HTST) processes involving a combination of high temperature, pressure and shear processing (Table 8.7 and Fig. 8.7). The cooking process takes place within the extruder where the product produces its own friction and heat due to the pressure generated. The process can induce both protein denaturation and starch gelatinization, depending upon inputs and parameters. Extrusion has the following effects on food:

- Inactivation of raw food enzymes
- Destruction of certain naturally occurring toxins
- Reduction of microorganisms in final products
- Slight increase of iron-bioavailability
- Loss of lysine, and essential amino acid necessary for developmental growth and nitrogen management
- Increase of glycemic index of the processed food, as the "extrusion process significantly increased the availability of carbohydrates for digestion
- Denaturation of proteins

Table 8.7: Heat labile anti-nutritional factors inactivated by thermal processing (Source: Khokhar and Chauhan, 1986)

Anti-nutritional Factor	Common Food Sources	Effects of Anti-nutritional Factors
Avidin	Egg whites	Binds biotin, making it biologically unavailable
Hemagglutinnins	Red kidney beans, yellow wax beans	Induces red blood cell clumping
Lathyrogens	Chick pea	Disrupts collagen structure
Goitrogens	Sweet potatoes, beans, cabbage, turnips	Causes goitre by limiting iodine absorption
a-Amylase inhibitors	Cereal grains, peas, beans	Slows starch digestion
Trypsin inhibitors	Legumes, egg whites, potatoes	Inhibits activity of trypsin
Thiaminases	Fish, shellfish, brussel sprouts, red cabbage	Destroys thiamin

Germination

Germination is also one of the oldest method of reducing antinutrients (Figure 8.7). Germination/malting increases the activity of endogenous phytase activity in cereals, legumes, and oil seeds through de novosynthesis, activation of intrinsic phytase, or both. The phytic acid serves asan important reserve of phosphate generated by the actionof phytase during seed germination for the developing seedling. However, this conversion depends upon the germinating conditions. Tropical cereals such as maize and sorghum have a lower endogenousphytase activity than do rye, wheat, triticale, buck wheat, and barley (Egli *et al.*, 2002). Hence, a mixture of cereal flours prepared from germinated and ungerminated cereals will promote some phytatehydrolysis when prepared as a porridge for infant and young child feeding. The rate of phytate hydrolysis varies with the species and variety as well as the stage of germination, pH, moisture content, temperature (optimal range 45–57_C), solubilityof phytate, and the presence of certain inhibitors (Sandberg *et al.*, 1999; Egli *et al.*, 2002). Egli *et al.* (2002) observed that during germination, rice, millet, and mung bean had the largest reductions in phytate content. α-Amylase activity is also increased during germination ofcereals, especially sorghum and millet. This enzyme hydrolyzesamylase and amylopectin to dextrins and maltose, thus reducing the viscosity of thick cereal porridges without dilution withwater while simultaneously enhancing their energy and nutrient densities (Gibson *et al.*, 1998). Certain tannins and other polyphenols in legumes (e.g., Viciafaba) and red sorghum may also be reduced during germination as a result of the formation of polyphenol complexes with proteins and the gradual degradation of oligosaccharides (Camacho *et al.*, 1992). Such reductions in polyphenols may facilitate ironabsorption. Some methods for the removal of antinutrients in the food and feeds are enlisted in table 8.8.

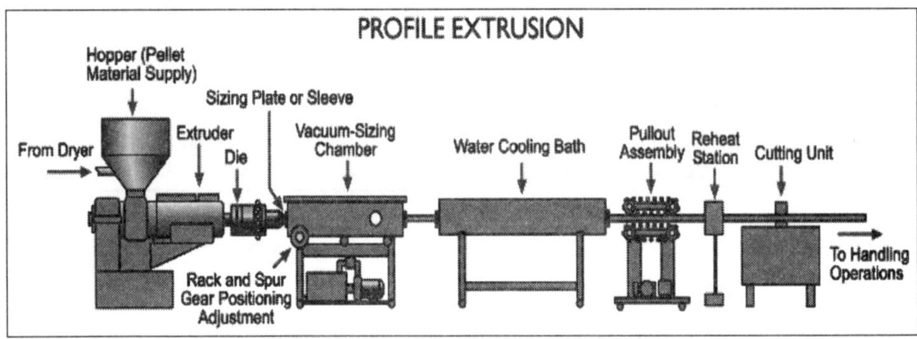

Fig. 8.7: Flow Diagram showing Extrusion Process

Fermentation

The use of fermentation as an integral partof food detoxification processes is widely practiced. A wide variety of fermented foods are produced and eaten around the world. Fermentation is also an effective means for food preservation. Fermented foods can be prepared at both, an industrial and household scale. Indeed, many fermented foods are prepared by very simple techniques and represent grass roots technology which is already widespread; a fact which facilitates their further refinement, transfer and adoption in underdeveloped countries for the detoxification of alternative food sources.

Table 8.8: Methods for removal of antinutritional factors

Physical Processing	Comments
Autoclaving, pressure cooking, steaming	Heating at ultrahigh temperature (>100°C) Performance dependent on temperature, Moisture, pressure relations.
Blanching	Mild boiling (75°C - 95°C) to inactivate endogenous enzymes and avoid cooking.
Ordinary cooking	Usually preceded by soaking or another domestic processing, de-hulling, germination, fermentation.
Extrusion	A form of high temperature short time (HTST) processing involving a combination of high temperature, pressure and shear processing.
Roasting	Dry heating at 120°C - 250°C
Soaking	Exposure to water and salt solution with or without additive to encourage ANF loss
Processing chemical and chemical modification	Treatment with thiols, sulphite, Cu-salts (± ascorbic acid). Chemical modification via acylation, succinylation

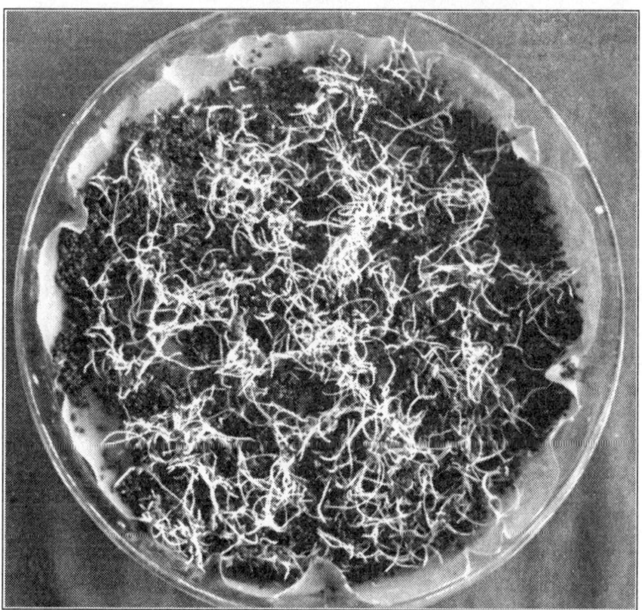

Fig. 8.8: Germination Process of Kidney Beans

Fermented cereal products are widely consumed in India and many countries of central and Southern Africa. Fermentation cause degradation of grain compounds, especially starch and soluble sugars by both grain and fermented media enzyme. Germination of grains of pearl millet increased the protein content and digestibility and fermentation of the germinated and course ground grains increases the protein content and thus protein digestibility greatly improves (Fig. 8.9).

Fig. 8.9: Multigrain Bread

Fermentation can induce phytate hydrolysis via the action of microbial phytase enzymes, which hydrolyzephytate to lower inositol phosphates. Such hydrolysis is important because myoinositol phosphates with, 5 phosphate groups (i.e., IP-1 to IP-4) do not have a negative effect on zinc absorption (Lo¨ nnerdal *et al.*, 1989), and thosewith, 3 phosphate groups do not inhibit nonheme iron absorption (Sandberg *et al.*, 1999; Hurrell, 2004).

The various Indian household preparation techniques for their effectiveness indetoxifying *L. sativus* and their methods which included afermentation step were the most effective in reducing ODPA levels, eliminating 95% of this toxin (Khokhar and Chauhan, 1986). Further, improvement in detoxifying is likely to be made with selection for better ODAP degradation. Such methods can, in principle, also beused for the post harvest detoxification of Vicia seeds, thus providing an alternative approach to the wider utilization of these grains without the need for genetic removal of their low molecular weight anti-nutritive and unpalatability factors. The incorporation of fermentation processes into other simple food technologies also offer good prospects for a detoxification of food source while simultaneously giving flexibility in the manipulation offlavour, texture and colour of the raw material (Jansman *et al.*, 1998).

Fermentation increases protein and amino acid content, and degrades protein into small functional peptides. During fermentation, microorganisms digest the carbohydrates in soybean or soy meal anduse for their own growth. The decreased dry matter and increased microorganisms weight ratio result in enhanced protein content (Song *et al.*, 2008; Chen *et al.*, 2010; Hong *et al.*, 2004). In reference (Song *et al.*, 2008), fermented soy meal with *S.cerevisae* increased its protein level from 47% to 58%, while with *L. plantarum* and *B. lactis*, protein level increased to 52.08% and 52.14%. Microorganisms used for soybean fermentation have been reported to secret protease during fermentation (Kim *et al.*, 2010). In Cheonggukjang, the *Bacillussubtilis* fermented traditional soybean food in Korea, the acidic protease activity level could be as high as 590.24±2.92 ¼g/ml. Neutral protease activity level could achieve 528.13±3.11 ¼g/ml (Kim *et al.*, 2012). Because of protein degradation during fermentation, fermented soybean products are easier to digest.

Microbial phytases originate either from the microflora on the surface of cereals and legumes or from a starter culture inoculate (Sandberg, 1991). The extent of the reduction in higher inositol phosphate levels during fermentation varies; sometimes 90% or more of phytate can be removed by fermentation of maize, soybeans, sorghum, cassava, cocoyam, cowpeas, and lima beans. In cereals with a high tannin content (e.g., bulrush millet and red sorghum), phytase activity is inhibited, making fermentation a less-effective phytate-reducing method for these cereal varieties (Sandberg, 1991). Fermentational so improves protein quality and digestibility, vitamin Bcontent, and microbiological safety and keeping quality. Low-molecular-weight organic acids (e.g., citric, malic, lacticacid) are also produced during fermentation and have the potential to enhance iron and zinc absorption via the formation of soluble ligands while simultaneously generating a low pH that optimizes the activity of endogenous phytase from cereal orlegume flours (Teucher *et al.*, 2004).

Finger millet known as ragi in India source of carbohydrate, protein and mineral that is comparing to other common cereal grain antinutrients like phytate and tannin reduce the nutrient bioavailability which can be improved by suitable processing methods such as germination and fermentation. Major biochemical changes in finger millet occurred during fermentation as compared to germination. The phytate contents decreases by 60% with an increase in HCL extractable minerals 47% and antinutrient level also decreases (Sripriya *et al.*,1997). Fermentation reduced cyanide in soaked seeds. Cooking and fermentation reduced cyanide in soaked seeds tosafe levels. The HCN is soluble in soaking water as such was leached out in the atmosphere. They further reported that cooking and fermentation synergistically reduced tannins. Cooking and fermentation broke down tanninenzyme and protein-tannin complexes and released freetannins which subsequently leached out the products. Ikemefuna *et al.* (1991) concluded that soaking, sprouting, cooking and fermentation appeared to have beneficial effects as methods of processing. Combinations of cooking and fermentation improved the nutrient quality and reduced the anti-nutritional factors inherent in sprouted cereal products to safe levels much greater than any of the other processing methods tested. The most effective treatments are fermentation and sprouting to improve the extractability of minerals but their application remains limited because of additional workload they imply or the particular organoleplic characteristics they produce. Fermentation decreases the level of anti-nutrients in food grains and increases mineral extractability (Badau *et al.*, 2005).

Adeniran *et al.* (2013) analyzeda decrease in anti-nutients of food with fermentation time. Tannin content decreased 2.0 mg/kg at 72 *h*and from 9.50 at 0 *h* to 3.06 mg/kg at 72 *h* of fermentation in lima beans and locust beans respectively. Whereas, phytate content from 22.0 at 0 *h* to 7.0 mg/kg at 72 *h* in lima beans. Cyanide content decreased from 0.97 at 0 *h* to 0.25 mg/kg at 72 *h* and from 15.0 at 0 *h* to 0.29 mg/kg at 72 *h* of fermentation in lima beans and locust beans respectively. Tryps in inhibitor content also decreased from 4.40 at 0 *h* to 1.76 mg/kg at 72 *h* and from 0.24 at 0 *h* to 0.10 TIU/g at 72 *h* of fermentation in lima beans and locust beans respectively.

ELIMINATION OF ANFS THROUGH GENETIC MODIFICATION

Genetic modifications are promising techniques for the elimination of anti-nutritional factors in various crops (Fig. 8.10). This identification now allows for the selection of genotypes with low levels of these factors, thus enabling the development of more palatable and less toxic cultivars. The selection of genetic material with contrasting levels of anti-nutritional factors is also ideally suited for the elucidation of their biological functions. The general aim isa selection of non-toxic and palatable genotypes requiring efficient screening techniques to expedite the quantitative detection of individual ANFs for the selection of improved grain legume cultivars. Such techniques should be suitable for testing large numbers of samples to facilitate the screening of the available germplasm and material generated through breeding or artificial mutagenesis. Sometimes simple colour reagents might work for an initial test, such as Reifers reagentfor quinolizidine alkaloids in lupins (it produces a brown precipitate with alkaloids; Wink, 1993). Immunological methodssuch as ELISA to detect specific proteins can also be established for low molecular weight compounds (Wink 1993). Substantial progress has recently been achieved for *Vicia*and *Lathyrus* employing DRUID-IR for the screening of g-glutamyl-g-cyanoalanine, and Capillary zone electrophoresis for ODAP, GEC, canavanine and vicine (Eichinger *et al*). Furthermore, an enzyme based method has been shown to be highly effective for ODAP screening. ICARDA routinely screens genotypes by Near-IR; TLC is used to screen *Trifoliumsubterraneum* for isoflavones. A careful selection of plants attacked by generalist herbivores might provide a clue to plants with lower ANF levels. A snail (*Helix aspersa*) bioassay on 24 welltissue culture plates may prove useful for the detection of phenolic compounds (Enneking, unpublished). Mass screening is still a labour and capital intensive strategy. With an increased understanding of ANF biology new opportunities, no doubt, will arise for the use of natural selection pressures in the screening for ANFs, either to improve crop resistance or to eliminate a particular factor and replace it with ANFs which are of no detrimental consequence for a particular end-use. Tolerance levels for individual ANFs and applications need to be known so that plant breeders can define target levels in their breeding programs.

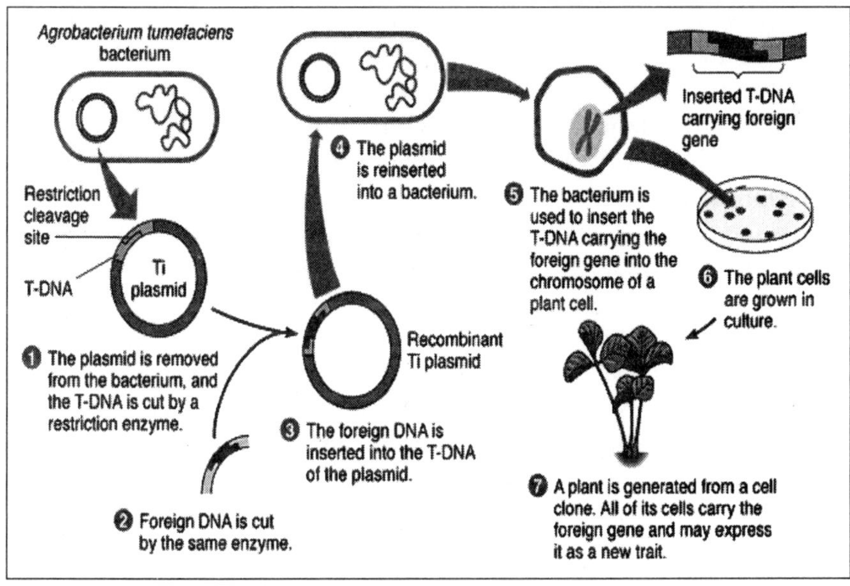

Fig. 8.10: Genetic Modification Process (Diels *et al.*, 2007)

Genetic engineering allows modifications in the gene level of particular organism. Insertion and deletion of particular gene, or some nucleotide base pair lead to modification at gene level. For example, if the gene is known which encodes a toxic protein (e.g., a lectin) or the key enzyme of a biosynthetic pathway leading to alkaloids, saponins, phytic acid, protease inhibitors, NPAAs etc., genetic engineering offers a set of methodologies at present to down regulateor to knock out the respective activity. Strategies include the expression of antisense mRNA, of gene targeting, and of synthetic oligonucleotides or ribozymes. Also the introduction of new traits into a crop plant, such as new lectins or proteins rich in methionine/cysteinecan be achieved by appropriate molecular techniques. Obstacles are often encountered in that relevant genes have not been detected so far which is usually the situation for biosynthetic enzymes of ANFs. If a time-, developmental and organ specific expression is required then promotor sequences need to be known for aparticular plant - and again these data are usually not available for the crop of interest. Transformed plants need to be regenerated which is a severe problem in most legumes. Several target enzymes could be envisaged for NPAAs or alkaloids, but since the genes are still unknown.

Seed Specific Deletion of ANFs

Though genetic engineering process, it might be possible to select strains of legumes, grains whichno longer accumulate ANFs in their seed, but still maintain their synthesis in the rest of the plant. In this case only theseeds and seedlings need additional protection but not the whole plant. This selection would work in instances in which ANFs are produced in the leaves but transported to the seeds or in which all parts of a plant produce a certain ANF but not for a seed specific synthesis. In the first instance, selection is directed towards plants inwhich the translocation via the phloem is blocked and the other instances towards an organ specific inhibition of biosynthesis.

Other Methods

The use of ammonia-heat treatments has shown effective reduction of aflatoxin (Jorgensen and Price, 1981; Schoerder *et al.*, 1985).Other chemicals such as monomethylamine, sodium hydroxide, sodium hypochlorite, and hydrogen peroxide also have resulted in acceptable detoxification in several commodities (Park *et al.*, 1981; Lillehojand Lagoda, 1979). During fermentative production of ethanol, little degradation of the toxin was achieved (Lillehoj and Lagoda, 1979). Other decontamination approaches include food and feed processing such as thermal inactivation, irradiation, solvent extraction, mechanical separation, density segregation, and reduction in bioavailable aflatoxin by selective chemisorption. Biocontrol methods and microbial inactivation have been suggested as well as decontamination procedures (Philips, 1994).

CONCLUSION

The health hazardous impact of ANF alongwith nutritional importance of plant based foods have been reviewed in this paper. The presence of secondary plant compounds such as phytic acids, protease inhibitors, tannins and hydrolysable phenolics, generally interfere with the level of protein and fibre contents of food which are used as indicators of high nutritional value. Keeping in view the harmful nature of ANF described, it is very important to elevate anti nutrients from the food for the proper intake of nutrients. The processing of various foods through roasting, cooking, fermentation and germination improves nutritional attributes by reducing anti nutritional factors.There is also a need to focus on recent techniques like genetic engineering for complete elevation of ANF's from food as well as increasing bioavailability of different nutrients present in food.

REFERENCES

Adeniran, H.A, Farinde, E.O and Obatolu, V.A. (2013). Effect of Heat Treatment and Fermentation on Anti-Nutrients Content of Lima Bean (*Phaseoluslunatus*) During Production of *Daddawa* Analogue. *Annual Review & Research in Biology,* 3(3): 256-266.

Alabaster, O., Z. Tang, and N. Shivapurkar. (1996). Dietary Fiber and the Chemo Preventive Modelation of Colon Carcinogenesis. *Mutation Research* 350: 185-197.

Arranz, M. Derbyshire, K. Kroger, C. Mischke, J. Stroka, and E. Anklam, J. (2005). AOAC *Internat* 88, 518.

Badau, M.H., Nkama, I. and Jideani, I.A. (2005). Phytic Acid Content and Hydrochloric Acid Extractability of Minerals in Pearl Millet as Affected by Germination Time and Cultivar. *Journal of Food Chemistry* 92(3): 425-435.

Bradbury, M.G, Egan, S.V, Bradbury J.H. (1999). Determination of all Forms of Cyanogens in Cassava Roots and Cassava Products using Picrate Paper Kits. Journal of Science Food and Agriculture,79: 593-601.

Brouwer, I.A., Dusseldorp, M.V., West,C.E., Meyboom, S., Thomas, C.M.G., Van Het Hof, K., Eskes,T.K.A.B., Hautvast, J.G.A.J. and Theumissen, R.P.M.S. (1999). Dietary Folate from Vegetables and Citrus Fruits Decreases Plasma Homocysteine Concentration in Humans in a Dietary Controlled Trial. *Journal of Nutrition* 129: 1135-1139.

Brunner, J.H. (1984). Direct Spectrophotometric Determination of Saponin. *Analytical Chemistry* 42: pp. 1752-1754.

Camacho L, Sierra C, Campos R. Guzman, Marcus D. Nutritional Changes Caused by Germination of Legumes Commonly Eaten in Chile. Arch LatinoamNutr. 1992; 42: 283-90.

Chen, C.C., Shih, Y.C., Chiou, P.W.S., *et al.* (2010). Evaluating Nutritional Quality of Single Stage-and Two Stage-fermented Soybean Meal. *Asian-Australasian Journal of Animal Science,* 23(5), 598-606.

Cheryan, M. (1980). Phytic Acid Interactions in Food Systems. *CRC Critical Reviews in Food Science and Nutrition*. 13: 296-335.

Cigic, Strlic, M., Schreiber, A., Kocjancic, M., and Pihlar, B. (2006). *Analytical Letters*. 39, 1475.

Cordier, C., Gruselle, M., Jaouen, G., Hughes, D.W., and McGlinchey, M.J. (1990). Structures of Zearalenone and Zearalanone in Solution: A High-field NMR and Molecular Modeling Study. *Magnetic Resonance Chemistry,* 28, 835.

Davidsson, L., Ziegler, E.E., Kastenmayer, P., van Dael, P., Barclay, D. (2004). Dephytinization of Soy Isolate with Low Phytic Acid Content has Limited Impact on Mineral and Trace Element Absorption in Healthy Infants. *British Journal of Nutrition*. 91: 287-93.

Dawra, R.K., Makkar, H.S.P. and Singh, B. (1988). Protein Binding Capacity of Microquantities of Tannins. *Analytical Biochemistry* 170: 50-53.

Delage,N., d'Harlingue, A., Colonna, B., Ceccaldi, B.C. and Bompeix, G. (2003). Occurrence of Mycotoxins in Fruit Juices and Wines. Food Control. 14: 225-227.

Diels, J., Cunha, M., Manaia, C., Sabugosa-Madeira, B., & Silva, M. (2011) Association of Financial or Professional Conflict of Interest to Research Outcomes on Health Risks or Nutritional Assessment Studies of Genetically Modified Products. *Food Policy,* 36: 197-203.

Egli, I., Davidsson, L., Juillerat, M-A., Barclay, D., Hurrell, R. (2002). The Influence of Soaking and Germination on the Phytase Activity and Phytic Acid Content of Grains and Seeds Potentially Useful for Complementary Feeding. *Journal of Food Science*. 67: 3484-8.

Egli, I., Davidsson, L., Zeder, C., Walczyk, T., Hurrell, R. (2004). Dephytinization of a Complementary Foods based on Wheat and Soy Increases Zinc, but not Copper Apparent Absorption in Adults. *Journal of Nutrition* 134: 1077-80.

El-Adawy, T.A. (2002). Nutritional Composition and Anti-nutritional Factors of Chickpeas (*Cicer arietinum L.*) Undergoing Different Cooking Methods and Germination. *Plant Foods for Human Nutrition (formerly Qualitas Plantarum)*, 57(1): 83-87.

Elsheikh, E.A.E., I.A. Fadul and A.H. El Tinay. (2000). Effect of Cooking on Antinutritional Factors and *in vitro* Protein Digestibility of Faba Bean Grown with Different Nutritional Regimes. *Food Chemistry*. 68: 211-212.

Enneking, D., Giles, L.C., Tate, M.E., Davies, R.L. (1993). *Journal of the Science of Food and Agriculture* 61: 315-325.

Erdman, J.W., Pneros-Schneier, A.G. (1994). Factors Affecting Nutritive Value in Processed Foods. In: Shils ME, Olson JA, Shile M, Editors. Modern Nutrition in Health and Disease. Philadelphia: Lea & Febiger, 1569-78.

Fasset, D.W. (1996). Oxalates. In: Toxicants Occurring Naturally in Foods. National Academy of Science Research Council, Washington D.C, U.S.A.

Gibson, R.S., Yeudall, F., Drost, N., Mitimuni, B., Cullinan, T. (1998). Dietary Interventions to Prevent Zinc Deficiency. *American Journal of Clinical Nutrition* 68(2 Suppl): 484S–7S.

Hambidge, K.M., Huffer, J.W., Raboy, V., Grunwald, G.K., Westcott, J.L., Sian, L. (2004). Miller LV, Dorsch JA, Krebs NF. Zinc Absorption from a Low-phytate Hybrids of Maize and their Wild-type Isohybrids. *American Journal of Clinical Nutrition* 79: 1053-9.

Hambidge, K.M., Krebs, N.F., Westcott, J.L., Sian, L., Miller, L.V., Peterson, K.L., Raboy, V. (2005). Absorption of Calcium from Tortilla Meals Prepared from Lowphytate Maize. *American Journal of Clinical Nutrition* 82: 84-7.

Henry, T.A. (1973). Organic Analysis of Alkaloids. 6: 163-187.

Hernandez-Infante, M., Sousa, V., Montalvo, H., Tena, E.(1998). Impact of Microwave Heating on Hemagglutinins, Trypsin Inhibitors and Protein Quality of Selected Legume Seeds. *Plant Food Human Nutrition* 52, 199-208.

Hong, K.J., Lee, C.H., & Kim, S.W. (2004). Aspergillus Oryzae GB-107 Fermentation Improves Nutritional Quality of Food Soybeans and Feed Soybean Meals. *Journal of Medical Food*, 7(4), 430-435.

Hotz, C., Gibson, R.S. (2001). Assessment of Home-based Processing Methods to Reduce Phytate Content and Phytate/zinc Molar Ratios of White Maize (Zea mays). Journal of Agricultural Food Chemistry. 49: 692-8.

Hurrell, R.F. (2004). Phytic Acid Degradation as a means of Improving Iron Absorption. *International Journal of Vitamin Nutrition Research* 74: 445-52.

Hussein, H.S. and Brasel, J.M. (2001). Toxicity, Metabolism, and Impact of Mycotoxins on Humans and Animals. *Toxicology*. 167(2): 101-134.

Igile, G.O. (1996). Phytochemical and Biological Studies on some Constituents of *Vernoniaamygdalina* (compositae) Leaves. Ph.D Thesis, Department of Biochemistry, University of Ibadan, Nigeria.

Ikemefuna, C., Obizoba, J., Atii, J.V. (1991). Effects of Soaking, Sprouting, Fermentation and Cooking on Nutrient Composition and some Antinutritional Factors of Sorghum (*Guinesia*) Seeds. *Plant Foods for Human Nutrition*, 41: 203-212.

Jaffe, W.G. (1979). Haemagglutinin in Toxic Constituents of Plant Foodstuff (Liener JE Ed.) Academy Press. N.Y. p. 71.

Jansman, A.J., Hill, G.D., Huisman, J. and Vander Poel, A.F. (1998). Recent Advances of Research in Anti-nutritional Factors in Legumes Seeds. Wageningen. The Netherlands: WageningenPers, p. 76.

Jayaramachandran, R., Ghadevaru, S. and Veerapandian, S. (2013). Survey of Market Samples of Food Grains and Grain Flour for Aflatoxin B1 Contamination. *Interantional Journal of Current Microbiology and Applied Sciences*, 2 (5): 184-188.

Jorgensen, K.V. and Price, R.L., (1981) Atmospheric Pressure-ambient Temperature Reduction of Aflatoxin B1 in Ammoniated Cottonseed, *Journal of Agricultural Food Chemistry*, 29(3): 555.

K.K. Sinha and A.K. Sinha. (1991). Monitoring and Identification of Aflatoxins in Wheat, Grain and Maize Flours in Bihar State (India). *Food Additive and Contaminants*. 8: 453-457.

Kersten, G.F, Spiekstra, A., Beuvery, E.C., Crommelin, D.J. (1991). On the Structure of Immune-stimulating Saponin-lipid Complexes (iscoms). *Biochimicaet. BiophysicaActa* 1062(2): 165-171.

Khalil, A.H., and Mansour, E.H. (1995). The Effect of Cooking, Autoclaving and Germination on the Nutritional Quality of Faba Beans. *Food Chemistry*, 54, 177-182.

Khokhar, S. and Chauhan, B.M. (1986). Anti-nutritional Factors in Moth Beans (Vigna*aconitifolia*): Varietal Difference and Effects of Methods of Domestic Processing and Cooking. *Journal of Food Science* 51(3): 591-594.

Khoury, A. and Atoui, A. (2010). Ochratoxin A: General Overview and Actual Molecular Status. *Toxins* 2: 461-493.

Kim, J., Hwang, K., & Lee, S. (2010). ACE Inhibitory and Hydrolytic Enzyme Activities in Textured Vegetable Protein in Relation to the Solid State Fermentation Period using Bacillus Subtilis HA. *Food Science and Biotechnology*, 19(2), 487-495.

Kim, M., Han, S., Ko, J., and Kim, Y. (2012). Degradation Characteristics of Proteins in Cheonggukjang (fermented Unsalted Soybean Paste) Prepared with Various Soybean Cultivars. *Food Science and Biotechnology*, 21(1), 9-18.

Krupa, U. (2008). Main Nutritional and Antinutritional Compounds of Bean Seeds – A Rewiev. *Polish Journal of Food and Nutrition Sciences* 58 (20: 149-155.

Lestienne, I., C.M. Rivier, C.I. Verniere, I. Rochette, and S. Treche. (2005). The Effects of Soaking of whole, Dehulled and Ground Millet and Soybean Seeds on Phytatedegradation and Phy/Fe and Phy/Zn Molar Ratios. *International Journal of Food Science and Technology* 40(4): 391-399.

Liener, I.E. (1979). Determination of Antitryptic Activity of Soybean. *Journal of Science and Agriculture* 16: 602-609.

Lillehoj, E.B. and Lagoda, A., The Fate of Aflatoxin in Naturally Contaminated Corn during the Ethanol Fermentation., *Cannadian Journal of Microbiology*, 25(911): 1979.

Lo¨nnerdal, B., Sandberg, A-S., Sandstro¨m, B., Kunz, C. (1989). Inhibitory Effects of Phytic Acid and other Inositol Phosphates on Zinc and Calcium Absorption in Suckling Rats. Journal of Nutrition 119: 211-4.

Logrieco, A., Arrigan, D.W.M., Brengel-Pesce, K., Siciliano, P. and Tothill, I. (2005) DNA Arrays, Electronic Noses and Tongues, Biosensors and Receptors for Rapid Detection of Toxigenic Fungi and Mycotoxins: A Review. *Food Addition and Contamination*. 22, 335-344.

Lopez-Garcia, R. and Park, D.L., Effectiveness of Post-harvest Procedures in Management of Mycotoxin Hazards, in *Mycotoxins in Agriculture and Food Safety*, Sinha, R.N. and Bhatnagar, D., Eds., Marcel Dekker, New York, 407, 1998.

Maga, J.A. (1983). Phytate: Its Chemistry, Occurrence, Food Interaction, Nutritional Significance and Methods of Analysis. *Journal of Agricultural Food Chemistry*, 30: 1-9.

Makun H.A., Gbodi T.A., Akanya H.O., Sakalo A.E., and Ogbadu H.G. (2007). Fungi and some Mycotoxins Contaminating rice (*Oryzasativa*) in Niger state, Nigeria. *African Journal of Biotechnology*, 6: 99-108.

Maragos C.M. and Thomson V.S. (1999). Fiber-optic Immunosensor for Mycotoxins. *Natural Toxins* 7, 371-376.

Mendoza, C. Viteri, Fe, Lo¨ nnerdal, B., Young, K.A., Raboy, V., Brown, K.H. (1998). Effect of Genetically Modified Low Phytic Acid Maize on Absorption of Iron from Tortillas. Am *Jourmal of Clinical Nutrition* 68: 1123-7.

Mosha, T.C., Gaga, H.E., Pace, R.D, Laswai, H.S, Mtebe, K. (1995). Effect of Blanching on the Content of Antinutritional Factors in Selected Vegetables. Plant Foods for Human Nutrition 47(4): 361-367.

Oakenfull, D., Sidhu, G.S. (1989). Saponins: In Toxicants of Plant Origin, Vol. II, Glycosides, (Eds). PR Cheeke, CRC. Press Inc. Florida. p. 97.

Park, D.L., LaFarge-Frayssinet, D., and Yvon, M.(1981). Decontamination of Aflatoxin Contaminated Peanut Meal Using Monomethylamine: Ca(OH)2, *JAOCS*, 12, 995.

Perlas, L., Gibson, R.S. (2002). Use of Soaking to Enhance the Bioavailability of Iron and Zinc from Rice-based Complementary Foods used in the Philippines. *Journal of Science Food Agriculture* 82: 1115-21.

Phillips, T.D., Clement, B.A., and Park, D.L.(1994). Approaches to Reduction of Aflatoxins in Foods and Feeds, in *The Toxicology of Aflatoxins: Human Health and Agricultural Significance*, Eaton, D.L. and Groupman, J.D., Eds., Academic Press, London, chap. 18.

Pratt, D.A. (1992). Natural Antioxidants from Plant Material. In: Huang, M.T. *et al.* (Eds.), Phenolic Compounds in Food their Effects on Health. Antioxidants and Cancer Preventation. ACS Symposium Series, American Chemistry Society, Washington, DC, 507: 540.

Preuss, H.G. (2009). "Bean Amylase Inhibitor and Other Carbohydrate Absorption Blockers: Effects on Diabesity and General Health". *Journal of American College Nutrition.* 28 (3): 266-76.

Rai, M. and Ajit, V. (Ed.). (2010). "Mycotoxins in Food, Feed and Bioweapons", Springer Heidelberg, Germay. pp. 137-242.

Reddy K.R.N., Reddy C.S., and Muralidharan K. (2009): Detection of *Aspergillus* spp. And Aflatoxin B1 in Rice in India. *Food Microbiology*, 26: 27-31.

Reddy, N.R., C.V. Balakrishnan and D.K. Salunkhe. (1978). Phytate Phosphorus and Mineral Changes during Germination and Cooking of Black Gram (Phaseolus mungo) Seeds. *Journal of Food Science* 43: 540-543.

Reddy, N.R., M.D. Pierson, S.K. Sathe and D.K. Salunkhe. (1989). Occurrence, Distribution, Content and Dietary intake of Phytate. In N.R.Reddy, M.D. Pierson, S.K. Sathe and D.K. Salunkhe (eds.) Phytates in Cereals and Legumes. CRC Press, Boca Raton, FL, USA. P. 39-56.

Saharan K., N. Khetarpaul and S. Bishnoi. (2001). HCl Extractability of Minerals from Ricebean and Fababean: Influence of Domestic Processing Methods. *International Food Science and Emerging Technology* 2(4): 323-325.

Sandberg, A.S. (2002). Bioavailability of Minerals in Legumes. *British Journal of Nutrition* 88(3): S281-S285

Sandberg, A-S., Brune, M., Carlsson, N-G., Hallberg, L., Skoglund, E., Rossander-Hulthen L. (1999). Inositol Phosphates with Different Numbers of Phosphate Groups Influence Iron Absorption in Humans. *American Journal of Clinical Nutrition* 70: 240-6.

Sandsteed, H. (2000). Causes of Iron and Zinc Deficiencies and their Effects on Brain. *Journal of Nutrition* 13: 347-349.

Schnerr H., Vogel R.F. and Niessen L.: A Biosensor-based Immunoassay for Rapid Screening of Deoxynivalenol Contamination in Wheat. Food Agric. Immunol. 14, 313-321 (2002).

Schoerder, T., Zweifel, U., Sagaelsdorff, P., Friederich, U., Luthy, J., and Schlatter, C.(1985). Ammoniation of Aflatoxin-containing Corn: Distribution, *in vivo* Covalent Deoxyribonucleic Acid Binding, and Mutagenicity of Reaction Products, *Journal of Agricultural Food Chemistry*, 33, 311.

Shahidi, F. (2004). Functional Foods their Role in Health Problems and Disease Prevention. *Journal of Food Science* 69(5): 146-149.

Silva, J.A., Pompeu, D.G., Costa, O.F.D., Goncalves, D.B., Spehar, C.R., Marangoni S, Granjeiro P.A. (2015). The Importance of Heat Against Antinutritional Factors from Chenopodium Quinoa Seeds. *Food Science and Technology* 35(1): 74-82.

Soetan, K. O. (2008). Pharmacological and Other Beneficial Effects of Antinutriional Factors in Plants. –A Review. Afr. J. Biotechnol. 7(25): 4713-4721.

Song, Y.S., Frias, J., Martinez-Villaluenga, C., *et al.* (2008). Immunoreactivity Reduction of Soybean Meal by Fermentation, Effect on Amino Acid Composition and Antigenicity of Commercial Soy Products. *Food Chemistry*, 108, 571-581.

Sripriya, G., Antony, U. and Chandra,T.S. (1997). Changes in Carbohydrate, Free Aminoacid, Organic Acids, Phytate and HCL Extractability of Minerals during Germination and Fermentation of Finger Millet (Eleusinecoracana). *Journal of Food Chemistry* 58(4): 345-350.

Sugano, M., Goto, S., Yaoshida, K., Hashimoto, Y., Matsno, T., Kimoto, M. (1993). Cholesterol-lowering Activity of Various Undigested Fractions of Soybean Protein in rats. *Journal of Nutrition* 120(9): pp. 977-985.

Teucher, B., Olivares, M., Cori, H. (2004). Enhancers of Iron Absorption: Ascorbic Acid and Other Organic Acids. *International Journal of Vitamin Nutrition Research*. 74: 403-19.

Tüdös A.J., Lucas-van den Bos E.R. and Stigter E.C.A.(2003). Rapid Surface Plasmonresonance based Inhibition Assay of Deoxynivalenol. *Journal of Agricultural Food Chemistry* 51, 5843-5848.

Van der Gaag B., Spath S., Dietrich H., Stigter E., Boonzaaijer G., van Osenbruggen T. and Koopal K. (2003). Biosensors and Multiple Mycotoxin Analysis. *Food Control* 14, 251-254.

Ware, G.M., Thorpe, C.W., and Pohland, A.E., Assoc. J. (1974). *Analytical Chemistry*, 57, 1111

Weaver, C.M. and S. Kanna. (2002). Phytate and Mineral Bioavailability In: N.R. Reddy and S.K. Sathe, Editors Food Phytates. CRC Press Bocaraton. P. 211-224.

Wink, M. 1993a In: The Alkaloids 43: 1-117 (Ed. G. Cordell), pp. New York: Academic Press.

Zenk, H. M. (1991). Chasing the Enzymes of Secondary Metabolism: Plant Cell Cultures as a Pot of Goal. Phytochemistry, 30(12), pp. 3861-3863. ZessNaukUMKTornu, 13: 253-256.

Pages: 156-173

MICROBIOLOGICAL AND PHARMACOLOGICAL ASPECTS OF BIODIVERSITY

Edited by: Dr. Pankaj Sharma; Dr. Neha Gautam Sharma & Dr. Pankaj Sharma

ISBN: 978-93-5056-878-1

Edition: **2017**

Published by: **Discovery Publishing House Pvt. Ltd., New Delhi (India)**

Pharmacological and Toxicological Aspects of *Datura stramonium* L.

Showkat Ahmad Bhat[1]; Sabhiya Majid[2]; Tehseen Hassan[2]
Hilal Ahmad Wani[2]; N.A. Naikoo[2]

ABSTRACT

Datura is well-known as a medicinal plant and plant hallucinogen all over the world. It has a very special place in Ayurveda since all parts of the plant namely leaves, flowers, seeds, roots, have been used for a wide range of medication such as treatment of leprosy, rabies, insanity, etc. The extract of Datura, however, is a potent poison and its indiscriminate use may lead to delirium and acute poisoning that may lead to death. The active constituents in Datura include scopolamine, atropine, hyoscyamine, withanolides (lactones) and other tropanes. Recently, with anolide compounds have shown significant antitumor, cytotoxic, anti-inflammatory, antibacterial, hepatoprotective, sedative, cytostatic and immunosuppressive activity. The present review includes phytochemical investigations and biological activities of various Datura species wherein several novel compounds have been isolated, characterized and screened for their biological activities. *Datura stramonium* is one of the important Datura species, a wild-growing plant, widely distributed and easily accessible. It contains a variety of toxic tropane alkaloids such as atropine, hyoscamine, and scopolamine. In Eastern medicine, especially in Ayurvedic medicine, it has been used for curing various human ailments, including ulcers, wounds, inflammation, rheumatism and gout, sciatica, bruises and swellings, fever, asthma and bronchitis, and toothache. Its few previous studies have reported that on the pharmacological effects of however, complete information regarding the pharmacology, toxicity,

[1] Division of Veterinary Biochemistry, Faculty of Veterinary Sciences & Animal Husbandry, Sher-e- Kashmir University of Agricultural Science & Technology (SKUAST-K), Srinagar (J & K) (India)

[2] Department of Biochemistry, Government Medical College, Srinagar (J & K) (India)

ethnobotany and phytochemistry remains unclear. Ethnomedicinally, the frequent recreational abuse of *D. stramonium* has resulted in toxic syndromes. *Datura stramonium*, in the form of paste or solution to relieve the local pain, may not have a deleterious effect; however, oral and systemic administration may lead to severe anticholinergic symptoms. For this reason, it is very important for individuals, mainly young people, to be aware of the toxic nature and potential risks associated with the use of this plant. This chapter includes information on botany, phytochemistry, pharmacology, toxicology and ethnomedicinal uses of Datura.

Keywords: Datura, chemical constituents, alkaloids, biological activities, therapeutic usage.

Datura is a wild weed belonging to family Solanaceae, its name derived from Sanskrit word "Dhutra" (divine inebriation) is used for its healing properties. Various species of Datura are known and widely employed for their medicinal and toxic properties that are based upon more than 30 alkaloids. Because of their funnel form, fragrant nocturnal blooms, species such as *Datura inoxia, Datura metel, Datura stramonium* and *Datura wrightii* are cultivated as ornamental plants with all but *D. metel* known from wild populations. Navajos chewed dried roots to reduce fever. Zunis made poultice from it to treat inflammation and bruises. In China, it is known as "Yangjinhua" and used for the treatment of asthma, convulsions, pain, and rheumatism. Flos Daturae has an effect on the treatment of psoriasis for clinical use in China. It is used in Italy to remove lice from hen bundles. *D. stramonium* seeds are used for acne and bronchitis in Sakarya province of North-west Turkey and locally called "Tatala", while the petroleum ether extract is also found to possess antimicrobial activities against *Esherichia coli* and *Trachystemon orientalis*. It is also used commonly in ethno veterinary practices in Nepal and by Gujjar community in India. In Ayurveda, Datura plant parts are sed to treat various disorders including asthma, skin disorders, jaundice, piles, and diabetes. Datura seeds have been used as a prophylactic measure to treat animal bites, especially dog bites. Person bitten by mad dog is administered with juice of Datura along with butter milk and jaggery. Also, the site of bite is smeared with a paste of the fruit. Extensive research has been carried out since 1925 for the isolation and characterization of the total alkaloid contents in Datura species. That The total alkaloid content in Datura varies from 0.02 to 0.52% and scopolamine from 0.0029 to 0.32% relative to the dried material, depending on the geographical area, the part of the plant studied and the stage of growth.(Del Pozo, 1966; Pan *et al.*, 2007; Guarrera, 1999; Uzun *et al.* 2004; Raut and Shreshtha, 2012; Gaur *et al.*, 2010; Dash and Kashyap, 1991; Papadoyannis, 1995; Berkov *et al.*, 2006; Dovelana *et al.*, 2006; Vitale *et al.* 1995).

Atropine is the racemic form of hyoscyamine. It binds competitively to muscarinic receptors blocking parasympathetic cholinergic neurons. It acts on both peripheral and central muscarinic receptors. In lower doses, it affects cardiovascular system causing bradycardia. Atropine increases acetylcholine release (cholinesterase inhibitors) and hence used as an antidote to treat organophosphate poisoning, to dilate the pupil, decrease the salivation and to reduce the gastrointestinal activity. Hyoscyamine and scopolamine act as anti muscarinic compounds and act on both CNS and peripheral nervous system. Scopolamine is used as CNS depressant in small doses and used to treat motion sickness. Apart from this, other therapeutic implications include antiemetic, antidysmenorrheal, and gastric anti spasmodic. Hyoscyamine is used as an adjunct in Zollinger-Ellison syndrome. Typical findings in Datura poisoning are dryness of the mouth, thirst, flushing, fever, amnesia, urinary retention, decreased salivation, papillary dilation, tachycardia, hallucinations (which are frightening), palpitation, ataxia, delirium leading to coma, cardiac and respiratory arrest and death (Bliss, 2001).

BOTANY OF *DATURA STRAMONIUM*

Scientific Name and Classification

In Nepal, *D. stramonium* L. is commonly known as Dhaturo, Seto Dhaturo, Dhattur, and Madak. In Sanskrit language, it has several names such as Dhatturdhurtadhustura Unmatta, Kanakahwaya, Dewatakitawasturi Mahamohi Shivapriya, and Matulo Madanashchasya phale Matulaputraka. Other common names of *D. stramonium* include, Estramonio (Brazil); Chan K'iue Tse (Chinese); Thorn apple, Jimson weed, Mad Apple (English); Chasse-taupe (French); and Trompetilla (Spanish). D. inermis Juss.ex Jacq., D. chalybea W. D. J. Koch and D. tatula (L.) Torr.are the synonyms of D. stramonium. It can be classified as Kingdom: Plantae - Plants; Subkingdom: Tracheobionta - Vascular plants; Superdivision: Spermatophyta - Seed plants; Division: Magnoliophyta - Flowering plants; Class: Magnoliopsida - Dicotyledons; Subclass: Asteridae; Order: Solanales; Family: Solanaceae - Potato family; Genus: Datura L.; and Species: D. stramonium L. (Figure 9.1).

DISTRIBUTION

D. stramonium is native to deserts of the North American Southwest, Central and South America, Europe, Asia, and Africa. It is mainly distributed in the Himalaya region from Kashmir to Sikkim up to 2700 m, in the hilly district of central and south India.

BOTANICAL DESCRIPTION

D. stramonium is a large and coarse shrub of about 3 to 4 feet in height. On rich soil, it may even reach the height of 6 feet. The root is large, whitish in color, with a taproot system giving off many fibers. The stem is green or purple, hairless, cylindrical, erect and leafy, smooth, branching repeatedly in a forked manner. Leaves and a single, erect flower arise through the forks of the branches. The alternate leaves are ovate in outline, but pinnately lobed. These lobes are somewhat shallow and point at their tips; there are usually 2 to 3 of these lobes on each side of the leaf blade. Leaves are cauline and ramal, exstipulate, up to 8 cm long and 6 cm across, petiolate, simple, dissected, acute, glabrous, unicosted, and arranged in reticular venation. The upper surface is dark and grayish- green, generally smooth, whereas the underside is paler, and when dry, minutely wrinkled. Leaves, when bruised, exude a rank, heavy, and somewhat nauseating narcotic odor. The flowers are ebracteate, ebracteolate, pedicellate, actinomorphic, bisexual, complete, regular, pentamerous, except fourth whorl and are hypogynous. They are sweet- scented, and can produce stupor if breathed for a prolonged period of time. Each flower is replaced by a hard fruit that is dry and spiny, and spheroid-ovoid in shape. Underneath, each fruit is a truncated remnant of the calyx that curves sharply down. These fruits are initially green, but become brown with maturity; they divide into four segments to release the seeds. The seeds are dull, irregular, and dark-colored; their surface may be pitted or slightly reticulated (Preissel *et al.*, 2002 & Das *et al.*, 2012).

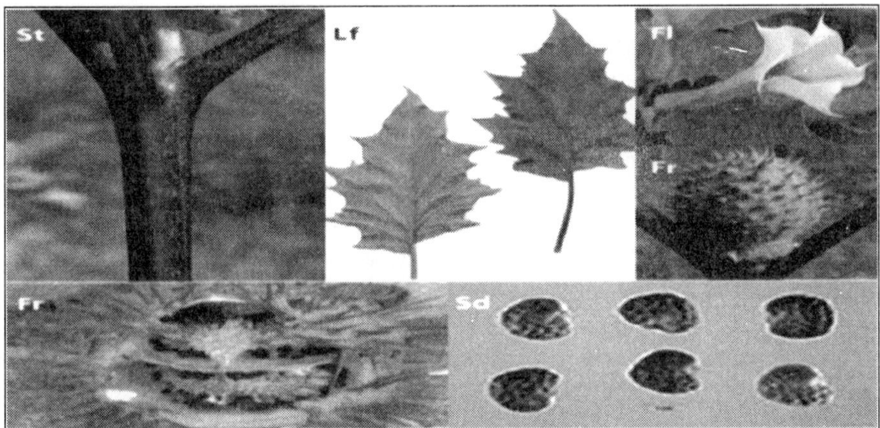

Fig. 9.1: Different Parts of Datura Stramonium St: Stem; Lf: Leaf; Fl: Flower; Fr: Fruit; Sd: Seed

PROPAGATION

D. stramonium is germinated via seeds. It is essentially a temperate plant but is found growing in the vicinity of cultivation, on rank soil, in all parts of the world. The seed usually germinates in 3 to 6 weeks at 15° C. Seeds can remain viable for several years in storage.

ETHNO-MEDICINAL USES

In Western Nepal, leaves of Datura along with the leaves of Cannabis sativa and stem of Neopicrorhiza scrofulariflora, are pounded with water and applied to treat headaches. Datura seeds are crushed with grains of rice and taken orally to relieve indigestion. In parts of Central Nepal, fresh leaves are warmed and placed on a sprained body part repeatedly, before going to bed, for the alleged analgesic effect. Juice from the leaves is given with warm milk to expel intestinal worms, specifically tapeworm. In Nigeria, the seeds are mixed with palm oil and applied to severe cases of insect bites and stings. In India, the seeds are used as a tonic and febrifuge; the leaves are roasted and applied locally to relieve pain. Women in Pakistan warm up 5 to 8 leaves in low fire, and then tie onto sagging breasts to bust them up. Two to five seeds are added to a cup of green tea to relieve headache. Native Americans used Datura seed for many years as a euphoric agent. Since the 1800s, it was used as a therapeutic agent in Great Britain (Gorsi *et al.*, 2002; Hussain *et al.*, 2006).

PHYTOCHEMISTRY

Phytochemical studies of *D. stramonium* have been conducted since the early 1930s. The major phytochemicals isolated are tropane alkaloids, atropine and scopolamine. It is reported that the whole plant contains 0.26% alkaloids. Its seeds contain the alkaloid daturine, first isolated, purified and crystallized by Geiger and Hesse, in 1833. Von Planta (1850) pronounced daturine to be identical with atropine, the principal belladonna alkaloid; later, Ladenburg differentiated daturine into atropine and hyoscyamine, the latter alkaloid predominating. Schmidt, however, contended that atropine predominates. The seeds contain fatty oil (25%), from which a new fatty acid, daturic acid ($C_{17}H_{34}O_2$), was isolated. Dohme concluded that the stems contain more alkaloids (0.3% to 0.4%, volumetrically) than even the seeds (0.25% to 0.29%), and the seeds contain more alkaloid than the leaves (0.21% to 0.23%, and 0.27% for green leaves). Berkov *et al.* (2006) suggested hyoscyamine as the main alkaloid in both diploid and tetraploid hairy root cultures of *D. stramonium*. Iranbakhsh *et al.* (2006) reported the percentage of atropine and scopolamine in different developmental stages and the parts. Their study suggested that the root contained lower levels of scopolamine than that of atropine and the same goes for the stem. In stems, atropine was almost three times higher than scopolamine. However, leaves and seeds contained higher level of scopolamine than that of atropine. Various workers reported the different alkaloids from *D. stramonium* seeds such as N-trans-feruloyl tryptamine, hyoscyamilactol, scopoletin, umckalin, daturaolone, daturadiol, N-trans-ferulicacyl- tyramine, cleomiscosin A, fraxetin, 1-acetyl-7-hydrox- beta-carboline, and 7-hydroxy-beta-carboline-propionic acid (Berkov *et al.*, 2003; Iranbakhsh *et al.*, 2006; Li *et al.*, 2012; Charpin *et al.*, 1979; Pretorius *et al.*, 2006).

D. stramonium contains a variety of alkaloids, including atropine and scopolamine, having anticholinergic and bronchodilating activity. Atropine and scopolamine act on the muscarinic receptors by blocking them (particularly the M2 receptors) on airway smooth muscle and submucosal gland cells, which dilate bronchial smooth muscle and ease asthmatic attacks. Charpin *et al.* (1979) reported that using *D. stramonium* as an antiasthmatic cigarette is an effective bronchodilator in asthmatic patients with mild airway obstruction. However, the exposure of *D. stramonium* to the fetus when a mother uses it for asthma will cause a continuous release of acetylcholine, resulting in the desensitizing of nicotinic receptors, which could ultimately result in permanent damage to the fetus. Though the antiepileptic activity of D. stramonium has not been reported yet, combination therapy with other herbs has the protective effect on status epilepticus. An experimental model of status epilepticus was induced in male rats by a single systemic injection of lithium (3mmol/kg) and pilocarpine (30 g/kg). Rats were then treated with herbal mixture containing D. stramonium. One week after the induction of status epilepticus, the rat group treated with extracts of Scutellaria lateriflora (Skullcap), Gelsemium sempervirens (Gelsemium) and *D. stramonium* displayed no seizure during treatment. The results of this experiment strongly suggest that the appropriate combination of herbs with *D. stramonium* may be helpful as adjunctive interventions to treat epilepsy. Since *D. stramonium* contains atropine and other anticholinergic compounds, it is a useful remedy for the central cholinergic symptoms of organophosphate (OP) poisoning. Bania *et al.* (2004) determined the beneficial effect of Datura seed extracts following a severe poisoning. According to their experiment, *D. stramonium* seeds were heated in water to make 2 mg/mL atropine solution and administered to male rats as a single intraperitoneal injection 5 min before the subcutaneous injection of 25 mg/kg of dichlorvos. Pretreatment with Datura seed extracts significantly increased survival in a rat model of severe OP poisoning. (Peredery *et al.*, 2004; Bania *et al.*, 2004)

The methanol extracts of aerial parts of *D. stramonium* showed the bactericidal activity against Gram-positive bacteria in a dose-dependent manner. However, little or no antibacterial activity was found against *Escherichia coli* and *Pseudomonas aeruginosa.* Ethanol extract exhibited the highest inhibitory activity against *Klebsiella pneumoniae* followed by *Staphylococcus aureus*, with the least activity against *Salmonella typhi*. The aqueous extract showed activity on only *S. aureus*, while *Neisseria gonorrhea* was resistant to both extracts. *D. stramonium* was very effective as vibriocidal against various strains of *Vibreo cholera* and *Vibreo parahaemolyticus*. The minimum inhibitory concentration (MIC) value of acetone extracts of *D. stramonium* was in the range of 2.5 to 15 mg/mL serving as broad-spectrum vibriocidal agents.Acetone extracts of *D. stramonium* have been reported to have antifungal activity against several fungi including *Penicillium expansum, Aspergillus niger, Aspergillus parasiticus, Colletotrichum gloeosporioides, Fusarium oxysporum, Trichoderma harzianum, Phytophthora nicotiana, Pythium ultimum and Rhizoctonia solani*. The MIC of *D. stramonium* extracts ranges from 1.25 to 2.5 mg/mL. The fungicidal effects of the extracts indicate the potential of *D. stramonium* seeds as a natural source of antifungal agent. The ethanolic extract of *D. stramonium* leaf showed significant anti-inflammatory activity against carrageenan- induced paw edema in rats. In one experiment, 39.43% inhibition of the edema was observed after 3 h of oral administration of 200 mg/kg extracts. Maximum activity was observed when the extract was administered in doses of 3-hour intervals. Since the extract of *D. stramonium* inhibited the carrageenan-induced edema that involves the release of histamine and serotonin in the first phase, the inhibitory effect of the extracts could be partly due to inhibition of mast cell mediator release. (Mdee *et al.*, 2009; Sonika *et al.*, 2010; Kurnal *et al.*, 2010)

Datura plant generates a characteristic odor that acts as repellent for various insects and pests. Kurnal *et al.* (2010) have reported that the ethanol extracts of *D. stramonium* leaf and seed showed potent acaricidal, repellent, and oviposition deterrent activity against adult two-spotted spider mites (Tetranychus urticae) under laboratory conditions. Leaf and seed extracts, which were applied in 167.25 and 145.75 g/L concentrations (using a Petri leaf disc-spray tower method), caused 98% and 25% mortality among spider mite adults after 48 h, respectively. These results suggest that *D. stramonium* could be used to manage the two-spotted spider mite.*D. stramonium* was reported to have anticancer effect against human epidermal carcinoma of the nasopharynx at a therapeutic dose of 0.05 to 0.1 g. However, precaution should be taken while using it as an anticancer agent since adverse anticholinergic effects may occur. The half lethal dose (LD50) for ethanolic extracts of *D. stramonium* leaves showed potential larvicidal and mosquito repellent activities against *Aedes aegypti* (LD50: 86.25 mg/L), *Anopheles stephensi* (LD50: 16.07 mg/L) and *Culex quinquefasciatus* (LD50: 6.25 mg/L). *D. stramonium* is generally administered at a dose of 60 to 185 mg powder for leaf and 60 to 120 mg powder for seed (Swathi *et al.*, 2012; Hirschmann *et al.*, 1990; Spina *et al.*, 2007.

D. stramonium is mostly studied for its toxicological properties. Datura poisoning is very common in India, usually involving the seeds. Many cases of unintentional poisoning by *D. stramonium* species have been reported when taken accidentally, or as decoction prepared from herbal prescription. General symptoms of poisoning include delirium, agitation and seizures, mydriasis, blurred vision, photophobia, dry mouth and mucous membranes, extreme thirst, tachycardia, nausea and vomiting, decreased bowel sounds, difficulty swallowing and speaking, hyperthermia, hypertension, loss of consciousness and coma. Dugan *et al.* (1989) have reported that ingestion of *D. stramonium* seed at concentrations of 0.5% or more in the diet produced adverse physiological changes in rats. Bouzidi *et al.* (2011) reviewed the acute, sub-acute and chronic toxicity studies of alkaloids from the seeds of *D. stramonium*. According to them, single dose acute toxicity of 100 mg/kg *D. stramonium* includes decreases in the weight of the liver, spleen and brain, and significant increases in the levels of red blood cells (RBC), hematocrit (HCT), hemoglobin (HGB), and white blood cells (WBC). Similarly, RBC, HGB, HCT and platelet levels were increased in 4-week subacute toxicity studies. However, the 120-day chronic toxicity study of *D. stramonium* alkaloids showed decreased levels of RBC, HCT, HBG and WBC, with a significant increase in liver enzymes. Fatal dosages of *D. stramonium* toxins occured with amounts exceeding 10 mg for adults, and mg for children. The amount needed to poison an adult is about 20 seeds, and the estimated LD in an adult is >10 mg atropine or >2 to 4 mg scopolamine. Almost all the parts of *D. stramonium* are reported to have toxic effects, and the toxicity of this plant is mainly due to the tropane alkaloids. Each part varies in the concentrations of alkaloids and other active substances. For this reason, it is very important for individuals, especially young people, to be aware of the toxicity and potential risks associated with the "recreational" use of this plant. *D. stramonium* in the form of a paste or solution to relieve local pain may not have a deleterious effect; however, its oral and systemic administration may lead to severe anti-cholinergic symptoms. Various cases of toxic delirium and psychiatric symptoms have been reported after its ingestion indicating the necessity of extreme precaution while using this plant (Oberndorfer *et al.*, 2002; Dugan *et al.*, 1989; Bouzidi *et al.*, 2011; Kurzbaum *et al.*, 2001; Karada *et al.*, 2001; Karada *et al.*, 2011)

ANALGESIC EFFECT

Aqueous extract of *D. fastuosa* leaves and seeds (10% w/v) were taken to evaluate the analgesic effect on acetic acid induced writhing pain and hot plate reaction in mice. Oral treatment of 400 and 800 mg/kg proved effective and showed significant analgesic effect. Upon naloxone administration, analgesic effect was reduced in leaf extract while the seed extract remained unaffected. Swiss mice under standard environment conditions were subjected to i.p. acetic acid injection (0.6%, 10 ml/kg) and hot plate to check the analgesic effect. Aqueous seed extract of *D. metel* L. was found not to possess analgesic activity on acetic acid induced model as well as the radiant heat tail-flick model (Abena *et al.*, 2003; Wannang *et al.*, 2009).

ANTIVIRAL

Atropine inhibited only the growth of enveloped viruses independent of the nucleic acid content of the virus. The activity of atropine was checked by plaque reduction test and one step growth experiments. The test viruses included Herpes Simplex Virus, Influenza virus, New Castle Disease Virus, Sindbis, Vaccinia, Adenovirus, Japanese encephaitis Virus. Viruses were cultivated on primary chick embryo (CE), HeLa S3, primary monkey kidney cells (MK). Atropine also blocks the glycosylaton of viral proteins of Herpes virus and hence the production of new infectious virus particles (virions). Virions formed in the presence of atropine are noninfectious (Yamazaki and Tagaya, 1980; Alarcon *et al.*, 1984).

ANTICANCER ACTIVITY

Chemical investigation of a methanol extract of the flowers of D. metel has led to the isolation of new withanolides I-P, 1-10-seco-withametelin B and 12 ″-hydroxy-1,10-seco-withametelin B together with seven known withanolides. The structures where elucidated using spectroscopic data, while single crystal X-ray analysis was done for structure 9. The compounds where screened against various cancer cell lines including A549 (lung), BGC-823 (gastric) and K562 (leukemia). Compounds 1, 3, 4 and 6 exhibited cytotoxic activities with their IC50 values ranging from 0.05 to 3.5 μM. Sasaki *et al.* (2002) have found that *D. stramonium* agglutin (DSA (lectin)) induced irreversible differentiation in C6 glioma cells. The differentiated cells had long processes, a low rate of proliferation and a high content of glial fibrillary acidic protein. Experiments with several other lectins indicated that both recognition of inear Nacetyllactosamine repeats and recognition of multiantennary units of cell-surface glycans were required for the inhibition of C6 proliferation. Proliferation of four human glial tumor cells was also inhibited by DSA, which suggests its usefulness as a new therapy for treating glioma without side effects. Li *et al.* (2005) isolated endophytic fungi from D. stramonium and tested for the antitumor activities by MTT assay on human gastric tumor cell line BGC-823, which exhibited 100% growth inhibition rate. Iman Ahmad *et al.* (2009) recently carried out studies on human cancer cell lines in vitro on MDA-MB231 (breast), and FaDu (neck). The treatment with *D. stramonium* aqueous leaf extract for 24 and 48 h showed increase in GSSG in FaDu cells indicating oxidative stress in treated cells.

WOUND HEALING PROPERTIES

In vivo healing potential of *Datura alba* alcoholic extract on burn rat wounds were studied (Shanmuga *et al.*, 2002). A 10% w/w ointment was prepared and applied topically on thermal wounds. Complete wound healing was observed within 12 days in treated rats against control rats which required about 30 days for healing. Apart from antimicrobial activity, studies were carried out to check rate of wound contraction and histochemical analysis to examine cellular infiltration. Biochemical assays to check collagen and hexosamine content of tissue on various days were carried out by using gelatin zymography. The antimicrobial assay done by disc diffusion method of the crude extract showed antimicrobial activity on pathogenic organisms obtained from burn patients. Silver sulfadiazine (1 mg/ml), DMSO and solvents used for fractionation were also tested simultaneously. The pathogens isolated from Burn ward unit, Child Trust Hospital, Chennai were *Staphylococcus* sp., *Klebsiella* sp., *E. coli*, *Streptococcus* sp., *Pseudomonas* sp., *Salmonella* sp. and *Vibrio* sp. Wound healing was increased due to enhanced epithelialisation. The crude extract has enhanced chemotactic effect which attracted inflammatory cells towards the wound site and cellular proliferation was observed by hematoxylin and eosin staining. Increase in cellular proliferation may be due to mitogenic effect of the plant extract. Increase in hydroxyproline content was observed which indicates the increase in collagen synthesis which is essential for wound healing. Matrix metalloproteases

(MMP's) such as MMP 9 were expressed in early days, and MMP 2, a 72 kDa gelatinase were also observed. MMP's are helpful in removal of fibrin and eschar which results in formation of peptides which are known to have angiogenic and chemotactic properties. The presence of gelatinase indicates progression of wound healing process.

ANTI-PERSPIRANT ACTIVITY

Anti-cholinergic compounds have antiperspirant action (Mac Millan *et al.*, 1964). Various compounds have been studied and esters of cholinergic compounds have been found to be more effective. Scopolamine hydrobromide is found to be most effective due to its skin penetration ability.

ANTI-QUORUM SENSING ACTIVITY

One of the way to check anti pathogenic effect of medicinal plant is to check anti-quorum sensing activity of the extracts (Adonizio *et al.*, 2006). A wide range of plants were selected of different families for their anti-quorum sensing activity. Plant chosen from Solanaceae was D. metel L. Double purple, *c.v.* from South Florida. Ethanolic and aqueous extract of flowers and leaves were used to check the activity. Biomonitor organisms used were *Chromobacterium violaceum* and *Agrobacterium tumefaciens* NTL4 (pZLR4). Bioassay was done using disk diffusion method where C. violaceum (wt), CV026 supplemented with AHL and *A. tumefaciens* NTL4 supplemented with AHL and X-gal. The plates were incubated overnight and QS was observed by a ring of colourless but viable cells around the disc. D. metel did not show anti-QS activity, but the extracts are known to have anti-microbial activity which indicates other mechanism of inhibition.

HYPOGLYCEMIC EFFECT

In vivo hypoglycemic and anti-hyperglycemic effect of *D. metel* seeds were studied (Krishnamurthy *et al.*, 2004). Experiments were carried out on normal and alloxan induced diabetic rats. Alloxan is a cytotoxin and induces diabetes chemically through the damage of insulin secreting cells. Seed powder extract were tested on both normoglycemic as well as alloxan induced hyperglycemic rats to compare whether excess hypoglycemic effect is hypoglycemic effect is lethal. Gliclazide was used as control to reduce blood glucose level. Histopathological studies were not performed and hence detail mechanism of action could not be studied. Effect of seed powder showed rapid normalization of blood glucose level. Possible mechanism could be that some of the "-cells might have survived the damage and secreted insulin when treated with seed extract. Further studies need to be carried out to check the exact mode of action and the active component participating from the seed extract and to check the synergistic action of the components present in the seed extract. Investigation on Insulin release and enzyme inhibition activity also needed to be studied.

IMMUNOMODULATORY ACTIVITY

Phytochemical investigations of *D. quercifolia* has led to the isolation and characterization of several Datura lactones, which are of withanolide skeleton by Bhat *et al.* (2005). Phytochemical investigation yielded a new Datura lactone, 1",5!,12!-trihydroxy-6!,7!, 24!, 25!-diepoxy- 20S, 22R with 2-enolide (5) along with two known compounds, 3 and 4. These compounds were evaluated for their immunomodulatory activity by observing the B and T-cell activation and cytokine production from splenocytes. Of the three compounds isolated, Compound 4 showed dose related increase in primary and secondary antibody production, while Compound 5 act as a suppressor where levamisole was use as standard which increases primary and secondary antibody production. Compound 3 showed higher SRBC induced DTH response at a dose of 0.1 mg/kg p.o. BMS (Betamethasone) was used as standard. Compound 3 was checked for the activation of spleen Tcell sub types, CD4 and CD8, selective release of cytokines, IL-2 and TNF! It stimulated and showed increase in CD4+ T-cell count and stimulated increase in IL-2 and TNF-! in dose dependent manner (0.01 mg/kg was found more effective) (Figure 9.1).

ANTI ULCER

Investigation was done to evaluate anti ulcer activity and its mechanism on various models on experimentally induced ulcers in rats (Falcao *et al.*, 2008). W.E. (20 mg/kg) reduced the ulcer and ulcer index significantly in rats. It decreased the volume of gastric secretion, acid and peptic output significantly; it did not affect the mucin secretion and total mucosal glycoprotein content in terms of total carbohydrate, protein gastric cell shedding or cell replication. It also augments prostaglandins.

ANTI-STRESS

Withanolides from *D. fastuosa* possess anti-stress activity (Manickam *et al.*, 1997; Ratan *et al.*, 2011). When administered with diazepam, it exhibited an axiolytic effect effect and inhibited the immobilization stress induced depletion of adrenal cortisone. Adrenal cortisone help organism to overcome annoying stimuli, but such responses can cause stress induced disorders.

Detailed study of varying doses, duration and mode of administration is essential to know the effectiveness as an anti-stress agent.

ANTI-MICROBIAL ACTIVITY

A new antibacterial agent, 5′, 7′ dimethyl 6′-hydroxy 3′, phenyl 3 !-amine ″-yne sitosterol (28) was isolated by Okwu and Igara (2009) from *D. metel* leaves. The structure was established using 13C, 1H NMR, IR and MS spectroscopic studies. This compound displayed antibacterial activity against *Staphylococcus aureus, Pseudomonas aeruginosa, Proteus mirabilis, Solmonella typhi, Bacillus subtilis and Klebsiella pneumoniae* but could not inhibit *Escherichia coli*. In vitro antibacterial activity of aqueous as well as organic extract from various plant parts of *D. innoxia* was checked. Gram negative bacteria such as *P. aeruginosa, E. coli, K. pneumonia, S. typhi, Enterococcus faecalis, Vibrio* sp., *Proteus vulgaris*, while the Gram positive: *B. subtilis, S. aureus, Bacillus cereus* were evaluated by Kaushik and Goyal (2008). It was found that the organic extracts from leaves are more potent inhibitors and displayed better antibacterial activity as compared to the stems and roots. Methanol extract shows more inhibition. While chloroform extract is found to be active against *Aspergillus flavus, Aspergillus niger, Aspergillus fumigatus. Candida albicans* (Eftekar *et al.*, 2005). Acetone extracts of *D. stramonium* plant parts were tested against *Vibrio cholerae* and *Vibrio parahaemolyticus* by Sharma and Patel (2009). The crude plant extracts exhibited a MIC of 2.5 to 15 µg/ml. The assays were done by disc diffusion method. Banso and Adeyemo (2006) have also assessed the phytochemical components and antimicrobial activity of *D. stramonium* ethanolic leaf extract against *P. aeruginosa, K. pneumoniae* and *E. coli*. It was recorded that higher concentrations of the extracts were required to inhibit growth. Antimicrobial substances may affect the synthesis of peptidoglycan around the bacterial cell, and the cell dies by osmotic shock. The MIC of the plant extracts ranged from 15 to 25% w/v.

ANTI-FUNGAL ACTIVITY

The hexane, chloroform, acetone and methanolic fractions of *D. metel* L. were investigated for antifungal properties against three species of *Aspergillus*, that is, A. fumigates, A. flavus, and *A. niger* (Rajesh and Sharma, 2002). The MIC of the chloroform extract was found to be 625.0 µg/ml by microbroth dilution method and 12.5 µg/disc by the disc diffusion assay. Although the chloroform extract of *D. metel* was 9.2 time less active than amphotericin B, it was 117.8 times less cytotoxic than the standard drug. A concoction brewed from D. stramonium, *Calotropis gigantean, Azadirachta indica* and cow manure was used against floral malformations caused by *Fusarium mangiferae* (Usha *et al.*, 2009). The study proved that the concoction is effective, inexpensive, easy to prepare and constitutes a sustainable and eco-friendly approach to control floral malformation in mango when it is sprayed at Aqueous extract of *D. alba* Rees was evaluated against *Rumex dentalus* L., a problematic weed of wheat. Application of aqueous extracts caused 68% reduction in germination, 62% in shoot length, 96% in root length and 68% in seedling biomass (Jamid *et al.*, 2009). Scopalamine has been shown to attenuate memory task. Grasby *et al.* (1993) have suggested that the acute blockade of cholinergic neurotransmission effects diverse brain areas, including components of visual and motor systems and in addition modulates memory task activation at distinct points in distributed network for memory function.

Datura stramonium L.

Datura stramonium, the most common species within this family, is native to Asia, but is also found in the United States, Canada, and the West Indies.

It is widespread with higher abundance in temperate, tropical and subtropical regions. Traditionally, *D. stramonium* has been used for mystic and religious purposes, and as an herbal medicine with narcotic effects or to treat asthma. The seed of *D. stramonium* is smoked to achieve hallucinogenic experiences as well. D. stramonium is toxic when consumed improperly. Accidental poisoning of humans and animals who consumed food sources contaminated with *D. stramonium* has been reported (Diker *et al.*,2007& Naude *et al.*, 2005). In areas where millet, wheat, rye, corn, and bean seeds are used for human consumption, and where *D. stramonium* is a common weed, the grain sometimes has been contaminated with Datura seeds. In Ayurvedic medicine, *D. stramonium* is described as a useful remedy for various human ailments including ulcers, wounds, inflammation, rheumatism and gout, sciatica, bruises and swellings, fever, asthma and bronchitis, toothache, etc. Many folk medicine remedies use *D. stramonium* therapeutically. In the Hindu religion, the seed of *D. stramonium* is believed to be associated with the God Shiva, which can promote misuse of the plant on religious occasions, such as Shivaratri and Swasthani Pujall In modern medicine, the therapeutic uses of *D. stramonium* are overshadowed by its toxic effects. The administration of large amounts of *D. stramonium* affects the central nervous system with symptoms such as confusion, bizarre behavior, hallucinations and subsequent amnesia. Though death by *D. stramonium* poisoning is rare, recovery may take several days. Therefore, a thorough understanding of the possible pharmacological and toxicological effects of *D. stramonium* is needed. This review focuses on the botany, phytochemistry, pharmacology, toxicology and ethnomedicinal uses of *D. stramonium* (Norton *et al.*, 2008; Kirtikar *et al.*, 1999; Gaire *et al.*, 2008).

CONCLUSION

Medicinal plants have formed the basis of health care throughout the world since the earliest days of humanity and are still widely used and have considerable importance in international trade. Plants are important for pharmacological research and drug development, not only when bioactive phyto-compounds are used directly as therapeutic agents, but also as starting materials or the synthesis of drugs or as models for pharmacologically active compounds. With latest advances in medicinal chemistry and knowledge of biosynthetic route for the development of lead compounds have opened a new perspectives in the field of drug chemistry. There is a need to design new molecules from natural sources to combat lethal diseases. Thus plants are proving as potential source for drug discovery. With anolides have known anticancer activity which needs to be further explored. However, the integration of herbal medicine into modern medicinal practises, including treatments for infections and cancer, must contemplate the related issues of quality, safety and efficacy. This review has been directed towards various interesting findings of the medicinal value of Datura, apart from its toxicity and ornamental importance to prove it as a potent chemotherapeutic agent. Thus concerted efforts in the relevant areas is still necessary to establish rational and sustainable exploitation of the worlds biodiversity. In Ayurveda, different parts of *D. stramonium* are used for various human ailments when applied both locally and through oral administration, but classic Ayurveda lacks specific knowledge on the toxicity of D. stramonium. The pharmacological effect of *D. stramonium* described above can be applied through modern or alternative herbal medicine approaches. *D. stramonium* should only be used therapeutically while under the care of knowledgeable health care professionals. The adverse effects of *D. stramonium* can be extremely severe and detrimental. Therefore, even in light of its many beneficial effects, the risk benefit ratio should be always taken into consideration before using *D. stramonium.*

REFERENCES

Abena AA, Miguel LM, Mouanga A, Assah HTH, Diatewa M (2003). Evaluation of Analgesic Effect of Datura Fastuosa Leaves and Seed Extracts. Fitoterapia 74: 486-488.

Adonizio AL, Downum K, Bennett BC, Mathee K (2006). Anti-quorum Sensing Activity of Medicinal Plants in Southern Florida. J. Ethnopharmacol. 105: 427-435.

Ahmad IM, Abdalla MY, Mustafa NH, Qnais EY, Abdulla FA (2009). Datura Aqueous Leaf Extract Enhances Cytotoxicity via Metabolic Oxidative Stress on Different Human Cancer Cells. Jordan J. Biol.Sci. 2(1): 9-14.

Alarcon B, Gonzalez ME, Carrasco L (1984). Antiherpes virus action of atropine. Antimicrob. Agents Chemother. 26(5): 702-706.

Bania TC, Chu J, Bailes D, O'Neill M (2004). Jimson Weed Extract as a Protective Agent in Severe Organophosphate Toxicity. Acad Emerg Med. 11(4): 335-338.

Banso A, Adeyemo S (2006). Phytochemical Screening and Antimicrobial Assessment of Abutilon Mauritianum, Bacopa Monnifera and Datura Stramonium. Biokemistri 18(1): 39-44.

Begum SA, Sahai M, Fujimoto Y, Asai K, Schneider K, Nicholson G, Suessmuth R (2006). A new kaempferol Diglycoside from Datura Suaveolens Humb. & Bonpl. Ex. Willd. Nat. Prod. Res. 20: 1231-1236.

Berkov S, Pavlov A, Kovatcheva P, Stanimirova P, Philipov S (2003). Alkaloid Spectrum in Diploid and Tetraploid Hairy Root Cultures of Datura Stramonium. Z Naturforsch C. 58(1-2): 42-46.

Berkov S, Zayed R, Doncheva T (2006). Alkaloid Pattern in some Varieties of Datura Stramonium. Fitoterapia 77: 179-182.

Bhat BA, Dhar KL, Puri SC, Qurishi MA, Khajuria A, Gupta A, Qazi GN (2005). Isolation, Characterization and Biological Evaluation of Datura Lactones as Potential Immunomodulators, Bio.Med. Chem. 13: 6672- 6677.

Bliss M (2001). Datura Plant Poisoning. Clin.Toxicol. Rev. 23: 6.

Bouzidi A, Mahdeb N, Kara N (2011). Toxicity Studies of Alkaloids of Seeds of Datura Stramonium and Synthesis Alkaloids in Male Rats. J Med Plants Res. 5(15): 3421-3431.

Broekaert WF, Allen AK, Peunes WJ (1987). Seperation and Characterization of Isolectin with Different Subunits Components from Datura Stramonium Seeds. FEBS Lett. 220:116-120.

Charpin D, Orehek J, Velardocchio JM (1979). Bronchodilator Effects of Antiasthmatic Cigarette Smoke (Datura stramonium). Thorax. 34(2): 259-261.

Cirigliano A, Velerio AS, Oberti JC, Burton G (1995). A 15!- Hydroxywithanolide from Datura ferox. Phytochemistry 40: 611-613.

D, Markovitz D, Rothman M, Sendovski U (2007). Coma as a Presenting Sign of Datura Stramonium Seed Tea Poisoning. Eur J Intern Med. 18(4): 336-338.

Das S, Kumar P, Basu SP (2012). Review Article on Phytoconstituents and Therapeutic Potentials of Datura stramonium Linn. J Drug Deliv Ther. 2(3): 4-7.

Dash B, Kashyap L (1991). Five Specialized Therapies of Ayurveda, Panchakarma: Based on Ayurveda; Concept Publishing Company New Delhi, 165. (b) Database on Medicinal Plants Used in Ayurveda, Vol. 2: Central Council for Research in Ayurveda and Siddha: 200. (c) Satyavati G.V, Rama M.K, Sharma M (1976). Medicinal Plants of India vol. 1, ICMR: New-Delhi p. 333.

Del Pozo EC (1966). Aztec Pharmacology. Ann. Rev. Pharmacol. 6: 9-18.

Desai NN, Allen AK, Neubergerr A (1981). Some Properties of Lectins from Datura Stramonium (Thorn Apple) and Nature of its Glycoprotein Linkages. Biochem. J. 187: 345-353.

DeWolf GP (1956). Notes on Cultivated Solanaceae 2 Datura. Baileya 4: 12-13.

Dhar KL, Kalla AK (1976). A 12-oxowithanolide from Datura Quercifolia Phytochemistry 15: 339. Eftekar F, Youxfardi M, Tafakori V (2005). Antimicrobial Activity.

Dugan GM, Gumbmann MR, Friedman M (1989). Toxicological Evaluation of Jimson Weed (Datura stramonium) Seed. Food Chem Toxicol. 27(8): 501-510.

Gaire BP (2008). Monograph on Datura Stramonium. Kaski, Nepal: Pokhara University Press. 1-114.

Gaur RD, Sharma J, Painuli RM (2010). Plants used in Traditional Healthcare of Livestock.

Gorsi MS, Shahzad R (2002). Medicinal uses of Plants with Particular Reference to the People of Dhirkot, Azad Jammu and Kashmir. Asian J Plant Sci. 1(3): 222-223.

Grasby PM, Frith CD, Friston KJ, Frackowiak, RJ, Dolan RJ (1993). The Effect of Muscarinic Antagonist Scopolamine on Regional Cerebral Blood Flow during Performance of a Network Task. Exp. Brain Res. 109: 337-348.

Guarrera PM (1999). Traditional Antihelmintic, Antiparasitic and Repellent Uses of Plants in Central Italy. J. Ethnopharmacol. 68: 183-192. Jamid A, Shafique S, Shafique S (2009). Herbicidal Activity of Withania Somnifera and Datura Alba Against Rumex dentatus. J. Agric. Res. 47: 37-45.

Hirschmann GS, De Arias AR (1990). A Survey of Medicinal Plants of Minas Gerais, Brazil.J Ethnopharmacol. 29(2): 159-172.

Hussain F, Badshah L, Dastagir G (2006). Folk Medicinal uses of some Plants of South Waziristan, Pakistan. Pak J Plant Sci. 12: 27-39.

Iranbakhsh A, Oshaghi MA, Majd A (2006). Distribution of Atropine and Scopolamine in Different Organs and Stages of Development in *Datura stramonium* L. (Solanaceae). Structure and Ultrastructure of Biosynthesizing Cells. Acta Biol Crac Ser Bot. 48(1): 13-18.

Jayaprakasam B, Zhang Y, Seeram NP, Nair MG (2003). Growth Inhibition of Humor Cell Lines by Withanolides from Withania somnifera Leaves. Life Sci. 74: 125-132.

Karada S, Selvi Y, §ahin M, Selvi F, Oncu R, Ozgokfe F (2011). Datura stramonium Intoxication: Report of a Case with Psychiatric Symptoms. Du^unen Adam: J Psychiatry Neuro Sci. 24(2): 152-154.

Kaushik P, Goyal P (2008). In vitro Evaluation of Datura innoxia (Thorn Apple) for Potential Antibacterial Activity. Indian J. Microbiol. 48: 353-357.

Kinghorn AD, Su BN, Kang YH, Park EJ, Pizzuta JM (2004). Induction of the Phase II Enzyme, Quinone Reductase, by Withanolides and Norwithanolides from Solanaceous species.Mini. Rev. Org. Chem. 1:115-123.

Kirtikar KR, Basu BD (1999). Indian Medicinal Plants. 2nd ed. Volume III. Dehradun: International Book Distributors. 1783-1787.

Kocor M, St. Pyrek J (1973). Triterpenes of Datura Innoxia Mill. Structure of Daturadiol and Daturaolone, J. Org. Chem. 38: 3685-3688.

Krishnamurthy B, Nauri S, Kota MK, Krishna Rao RV, Koteswara Rao N, Annapurna A (2004). Evaluation of Hypoglycemic and Antihyperglycemic Effects of Datura Metel (Linn) Seeds in Normal and Alloxan-induced Diabetic Rats. J. Ethnopharmacol. 91: 95-98.

Kurnal NA, Qobanoglu S, Yalcin C (2010). Acaricidal, Repellent and Oviposition Deterrent Activities of Datura Stramonium L. against Adult Tetranychus Urticae (Koch). J Pest Sci. 83(2): 173-180.

Kurzbaum A, Simsolo C, Kvasha L, Blum A (2001). Toxic delirium due to Datura Stramonium. Isr Med Assoc J. 3(7): 538-539.

Li H, Qing C, Zhang Y, Zhao Z (2005). Screening for Endophytic Fungi with Antitumor and Antifungal Activities from Chinese Medicinal Plants.World J. Micro Biotechnol. 21: 1515-1519.

Li J, Lin B, Wang G, Gao H, Qin M (2012). Chemical Constituents of *Datura stramonium* Seeds. Zhongguo Zhong Yao Za Zhi. 37(3): 319-322.

Mac Millan FSK, Reller HH, Synder FH (1964). The Antiperspirant Action of Topically Applied Anticholinergics. J. Investig. Dermatol. p. 363.

Manickam M, Awasthi SB, Sinha-Bagchi A, Sinha SC, Ray AB (1996). Withanolides from Datura tatula. Phytochemistry 41: 981-983.

Manickam M, Padma P, Chourasia JPN, Ray AB (1997). Evaluation of Antistress Activity of withafastuosin D, a withanolide of Datura fastuosa. Phytother. Res. 11: 384-385.

Manickam M, Srivastava A, Ray AB (1998). Withanolides from the Flowers of Datura Fastuosa. Phytochemistry 47: 1427-1429.

Mdee LK, Masoko P, Eloff JN (2009). The Activity of Extracts of Seven Common Invasive Plant Species on Fungal Phytopathogens. South Afr. J. Bot. 75:375-379.

Mohan R, Hammers HJ, Zhan XH, Herbstritt CJ, Ruiz A, Zhang L, Hanson AD, Commer BP, Rougas J, Priblude VS (2004). Withaferin A is a Potent Inhibitor of Angiogenesis. Angiogenesis 7: 115.

Naude TW, Gerber R, Smith RJ, Botha CJ (2005). Datura Contamination of Hay as the Suspected Cause of an Extensive Outbreak of Impaction Colic in Horses. J S Afr Vet Assoc. 76(2): 107-112.

Norton S. Toxic Effects of Plants (2008). *In*: Klaassen CD. Caserett and Doull's Toxicology, the basic Science of Poisons. 7th ed. New York: McGraw Hill. 1110.

Oberndorfer S, Grisold W, Hinterholzer G, Rosner M (2002). Coma with Focal Neurological Signs Caused by *Datura stramonium* Intoxication in a Young Man. J Neurol Neurosurg Psychiatr. 73(4): 458-459.

Okwu DE, Igara EC (2009). Isolation, Characterization and Antibacterial Activity of Alkaloid from Datura Metel Linn leaves. Afr. J. Pharm. Pharmacol. 3: 277-281.

Pan Y, Wang X, Hu X (2007). Cytotoxic Withanolides from the Flowers of Datura Metel. J. Nat. Prod. 70: 1127-1132.

Papadoyannis IN (1995). Determination of Datura Alkaloids by using Chromatographic Techmiques: Rev. Natl. Tox. 3: 310-316.

Peredery O, Persinger MA (2004). Herbal Treatment Following Post-seizure Induction in Rat by Lithium Pilocarpine: Scutellaria Lateriflora (Skullcap), Gelsemium Sempervirens (Gelsemium) and Datura stramonium (Jimson weed) may Prevent Development of Spontaneous seizures. Phytother Res. 18(9): 700-705.

Preissel U, Preissel HG (2002). Brugmansia and Datura: Angel's Trumpets and Thorn Apples. New York: Firefly Books. 106-129.

Pretorius E, Marx J (2006). Datura Stramonium in Asthma Treatment and Possible Effects on Prenatal Development. Environ. Toxicol.Pharmacol. 21: 331.

Pretorius E, Marx J (2006). Datura Stramonium in Asthma Treatment and Possible Effects on Prenatal Development. Environ Toxicol Pharmacol. 21(3): 331-337.

Rajesh C, Sharma GL (2002). Studies on Antimycotic Properties of Datura Metel. J. Ethnopharmacol. 80: 193-197.

Raut B, Shreshtha AP (2012). Ethenoveterinary Practices in Western Morang, Nepal. Int. J. Pharm. Sci Res. 3: 182-188.

Sasaki T, Yamazaki K, Yamori T, Endo T (2002). Inhibition of Proliferation and Induction of Differentiation of Glioma Cells with Datura Stramonium Agglutinin. Brit. J. Cancer 87: 918-923.

Savitharam N, Sulochana C, Rao KA (2007). Ethnobotanical Survey of Plants Used to Treat Asthma in AP, India, J. Ehthano. 113: 54-61.

Shanmuga PK, Gnanmani A, Radhakrishnan N, Mary B (2002). Healing Potential of Datura Alba on Burn Wounds in Albino Rats. J. Ethnopharmacol. 83: 193-199.

Sharma A, Patel VK (2009). In vitro Screening of the Antibacterial Activity and Identification of Bioactive Compounds from Plants Against Selected Vibrio spp. Pathogens Turk. J. Biol. 33: 137-144.

Sharma N, Trivedi PC (2002). Screening of Leaf Extracts of some Plants for their Nematicidal and Fungicidal Properties Against Meloidogyne Incognita and Fusarium Oxysporum. Asian J. Exp. Sci. 16: 21-28.

Siddiqui S, Sultana N, Ahmed SS, Haider SI (1986). Isolation and Structure of a New Alkaloid Datumetin from the Leaves of Datura Metel. J. Natural Prod. 49: 511-513.

Sonika G, Manubala R, Deepak J (2010). Comparative Studies on Anti-inflammatory Activity of Coriandrum Sativum, Datura Stramonium and Azadirachta Indica. Asian J Exp Biol Sci. 1(1): 151-154.

Spina SP, Taddei A (2007). Teenagers with Jimson Weed (Datura stramonium) Poisoning. CJEM. 9(6): 467-468.

Swathi S, Murugananthan G, Ghosh SK, Pradeep AS (2012). Larvicidal and Repellent Activities of Ethanolic Wxtract of Datura Stramonium Leaves Against Mosquitoes. Inter J Pharmacogn Phytochem Res. 4(1): 25-27.

Tosun F, Akyüz KC, Sener B, Vural M, Palittapogarnpim P (2004). Antimycobacterial Screening of some Turkish Plants. J. Ethnopharmacol. 95: 273-275.

Usha K, Singh B, Praseetha P, Deepa N, Agarwal DK, Agarwal R, Nagaraja A (2009). Antifungal Activity of Datura Stramonium, Calotropis gigantean and Azadirachta indica Against Fusarium Mangiferae and Floral Malformation in Mango. Eur. J. Plant Pathol. 124: 637-657.

Uzun E, Sariyara G, Adsersenb A, Karakocc B, Ötük G, Oktayoglua E, Pirildara S (2004). Traditional Medicine in Sakarya Province (Turkey) and Antimicrobial Activities of Selected Species. J. Ethnopharmacol. 95: 287.

Vitale AA, Acher A, Pomilio AB (1995). Alkaloids of Datura Ferox from Argentina. J. Ethanopharmacol. 49: 81-89.

Wannang NN, Ndukwe HC, Nnabuife C (2009). Evaluation of the Analgesic Properties of the Datura Metel Seeds Aqueous Extract. J. Med. Plants Res. 3: 192-195.

Wollenweber E, Dorsam M, Dörr M, Roitman JN, Valant-Vetschera KM (2005). Chemodiversity of Surface Flavanoids in Solanaceae. Z. Naturforsch. 60c: 661-670.

Yamazaki Z, Tagaya I (1980). Antiviral Effects of Atropine and Caffeine. J. Gen. Virol. 50: 429-431.

Pages: 174-182

MICROBIOLOGICAL AND PHARMACOLOGICAL ASPECTS OF BIODIVERSITY

Edited by: Dr. Pankaj Sharma; Dr. Neha Gautam Sharma & Dr. Pankaj Sharma

ISBN: 978-93-5056-878-1

Edition: 2017

Published by: Discovery Publishing House Pvt. Ltd., New Delhi (India)

Nirgundi (*Vitexnegundo* Linn.): A *Multipurpose Medicinal and Soil Amending Plant*

Jitender Kumar; K.K. Paramanick; A.K. Shukla
Santosh Watpade and Ranjeet Singh

ABSTRACT

Vitex negundo is widely cultivated and found mostly near bodies of water, recently disturbed land, grasslands, and forests. The present study was conducted to evaluate the soil amendment activities of leaves of *Vitex negundo* Linn. It is a multipurpose medicinal plant found throughout India.The evaluation of growth parameters of apple saplings and the values of pH and EC of nursery fields soil in present study indicated that the application of bio-control agent (*Trichoderma viride*) fortified with FYM (100g/kg), soil amendment with *Vitex negundo* leaves (1kg/m^2) in nursery field soil gave maximum values of growth parameters of apple saplings. The above combination of treatments with chopped Nirgundi leaves helped to grow vigorous and graft able apple sapling organically without using any chemical fertilizers. Such practices reduce the uses of chemical fertilizers which affect the nutrient ions concentration of soil, affect plant growth parameters negatively and minimized the physiological disorder symptoms caused by misbalanced use of chemical fertilizers. Different soil amendment techniques help directly or indirectly to improve the soil health.

Keywords: *Vitex negundo,* biocontrol agent, soil amendment, apple sapling, medicinal plant activity.

INTRODUCTION

Medicinal plants are available all over the country. But due to unawareness and shortage of knowledge of identification and medicinal values of these plants are sometimes left unused. *Vitex negundo* is multipurpose

ICAR-Indian Agricultural Research Institute, Regional Station (C&HC), Amartara Cottage, Shimla -171 004 (H.P.) (India)

widely cultivated herb to small tree (Fig. 10.1). The holistic system of Indian medicine is an integral part of our national heritage. The curative science, after years of neglect is on the path of resurgence today. It has become truer with the development of many wonderful drugs of synthetic origin. Taking advantage of tribal and illiterate people of villages, the merchants of medicinal plants, purchase all the plants without knowing its real value at cheap rates and sell these plants in market at very high prices. This practice is making these Indian systems of medicine very expensive. Keeping in view thescarcity of medicinal plants in the near future, it can be said that those who cultivate these herbs can set their own terms for sale which means that medicinal plant will fetch a better price than the cash crops. The ethanol and methanol extracts of Vitex leaves and petroleum ether and chloroform extract of Nirgundi bark exhibited significant antibacterial activity. It supports traditional use of the plant in the treatment of some diseases broad spectrum antibacterial agents (S.K.P, *et al.* 2009). Hippocrates, Dioscorides, and Theophrastus mention the use of Vitex for a wide variety of conditions, including hemorrhage following childbirth, and also to assist with the 'passing of afterbirth." Decovtions of the fruit and plant were also used in sitz baths for diseases of the uterus.The extract of leaves have insecticidal activity. The fresh leaves are burnt with grass as a fumigant against mosquitoes, particularly in cow shed during raining season when mosquitos' problem is at its peak and bite the animals (Hebbalkar *et al.* 1992). The leaves are used to prepare germinated grams which are used in religious functions in Himachal Pradesh. The covering soaked grains with vitex leaves prevent the development of putrefying bacteria. The leaves are used to repel insects in grain stores.

Fig. 10.1: Nirgundi Plant (*Vitex negundo*)

Distribution

Vitex negundo is one well known medicinal and aromatic shrub to small tree. It is growing in the Mediterranean area to western Asia. In India it is growing in different geographical regions of the country and used for different purposes in different localities by the local peoples. It is found growing throughout the greater part of India ascending to an altitude of 1500 m in outer Himalayas. In Himachal Pradesh it is found in almost all the districts except few such as LauhalSpiti and Kinnaur. It is popularly known as nirgundi or five-leaved Chaste tree or bana (Fig. 10.1) in India and belongs to Verbenaceae family. Vitex has effective role in health care and as a source of income in rural areas. All the plant parts are used for medicinal purposes. It contains many polyphenolic compounds, terpenoides, glycosidic, iridoids and alkaloids. In this article the plant characteristics, its distribution, various uses, chemical constituents etc. have been discussed in detail for the benefit of the researchers, teachers, local peoples, farmers, students and social workers. It is used to check soil erosion by growing outside the field.

Plant Description

Vitex negundo or five leaved Chaste treeis commonly known as Nirgundi or bana in India. The plant prefers to grow in light sandy and medium loamy soils. Vitex usually grows from three to nine feet tall, but under cultivation can develop to 20 feet tall. The bark is white felted. It requires well-drained soil and can grow even in nutritionally poor soils. The plant prefers acid, neutral and basic (alkaline) soils. It is often found growing next to streams and requires moist soil. It can be described as a cross between a shrub and a tree with a single woody stem. The overall plant growth varies from 2-5m height that grows slowly. The stem is medium in thickness which is not straight and grows in zigzag fashion covered with white-felted bark. Leaves are usually 5-7 foliate (Fig. 10.2), rarely with 3 leaflets. Opposite leaves are palmately compound (Fig. 10.2). Leaflets are lanceolate, entire, 4-10 cm long, slightly hairy underneath. It flowers from September to October.

Fig. 10.2: Nirgundi Leaves

Fig. 10.3: Nirgundi Lnflorescence

Panicles are terminal, slightly hairy, many-flowered, 10-20 cm long and additional axillary ones often present (Fig. 10.3). Flowers are pale lilac or rose- colored, 6-7 mm long, scented, corolla is two lipped from 6-9 mm long and hermaphrodite i.e have both male and female organs. Flowers blue to lavender and fruit globose, black when ripe, about 4mm in diameter. Pollination takes place mostly through insects. Fruits are small, hard, globose, drupe, gray-brown, and reddish-black when ripe, about 4mm in diameter with a persistent calyx.The flowers are used for medicinal purposes viz. diarrhoea, cholera and liver disorders.

Chemical Constituents and other Ingradients

The chemical constituents which are responsible for the medicinal and pesticidal properties of vitex has been isolated and characterized. Twelve compounds have been identified which include viridiflorol; squalene; beta-sitosterol; 5-hydroxy 3,6,7,3′, 4′-pentamethoxy flavones; 5-hydroxy 3, 7, 3′, 4′- tetramethoxy flavones; 5, 3′- dihydroxy 7, 8, 4′-trimethoxy flavanone; p-hydroxy benzoic acid; 3, 4 –dihydroxy benzoic acid; luteolin 7- glucoside; isoorientin; agnuside; and, 2′-phydroxy benzoyl mussaenosidic acid. Agnuside has been found to possess significant hepatoprotective activity, and viridiflorol exhibited antifeedant activity against Sitophilus oryzae and ovipositional activity against Callosobruchuschinensis (Gupta, *et al.* 2005).

OBJECTIVES

Different soil amendment techniques help directly or indirectly to improve the soil health and help to rejuvenate the disturbed land. Nirgundi plant is among those plants which help in rejuvenation of disturbed soil quickly. The huge vegetative growth of Nirgundi plant helps to overcome such conditions. *Vitex negundo* is good soil amending plant. In present study it was used as nursery soil amending in apple saplings production.

The organic way of apple saplings production helps to overcome the soil-borne diseases by improving the soil health. The healthy soil profile by using the soil amendment techniques improves the production of healthy apple nurseries.

The healthy apple saplings production in nurseries helps in the establishment of healthy orchards. Such organic ways of apple nursery production is easy and cost free methods in which all required materials are easily available and organic waste of fields are recycled.

MATERIALS AND METHODS

The present study was undertaken at Research Farm of ICAR-IARI, Regional Station, Shimla, in Himachal Pradesh. Depending upon the agro climatic conditions and the suitability of a particular area for the growing of specific fruit crops in that area, the state is broadly divided into four agro climatic zones viz. Low hill and valley areas near the plains (350-900 meters m.s.l & rainfall 60-100cms), Mid hills (Sub Temperate, 900-1500m m.s.l, rainfall

90-100cms), High Hills and Valleys in the interior (Temperate, 1500-2750m m.s.l, rainfall 90-100cms), Cold and Dry Zone (Dry Temperate, 2750-3650m m.s.l, rainfall 24-40cms) (Kishore *et al.*, 2006). The present study was carried at the elevation of 1900-2000 meter above mean sea level having average annual rainfall 20-40cms and the temperatures range from -4° C (24.8° F) to 31° C (87.8° F) over the year. The average temperature during summer is between 19° C & 28° C and between -1° C and 10° C in winter. Prior to laying out trials initial soil status of the nurseries was analyzed for pH, Electrical conductivity, Organic carbon/matter and microbial count etc.The treatments were applied subsequently. The bio-control agent was applied after mixing the spores with charcoal powder amounting to 10^{13} spores per hectare. The soil amendments by *Vitex* leaves were applied @ 1Kg/m^2 after chopping the fresh leaves into small pieces and mixing them into upper 10-15 cm depth of well prepared nursery beds (Fig. 10.4).

Fig. 10.4: Soil Amendments by Chopped Leaves of Nirgundi in Apple Nursery

Plant growth characteristics such as plant height, girth, leaf area, fresh and dry root weight were recorded for treatment at experimental sites. The plants were selected randomly and plant height was recorded from stem base to the tip of the seedlings. Plant girth was measured with the help of vernier clipper and recorded in millimeter. Leaf area measurements were recorded with the help of leaf area meter and expressed in square centimeter.

Ten leaves were taken from each treatment. Root weight was recorded after uprooting three plants at random from each treatment. The root portion was cut from the stem base, washed in tap water, air dried and fresh root weight was recorded in grams per plant.

RESULTS AND DISCUSSION

The present investigation was aimed at production of healthy and vigorous apple saplings in nurseries and evaluation for growth parameters viz. plant height, stem girth, fresh root weight, dry root weight and leaf area against soil amendment by *Vitex* leaves.The data on growth parameters viz. plant height (cm), plant girth (mm), fresh root weight (gm), dry root weight (gm) and leaf area (cm^2) of apple sapling at experimental sites after soil amendment techniques were recorded in dormancy period (October-February). The apple saplings growth parameters were affected by soil amendments in nurseries at present experimental sites (Fig. 10.5). The application of biocontrol agents and use of chopped leaves of Nirgundi leaves overcome the drawbacks of conventional method of apple nursery production and ensure organic nursery production also. Apple saplings growth parameters, health and vigorous were affected by soil amendments in nursery at experimental site.

Sanchez *et al.*, (2006) evaluated the effects of soil management on yield, growth and soil fertility in an organic apple orchard cv. Royal Gala/EM 26 and cover crop treatments were applied to the inter-row spaces planted at 4×2 m. Soil organic matter increased in the topsoil especially with permanent cover crops but decreased in the C treatment due to both annual soil tillage and less input of groundcover biomass. It is concluded that tree growth and yield are affected by soil management. Perennial cover crops perform better than annual common vetch. Disking is not a recommended practice because it may decrease the content of soil organic matter and lead to poor tree vigor that corresponds to low fruit bearing potential. However, even with the use of permanent cover crops the addition of organic fertilizers is necessary in order to sustain good yields and proper tree vigor.

Salam *et al*, 2009 conducted on the use of medicinal plant leaf extract have opened a new avenue for the control of plant disease. Medicinal plants are known to possess of various types of alkaloids with varying solubility in different solvents. These alkaloids are believed to have fungicitoxic properties. An effort was made to evaluate these alkaloids extracted from datura, neem, lemon grass, Karanj and *Calotropisprocera*. It concluded that the cold water, hot water and acetone extracts from these plants used to reduce sheath blight disease severity on rice.

The apple saplings growth parameters are affected by soil amendments in nurseries. The application of biocontrol agents and use of chopped leaves of medicinal plants along with soil heating by burning overcome the drawbacks of conventional method of apple nursery production and ensure organic nursery production also (Verma *et. al.*, 2015).

The less input along with organic waste recycling in the cultivation of apple nursery impact soil health and growth parameters of apple sapling. The application of soil amendments along with biocontrol agent i.e. *Trichoderma viride* regulate the population of soil micro flora and increase the organic carbon or matter contents also. Moreover, the soil treatments/amendments applied during the course of this study had residual impact even after one year of the application.Residual impact the soil amendments clearly suggests that it is not necessary to apply the soil amendments in the apple nurseries every year. These amendments can be applied every alternate year.

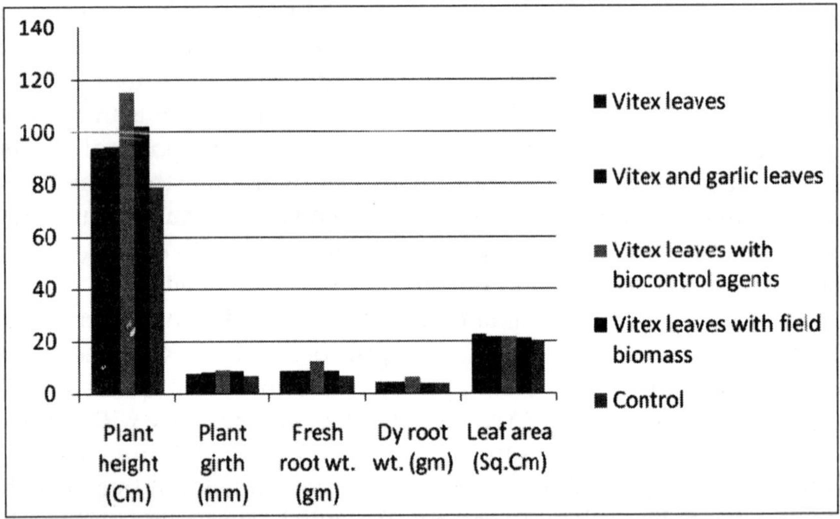

Fig. 10.5: The Growth Parameters of Saplings against Soil Amendments by *Vitex* Leave

OTHER USES OF VITEX NEGUNDO PLANT

Nirgundi is an ayurvedic herb which has been used since ancient times as a remedy herb. It is used as a drug of choice to manage pain, inflammation and other related diseases.

Parts utilized: Leaves, bark, roots and seeds. Leaves may be harvested three months after establishment.

Medicinal Uses

The leaves are astringent, febrifuge, sedative, tonic and vermifuge. It treats mild cuts and wounds. It is also an important cure for bruises and different kinds of skin infections (Sahni *et al.*, 2001). The whole plant is used for medicinal purposes. In tradition, it was also known as an important European remedy for controlling and regulating and Dysmenorrhoeal, it also helped ease menopausal problems and aided the birth process.

The dried fruit is vermifuge and is also used in the treatment of angina, colds, coughs, rheumatic difficulties etc.

The root is expectorant, febrifuge and tonic. It is used in the treatment of colds and rheumatic ailments. The plant is said to be a malarial preventative and is also used for the treatment of bacterial dysentery.

Nirgundi possesses potent snake venom neutralizing capacity (Alam and Gomes, 2003). Snake venom is neutralized by Indian medicinal plants *Vitexnegundo*and *Emblica officinalis* root extracts.

Nirgundi oil is herbal oil extracted from Nirgundi plant. This oil act as a mild painkiller and helps to relaxes the muscles and ensures good natural sleep. This oil is very useful for vatta dominant people. The study was conducted to assess the antioxidant activity of methanol and hexane extract and essential oil from *Vitex negundo* leaf using different *in vitro* antioxidant assays (M. Zargar, *et al.*, 2011).

As there are other varieties of Nirgundi so make sure to have the five leaved varieties for medicinal uses. The use of dried leaves as a regular tea helps to ease headaches related to migraines.

Edible Uses

Seed- Occasionally used as a condiment, it is a pepper substitute. When washed to remove the bitterness it can be ground in to a powder and used as a flour, though it is very much a famine food used only when all else fails.

A tea is made from the roots and leaves of the Nirgundi plant.

Preparation of Syrup

Clean fresh Nirgundi leaves and chopped with knife. Boil 4 tablespoons of minced Nirgundi leaves for 50 minutes in 4 glasses of water. Strain the liquid extract and add 1 part honey to 4 parts extracts. Boil this extract in an earthen pot/enamel lined saucepan for 15 minutes until the desired viscosity is attained and cool the extract before preservation. Among the herbal extracts, root extract of Vitex is very useful. The mature fresh leaves of *Vitex negundo* have anti-inflammatory and analgesic activities (Dharmasiri, *et al.* 2003).

Insecticidal and Pesticide Uses

The use of plant products in crop pest control is gaining importance because of their safety to non target organisms and the environment.The *Vitex* negundo leaf extract served as a potential larvicidal agent against Japanese encephalitis vector *C. tritaeniorhynchus* and additionally acted as a promising repellent against various adult vector mosquitoes (Chowdhury *et. al.*, 2011).

Uses in Preparing Valuable Items

The young stems are used in basket making and for making wattles.Nirmalakumari (2006) also reported on callus induction from bark of Vitex negundo on medium supplemented with combination 2.5 mg/L 2,4-D and 0.75 mg/L kinetin.

REFERENCES

Alam M.I., Gomes A (2003): Snake Venom Neutralization by Indian Medicinal Plants (*Vitexnegundo*and *Emblica officinalis*) Root Extracts. *J. Ethnopharmacol.* 86: 75-80.

Chowdhury N.Y., Islam W., and Khalequzzaman M., (2011): Insecticidal Activity of Compounds from the Leaves of *Vitexnegundo* (Verbenaceae) against Triboliumcastaneum (Coleoptera: Tenebrionidae). *International Journal of Tropical Insect Science*, Volume 31, Number 03, Page 174.

Dharmasiri MG, Jayakody JRAC, Galhena G, Liyanage SSP, Ratnasooriya WD (2003): Anti-inflammatory and Analgesic Activities of Mature Fresh Leaves of *Vitex negundo*. *J. Ethnopharmacol.* 87: 199-206.

Gupta A.K., Tandon N., Sharma M. (2005): Quality Standards of Indian Medicinal Plants. Indian Council of Medical Research, New Delhi, India.

Hebbalkar D.S., Hebbalkar G.D., Sharma R.N., Joshi V.S., and Bhat B.S. (1992): Mosquito Repellant Activity of Oils from Vitex Negundo Linn Leaves. *Ind. J. Med. Res.* 95: 200-203.

Kishore D.K., Sharma S.K., and Paramanick, K.K. (2006): A Text Book on Current Scenario of Temperate Fruits in H.P. New India Publishing Agency, Pitam Pura, New Delhi - 110 088.

Nirmala Kumari A., (2006): Effect of Phytohormones on the in-vitro Callus Formation in Vitex Negundo L. *Madras Agric. J.* 93 (7-12), 217-221.

Panda S.K., Thatoi H.N. and Dutta S.K. (2009): "Antibacterial Activity and Phytochemical Screening of Leaf and Bark Extracts of Vitex Negundo L. from Similipal Biosphere Reserve, Orissa." *Journal of Medicinal Plants Research,* Vol. 3 (4), 294-300.

Sahni Y.P., Srivastava D.N., and Gaidhani S.N. (2001): Protective Activity of some Indigenous Medicinal Plants on Gastric Ulceration in Albino Rats. *J. Med. Arom. Plant Sci.* 22: 89-90.

Salam D., Lakpale N., and Thrimurty V.S., (2009): Evaluation of Plant Extracts Against *Rhizoctoniasolani* Causing Sheath Blight of Rice. *J Myco Pl Pathol.*, 39(3): 523-525.

Sanchez, E.E., Cichon L.I., and Fernandez D., (2006): Effects of Soil Management on Yield, Growth and Soil Fertility in an Organic Appleorchard. *ActaHorticulturae*,721, 49-53.

Verma J.K., Sharma A. and Paramanick K.K. (2015): Biotic and Abiotic Factors of Apple Nursery. R.N. Kharwar *et al.* (eds.), *Microbial Diversity and Biotechnology in Food Security*, DOI 10.1007/978-81-322-1801-2_21, © Springer India 2014 pp. 243-249.

Verma J.K., Sharma A. and Paramanick K.K. (2015): To Evaluate the Values of Electrical Conductivity and Growth Parameters of Apple Saplings in Nursery Fields. *Int. Journal of Applied Sciences and Engineering Research,* Vol. 4(3), 321-332.

Zargar M., Azizah A.H., Roheeyati A.M., Fatimah A.B., Jahanshiri F., and Pak-Dek M.S., (2011): "Bioactive Compounds and Antioxidant Activity of Different Extracts from Vitex Negundo Leaf." *Journal of Medicinal Plants Research,* Vol. 5 (12), 2525-2532.

Pages: 183-202
MICROBIOLOGICAL AND PHARMACOLOGICAL ASPECTS OF BIODIVERSITY
Edited by: Dr. Pankaj Sharma; Dr. Neha Gautam Sharma & Dr. Pankaj Sharma
ISBN: 978-93-5056-878-1
Edition: 2017
Published by: Discovery Publishing House Pvt. Ltd., New Delhi (India)

Therapeutic Claims of Chyawanprash
An Ayurvedic Polyherbal Formulation

Dr. Rohit Sharma[1*]; Dr. Hetal Amin[2]; Mr. Atul Kabra[3]; Prof. PK Prajapati[4]

ABSTRACT

Chyawanprash (CP) is an Ayurvedic category of *Rasayana*- a super-concentrated mixture of vitamin-rich herbs and minerals designed to restore spent reserves of vital energy (*ojas*) and maintaining physique, vigour and vitality, while delaying the ageing process. CP is prepared by incorporating around 50 herbs including *Amla* (Indian gooseberry), the richest source of vitamin C. Herbs used in preparation of formulation are boiled in water, then dried extract is combined with honey followed by addition of aromatic (like cardamom, cinnamom, and clove) herb powders. The finished product, having fruit jam like consistency, is sweet, sour and spicy in taste. CP deserves a scientific exploration so as to comprehend its therapeutic utility. Scattered information exploring therapeutic potential of CP is accessible and there is need to assemble it. Therefore, an effort is made to assemble the scattered information in prehistoric Ayurvedic texts and other Ayurvedic treatises along with ethno-botanical and modern evidences highlighting the role of CP in therapeutics. Citations relevant to topic were screened.

Keywords: Chyawanprash, Ayurveda, *Amla*, Medicinal plants, Herbs, Traditional medicine

INTRODUCTION

Chyawanprash (CP) [also spelled chyavanaprasha, chyavanaprash, chyavanaprasam and chyawanaprash] comprise of two words, '*Chyawana*' and '*Prasha*'. The former stands for the name of a sage. The word also denotes 'degenerative change'. The latter word denotes a drug or diet, which is fit for ingestion. CP is a comprehensive 'metabolic'tonicthatcontains a variety of herbs,which is used in Ayurvedicmedicine to promote health and prevent disease. CP is an ancient Ayurvedic polyherbal formulation, prepared according to an ancient Ayurvedic formula, fortified with various herbs, herbal extracts and minerals, which is used to boost immunity and longevity. It is a magical name in man's quest for immortality, freedom from disease and delaying old age. Regarded by many connoisseurs as the ultimate health supplement, CP has been around for thousands of years. CP is a traditional Ayurvedic polyherbal jam prepared according to an ancient Ayurvedic formula with multiple health benefits. CP is very commonly used health supplement and medicine since centuries; and since the day of its inception to age of technology, it remained in the heart of Indians irrespective of political, cultural and scientific upheavals. Long before there were vitamins, minerals, and antioxidant supplements, there was CP, one of Ayurveda's most respected anti-aging foods.[1]

Rasayana is a branch of Ayurveda which deals with all specialized approaches aimed at prolonging life, preventing aging and disease, elimination of all degenerative processes and promoting excellent health. Among all the *Rasayana* formulations enumerated in the classical and medieval periods, the CP undoubtedly stands out as the monarch. This formulation has made major strides as an over the counter product since it was placed in the consumer market in the 1950's. CP is widely sold and consumed in India as a dietary supplement. It is highly appreciated to possess multiple health benefits and cover the preventive, promotive and curative aspects of health.

CP is made in *Amla/Amalaki* (*Phyllanthus emblica*/Indian gooseberry) base, which is the most useful *Rasayana* for maintaining homeostasis.[2] The formulation is an admixture of at least five tastes such as sweet, sour, bitter, pungent and astringent, due to *Amla*.[3] CP improves all aspects of health, when taken regularly.[4]

ORIGIN

Its rather unusual name is derived from the legend of *Chyavana Rishi*, a forest sage. Various Indian holy books like Mahabharat, Puranas etc., relate that *Ashwini Kumar* brothers, the twins, who were *Raj Vaidya* (royal physicians) to *Devas* (gods) during Vedic times, first prepared this formulation for *Chyawan Rishi* at his Ashram on Dhosi Hill near Narnaul, Haryana, India, hence the name CP. He practiced austerities to gain enlightenment, which made him old and weak. He used CP to regain his youth and rejuvenated his body.[5-8] The first historically documented formula for CP appears in Charaka Samhita, the ancient Ayurvedic treatise.Here it is appreciated as the foremost of all herbal rejuvenative tonics.[9]

COMPOSITION

CP falls, by virtue of its consistency and dosage form, under the category of *Awaleha-paka* group of Ayurvedic formulations.[10] Generally CP includes four class of herbal drugs: *Dashmula* class (ten roots); *Chaturjata* class (four aromatic plants); substitution of *Ashtavarga* (*Ashtavarga*: threatened medicinal herbs of north-west Himalaya, which are not commercially available in modern era);[11] and general class (other than former classes). The recipe of CP is mentioned in manuscripts written for ayurvedic method of treatment viz. Ashtanga Hridayam, Charaka Samhita, Sangandhara Samhita. The dominant ingredient is *Amla*, a long-living tree that produces an intensely sour citrus fruit; it is one of the most powerful rejuvenative herbs in Ayurveda. The main ingredients of CP with their botanical identities and specific therapeutic roles are detailed in Table 11.1.

All the ingredients in CP have been scientifically validated individually for their health benefits. The combination of these nutrients used in CP in a specific quantity and manner of blending creates a powerful synergy for optimum health benefits.[12,13] But nowadays many pharmaceutical and herbal companies deviate from the original formula given in Ayurveda. CP is lost somewhere in between the procedures of preparation and the methods of promotion to make it more special than competitors' product. If an ingredients other than traditional formula is added it can no more be called as CP.[14]

PREPARATION OF CP

In absence of standard operating procedure (SOP) in ancient times, the method of preparation, of CP varies from manufacturer to manufacturer and place to place.In Indian system of medicine, use of 500 number of *Amla* in many formulations in single lot has been described. However, numerical v/s quantitative variations in ingredients of CP (i.e. variation in size and quantity of available pulp) is the biggest limiting factor for the SOP (Standard Operative Procedure) and standardization. Weight of 500 fresh *Amla* varies from 2.5-25.25 kg.*Amla* collected and used in ancient times was mainly obtained from wild trees. Wild *Amla* fruit is comparatively richer in vitamin C content than cultivated varieties.[15] AFI (Ayurvedic Formulary of India) mentions use of 2.5 kg for 500 number of fresh *Amla* and 2.4 kg sugar for its preparation.[10] If cultivated *Amla* is available, 500 such fruits would weigh approximately 6.5 kg.

Standard method of preparation of CP is described as follows: 50g meach of the following plants, viz. *Bel, Arni, Gambhari, Arlu, Patla, Gokhru, Shalparni, Brihati, Kantakari, Kakdashingi, Munakka, Harde, Giloy, Bala, Bhumiamla, Adusa, Jivanti, Kachur, Pushkarmool, Nagarmotha, Magdaparni, Mashparni, Shalparni, Prishparni, Pippali, Kaknasa, Varahikand, Vidarikand, Punarnawa, Kanwal, Agar, Chandan, Shatavari* and *Ashwagandha*, are suspended in around 16l water. 500 *Amla* fruits (each weighing around 15-20 gm, total weight approximately 6.5 kg) are wrapped in a clean cloth and are dipped into the above ad mixture of plants. Mixture is heated until the volume is reduced to one quarter. After removing the cloth, seeds are discarded from *Amla;* rubbing the peels of *Amla* on a mesh, fibers are discarded and finally, *Amla pithi* (wet paste of *Amla*) is prepared. Decoction is filtered and mare is discarded.

Table 11.1: Ingredients of CP with their botanical identities and specific therapeutic roles

Plant Name	Common Name	Uses
Adhatodavasica Nees	*Adusa,Vasaka*	Cardiotonic, expectorant, diuretic, cardiac & respiratory disorders.
Aeglemannelos Correa	*Silva, Be*	Useful in chronic dysentery, diarrhoea & dyspepsia.
Aquilariaagallocha Roxb.	*Agar, Agarkashta*	Aromatic, neurotrophic, carrninative & aphrodisiac.
Bambusaanmdinacea Willd	*Vansh/ochan*	Stimulant, a stringent and aphrodisiac.
Boerhaal'iadiffusa Linn.	*Punarnawa, Punarnava, Gad-hapuran*	Cardiotonic, hematinic, diuretic & help sinanemia
Cinnamomum tamala Nees & Ebrrn.	*Tamalpatra, Tejpatra, Patra*	Helps in general debility, anorexia & indigestion, uterine stimulant.
Cinnamomumzeylanicum Breyn	*Dalchini*	Anemia, general debility, abdominal distension & anorexia.
Curcuma zedoaria Rose.	*Kachur, Sathikehora*	Stimulant, tonic, depurative, vertigo & during pregnancy.
Cypemsrotundus Linn.	*Nagarmotha, Mustak, Motha*	Neurotrophic, carrninative, helps in constipation, hepatoprotective.
Desmodiumbulbifera Desv.	*Shalparni, Sarivan*	General debility, nervine tonic, cardiac, blood & respiratory disorders
Elettariacardamomum Maton	*Elaichi, Cardamwn*	Generaltonic, useful in anorexia and flatulence.
Emblicaofficinalis Gaertn.	*Amalaki, Al/a. Awala,* Indian Gooseberry	Rejuvenative, neurotrophic, hepatoprotective, antioxdant, cardiotonic, rich source of vitamin C.
Gmelina arborea Roxb.	*Gambhari, Khambhari, Kash-marya*	Promotes lactation & helps in indigestion.
Leptadeniareticulata Wight& Am.	*JivanIi*	Cooling, eye tonic, nutrient and a phrodisiac.
Martyniadiandra Glox.	*Kaknasa, Kakakshi, Kauathodi*	Hepatotonic, cholagogue, laxative, anorexia, indigestion & constipation.
Mesuaferrea Linn.	*Nagkesar*	Nutrient, cardiotonic, brain tonic, carminative and appetizer.
Nelumbiwnspecioswn Willd.	*Kanwal. Neelkamal*	Neurotrophic, cardiotonic & helps in general debility.
Oroxylumindicum Vent.	*Arlu, Sonapatlw, Shyonak*	General debility, diarrhoea & dysentery.
Phaseolustrilobus-sensu Ait.	*Mudgparni, Van-mug, Mataki*	Aphrodisiac, mild sedating, fatigue, general debility, malnutrition.
Phyllanthusni111ri Linn.	*Bhumyaamalaki, Blmmi-amla, Bhueawala*	Apetizer, cholagogue, laxative, hepatoprotective & antiviral.

(Table Contd...)

Plant Name	Common Name	Uses
Piperlongum Linn.	*Pippali*	General debility, dyspepsia, flatulence, respiratory tract infection.
Pistacia integerrima Stewart-ex Brandis	*Kakdashingi, Karkatshingi, Shringi*	Expectorant, carminative, anorexia, cholagogue, cough & asthma.
Premnailltegrifolia Linn.	*Arni, Agnimantha*	Laxative, helps in indigestion & cough.
Ptertoc(//pussantalinus Linn.f.	*Lal Chandan*	Skin, blood & eye disorders, used as disinfectant tomucus membranes of genito-urinary & bronchialtracts.
Sesamumindicum Linn.	*Til* oil, Sesameoil	Cooking oil, tonic, nutrient, aphrodisiac, diuretic, curesdry cough, asthma, lung diseases, inflammation, ulcers, urinary diseases, migraine & vertigo.
Sidacordifolia Linn.	*Bala, Bariyara*	Cardiotonic, stomachic, aphrodisiac & generaltonic.
Solanumindicum Linn.	*Brihati, Barikateri, Vanbhantlw*	Cardiac tonic, astringent, carminative & helps in flatulence
Solanumxanthocaipum Schrad & Wendi.	*Kantakari, Chhotikateri, Kashta-kari*	Mucolytic, expectorant, allergic bronchitis, bronchial asthma, and common cold.
Stereospermum suaveolens Prodr.	*Paru/Patla, Patha, Padhal*	General debility, dyspepsia, blood disorders, cough & acidity.
Teramnuslabialis Spreng.	*Mashparni,Van-udadh, Mashvan*	Aphrodisiac, mildsedative, general debility, malnutrition & fatigue.
Terminaliachebula Retz.	*Harde, Haritaki, Harad, Abhaya*	Neurotrophic, carminative, infertility, cardiac and liver disorders.
Tinosporacordifolia Miersex Hookf. & Thoms.	*Guduchi, Giloy, Amrla*	Generaltonic, immunomodulator, helps indegenerative disorders.
Trib11!11sterrestris Linn.	*Gokhm. Gokshura*	Aphrodisiac, diuretic & cardiotonic
Urariapicta Desv.	*Prishniparni, Pithwan, Devala*	Generaldebility, nervinetonic, cardiac & blood disorders, antidote for snake venom.
Vitisvinifera Linn.	*Draksha, Munnaka*	Nutrient, stomachic, demulcent, laxative, anorexia, hepatoprotective, dyspepsia & constipation.
Animal fat	*Ghee*	Nutrient
Honey	Obtained from honey bees	Mildlaxative, bactericidal, sedative, antiseptic, useful for cold, cough, fever, soreeyes, throat, tongue, duo-denalulcers & liver diseases.

(Table Contd...)

Plant Name	Common Name	Uses
Sucrose	Sugar	Sweet eningagent.
Asparagusracemosus Willd	*Shatavari, Shatavar*, Substituent for *Medha, Mahamedha*	Aphrodisiac, nutrient, potent galactogogue, goodtonic for lactating mothers.
Dioscorea bulbifera Linn.	*Varahikand, Varahi*, Substituent for *Ridhi, Vridhi*	Aphrodisiac, useful in acidity & ulcers.
lpomoeadigitata Linn.	*Vidarikand*, Substituent for *Jeevak, Rishabh*	Aphrodisiac, tonic, helps in nervous debility, skin problems, hepatic disorders & constipation.
Withania somnifera Dunal	*Ashwagandha, Asgandh*, Substituent for *Kako/i, Ksheerkakoli*	Aphrodisiac, antioxidant, loss of memory, loss of muscular energy.
Ayurvedic Preparation	*Abhrak Bhasam*	General debility, useful in asthma & cough.
Ayurvedic preparation	*Shukti Bhasam*	As calcium supplement, neurotrophic, useful in cardi; and bone disorders.
Ayurvedic preparation	*Shring Bhasam*	Useful in pneumonia, rheumatic pain & cough.
Ayurvedic preparation	*Makardhawaj*	Aphrodisiac, nervine tonic and helps in rheumatic pain.
Eugeniacaryophyllus Linn.	*Lavang*, Clove	Antiseptic, aromatic, carminative, stimulant & flavoring agent.

Amlapithi is mixed with *Yamakadravyas* (500 gm ghee and 500 gm sesame oil) in an iron pan and fried untilred. Decoction of plants is added with sugar and sugar syrup is prepared. Fried *Amla pithi* is added to this decoction syrup and heated until ghee starts separating. After removing the pan from fire, *Prakshepa dravya* (powders of 150g *Vanshlochan,* 100g *Pippali* and 10 g each of *Nagkesar, Elaichi, Tamalpatra* and *Dalchini*) are mixed and stirring is continued till a homogenous mixture is obtained. After cooling, 250 g old honey is added and finally the finished product, which is dark shining brown in colour with fruit jam like consistency is prepared.

Some Ayurvedic additives, *Shukti Bhasm* 100 gm, *Abharak Bhasm* 100 gm, *Shring Bhasm* 100 gm, *Makardhawaj* 25 gm, *Lavang* (clove) 25 gm and *Rajata* (silverfoil) 75 in number, for special health benefits are added by some manufacturers.[1]

MODE OF ADMINISTRATION

CP can be consumed by people of all ages in all seasons, as it contains ingredients, which are weather friendly nullifying the unpleasant effects due to extreme environmental and climatic conditions.[16,2] CP is to be consumed in a quantity that does not influence the hunger and appetite for food.[17-21] CP (12-28 gm) is taken with 100-250 ml milk in the morning on empty stomach.[21,22]

It is advised to avoid milk and curd intake for individuals suffering from asthma/respiratory disorders.[22] In such cases the formulation can be advised with luke warm water. It is recommended to consume CP within a year from the manufacturing date as a study indicates that chemical degradation might take place during storage and may result in the loss of therapeutic activity of CP.[23]

TASTE AND APPEARANCE

CP is a polyherbal formulation with a semi-solid sticky mass was brownish black appearance, predominantly having sweet and pungent aroma, sweet and astringent after taste with smell of *Prakshepa dravya* (powder of seven herbs).[24,25] The taste is largely dominated by the flavours of honey, ghee (clarified butter) and *Triphala,* and the smell by ghee and other spices including sandalwood, cinnamon and cardamom.

THE 'VITAMIN C' CONTROVERSY

Amla, one of the richest sources of vitamin C (445 mg/100g), constitutes the main ingredient (35%).[26,27] Due to lack of suitable quality control standards of Ayurvedic drugs, it is difficult to ensure the uniformity of their composition and consequently the efficacy of final products.[28] Even though the official methods for quality assurance of CP[29] do not include vitamin C content, there are conflicting reports on the presence of Vitamin C in CP,[30,31] probably due to adoption of less sensitive and non-specific methods for its determination. A study in 1997 found that the tested samples of CP do not contain any vitamin C and it is probably destroyed during frying of *Amla* pulp with ghee in pharmaceutical process.[32] Though subsequent researchers reported that Vitamin C does not get deteriorated on heat exposure during preparation of CP,[33,23] where a study reported 34 mg/100 g Vitamin C in CP.[34]

NUTRITIONAL SUPPLEMENTATION

Along with rich vitamin, protein, dietary fibre, energy contents, carbohydrate and low fat contents (no trans fat and zero percent cholesterol), appreciable levels of major and minor trace elements (mg/100g)viz. Fe (21.1), Zn (3.1), Co (3.7), Cu (0.667), Ni (1.4), Pb (2.4), Mn (8.3), vitamin C (0.5), and tannic acid (20.2) are found in CP, that acts as micronutrients for health restorative purpose. The essential phtoconstituents it provides are namely flavonoids, alkaloids, saponins, antioxidants, piperine, phenolic compounds etc.Its rich nutritive composition and antioxidant potential is essential for immunomodulation, body building and health restoration.[35]

HEALTH BENEFITS

Ancient Claims and Contemporary Scientific Evidences

CP has been used in India as a health food and nutraceutical continuously with the same vigour and enthusiasm for the past 5000 years. CP has been in use for centuries and has survived due to the benefits that it offers. Many Ayurvedic scholars call CP as "Ageless Wonder". The recipe of CP has stood the test of time and is still beneficial to alleviate modern day health concerns. In context of CP, Charaka Samhitanarrates: 'It is the foremost of all rasayanas, especially good for alleviating cough and asthma; it nourishes the weak, the wounded, the old, and those that are of tender years as well.' Through the use of this Rasayana 'a person acquires intelligence, memory, comeliness of body, freedom from disease, longevity, strength of the senses, great pleasure in the companionship with women, great increase in the strength of the digestive fire, improvement of the complexion, and the restoration of wind to its normal course.'[3,36]

Ayurveda uses the 3 *doshas*, *Vata*, *Pitta*, and *Kapha*, to give a holistic view of your health. CP helps balance these doshas. The balances and imbalances of these 3 doshas give a great way to approach wellness in a way that ties together everything that may be happening with you.In Ayurvedic perspective, the specific actions of herbs in CP in the *poshaka rasa* level (nutrient supplement) *agni* level (metabolic appreciation) and *srotas* level (tissue nourishment) are well accepted.[37]

CP has passed the scrutiny of several scientific studies. Contemporary studies corroborate and validate the ancient claims and traditional beliefs of its therapeutic use. The spices and herbs of CP help improve the circulation in the body, thus removing the toxins from various tissues and internal organs. It creates a harmonious synergy in the body leading to better metabolism. All the ingredients in CP have been studied individually by scientific and medical community for their benefits. It is not always possible to find the active phyto-constituent and the rationality of a particular herb in terms of modern scientific methods. But all that is beyond the reach of scientific proof is not irrational and non-existing, as rightly depicted by Charaka Samhita, 'What is visible to human being is only a small fraction of this universe and what we cannot perceive is much more than that, which doesn't make that non-existent'. CP is beneficial for the health in a number of ways. It is anexcellent ergogenic (enhancing physical performance), tonic, rejuvenator, anabolic, immuno modulator and provides strength to stomach, intestines, liver, lungs, brain, heart, blood vessels, nerves, kidneysand reproductive organs.[38]

IMPROVES DIGESTION AND METABOLISM

CP is helpful in clearing the accumulated excreta by promoting digestion and excretion. It relieves nausea & vomiting and corrects hyperacidity, dyspepsia & flatulence. CP is helpful in gastritis, peptic ulcer, intestinal cramping, and improves the functioning of the gastro intestinal tract. It is also a great detoxifier and blood purifier, which are both vital for a healthy liver.[19, 1] It is hepato protective, strengthens liver and kidneys and streamlines the metabolism of fats and proteins.[39-43] The ingredients of CP such as *Nagkesar, Tamalpatra, Elaichi, Dalchini. Patla, Arni, Gambhari, Bel, Arlu. Shalparni. Draksha, Harde,* honey, *Bhumyaamalaki, Kachur, Pushkarmool, Nagarmotha, Kaknasa. Vidarikand* and *Agar* help in correcting digestive system related complaints.[44,45]

It is very common to add the nourishing honey and ghee (clarified butter) in certain Ayurvedic herbal formulations act as 'a carrier of herbs' called *Yogavahi* and probably promotes the quick absorption and assimilation of various herbal constituents deep into the tissues (Ayurveda strongly promotes lacto-vegan diet which includes milk and milk derivatives). In the case of CP, its sweet flavour favours its quick assimilation into the bloodstream, which helps to better facilitate its active ingredients into cell walls.[46,47]

PROTECT AND STRENGTHENS THE RESPIRATORY SYSTEM

The smooth functioning of the tracheo bronchial tree of the respiratory system is ensured by regular in take of CP. Adequate hydration is maintained in the respiratory system. It alleviates cough, asthma and broncho spasm of seasonal or non-seasonal origin, thereby strengthening the respiratory system. It is also useful in respiratory infections, common cold and tuberculosis. It is also used as an adjunct to anti-tubercular drugs as an add-on therapy.[48-50] *Pippali, Kantakari, Kakdashingi, Bhumyaamalaki, Vasaka, Pushkarmool, Prishniparni, Arni, Shalparni,*seasame oil and *Amla* help in nourishing the respiratory system.[44,45,51]

ANTIOXIDENT, ADAPTOGENIC AND IMMUNO-BOOSTER

For centuries it's been used to maintain youth and optimal health, and its adaptogenic properties make it an excellent anti-aging and anti-stress tonic. The rejuvenating and tonic properties of CP are considered majorly due to their antioxidant principles, which in turn are due to the presence of flarvonoid, tannis and phenolic constituents.[52-55] Experimental and clinical evidence are, however lacking. Recent studies have shown that polyphenols possess potential neuro protective and antioxidant properties.[56] CP is an effective adaptogenic.[57] Some clinical reports do suggest adaptogenic and antioxidant effect of CP on normal and depressive patients and its effect.[58]

A study evaluated and as certained highly potent free radical scavenging (based on the ability to scavenge the synthetic DPPH) and antioxidant activities of ethyl acetate extracts of various market brands of CP. The findings were close to the standard ascorbic acid (IC 50 20.693 µg/ml).[59]

CP strengthens immunity and facilitate shealing process.[60] Due rich *Amla* percentage, CP is loaded in high Vitamin C content and polyphenolics including flavonoids, it possess potent antioxidant and free radical scavenging activity, enhance the immune system and fight infections.[61] Vitamin C also help to retrieve or refill the energy lost by body.[62] Vitamin C is released into the body due to an inherent mechanism and is mainly conjugated to gallic acid and reducing sugars thus resulting to the formation of complex synergistic effect with other phyto conetituents.[63] Many of the natural antioxidants, hence, especially flavanoids exhibit a wide range of biological effects, including antibacterial, antiviral, and anti inflammatory, anti allergic, antithrombotic, and vasodilatory actions.[64]

NOOTROPIC POTENTIAL

CP Nourishes the brain cells, promotes coordination among various body parts, improves memory, and increases learning ability, storage, recall and intellect. It has a calming effect on Central Nervous System (CNS), thereby reducing anxiety and stress-induced psychiatric problems and imparts sound sleep. Researches also suggests its pro-cholenergic activity and antiamnesic potential.[65-67] The rich Amla and ascorbic acid contents play crucial role in such activities.[68,69] *Nagkesar, Guduchi, Nagarmotha, Vidarikand, Kanwal, Agar, Ashwagandha, Shalparni, Prishniparni* and*Amla* help to sharpen the CNS. Several of these ingredients possess antioxidant and anti-inflammatory properties.[44,45]

CARDIOTONIC VALUE

CP is a powerful cardiotonic and strengthens heart, improves force and rate of contraction of heart by improving the blood supply to cardiac muscles. It helps in purification of blood and elimination of toxins. CP also lowers cholesterol levels by improving blood lipid profile.[34,70] *Amla, Kanwal, Punarnawa, Pushkarmool, Kachur, Vasaka, Bala, Shalparni, Prishniparni, Brihati* and *Gokhru* help in streamlining the cardiovascular system (CVS). [44,45]

POTENT APHRODISIAC AND BALANCES THE ENDOCRINE SYSTEM

Regular intake of CP makes sexual life pleasuresome, enhances libido and fertility in both the sexes. It improves the functioning of gonads, strengthens endocrine system and balances the hormonal flow. It thickens semen in males and streamlines menstrual cycle in females.[71-73] *Gokhru, Varahikand,* seasameoil, *Shatavari, Vidarikand, Bala, Jivanti, Mudgparni, Mashparni, Ashwagandha* and *Vanshlochan,* have been found to act as aphrodisiacs and tonics.[44,45]

RADIOPROTECTIVE, CYTOPROTECTIVE, GENOPROTECTIVE, ANTIMUTAGENIC, AND ANTICARCINOGENIC EFFECTS

A study evaluated the radio protective effect of CP in mice exposed to lethal dose of gamma-radiation revealed that CP can provide good radio protection at a very low non-toxic dose. The best protection was seen for 15 mg/kg, where the highest number of survivors was observed at the end of 30 days post-irradiation.[74] A study investigated geno protective efficacy of CP (Dabur) against tobacco smoke on the somatic chromosomes of 25 male bidi smokers. 20 gms of CP was fed to bidi smokers for 2 months, twice a day. Bidi smokers were compared with CP-fed bidi smokers. Mitotic index (MI), chromosomal aberrations (CA), sister chromatid exchanges (SCE) and satellite associations (SA) were analysed. In CP-fed bidi smokers as compared with bidi smokers all the parameters showed a significant decrease ($P<0.01$). The frequency of CA (1.00) practically came down to the level of controls (0.88) indicating that CP can minimise the genotoxic risk caused by mutagenic agents present in tobacco smoke.[58] Due to rich Amla contents, it also exhibits cytoprotective (effective against metal clastogens), anti carcinogenic, anti mutagenic activities and neutralizes the side effects of chemotherapy and radiation.[75-80]

FAVOURABLE EFFECTS ON LIPID PROFILE AND GLYCEMIC LEVELS

Owing to rich sugar and honey contents, CP is generally considered to be contraindicated in diabetics, however, contrary to this widespread belief, CP is reported to reduce the postprandial glycemia in the oral glucose tolerance test and it also reduced blood cholesterol level to a significantly greater extent than vitamin C.[34]CP is also an efficient hypolipidaemic.[81] A study conducted on CP for evaluation of health promotion in elderly people reported decrease in cholesterol, Triglyceride, LDL and increase in HDL level within the normal range exhibits its ripple effects on particular indications those age cited in *Phalasruti* (beneficial effects) of this formulation.[82]

OTHER PREVENTIVE, PROMOTIVE AND CURATIVE HEALTH BENEFITS

CP helps in the absorption of calcium, strengthens bones and teeth by increasing absorption of calcium and improves muscle tone by increasing protein synthesis. It stimulates growth in children, helps to increase weight

Table 11.2: Comparative test performance scores of leading market brands of CP

Brand / Parameter	Wt %	Baidyanath Kesari Kalp	Apollo Pharmacy	Dabur	Humdard	Divya	Himalaya [Patanjali Yogpeeth]	Himani	Zandu (Sona Chandi)
(1)	(2)	(3)	(4)	(5)	(6)	(7)	(8)	(9)	(10)
Pack size, gm		1000	1000	1000	1000	1000	1000	1000	1000
MRP ₹	520	220	210	210	200	220	230	185	
Physico-chemical Tests									
Antioxidant	8	6.94	7.77	6.88	7.71	6.97	7.51	6.09	7.74
Phenolic Compound	5	4.02	4.67	3.99	4.5	4.05	4.42	3.78	4.49
Vitamin C	8	6.22	8	7	7.2	6.27	5.98	6.88	4.54
Piperine	4	3.48	3.4	3.56	4	3.44	3.72	2.8	3.36
Steroids	4	4	4	4	4	4	4	4	4
Fat	4	3.74	3.7	3.15	3.67	3.51	3.63	2.8	3.8
Protein	3	3	2.1	2.27	2.18	2.4	2.27	2.3	2.13
Carbohydrate	4	3.94	3.41	3.25	3.04	3.6	3.55	3.01	3.59
Calorific Value	3	2.55	2.79	2.61	3	2.6	2.66	2.58	2.73
Crude Fiber	2	1.88	1.4	1.89	1.98	1.69	2	1.93	1.59
Dietary Fiber	2	1.83	1.75	1.98	2	1.8	1.73	1.71	1.77
Pesticides	4	4	4	4	4	4	4	4	4
Heavy Metals	6	6	6	6	6	6	6	6	6
Aflatoxin	6	6	6	6	6	6	6	6	6
Sugar	3	2.83	2.46	2.82	2.85	2.72	2.45	2.84	2.4
pH	3	2.47	2.18	2.29	2.1	2.85	2.49	2.4	2.37

(Table Contd...)

(1)	(2)	(3)	(4)	(5)	(6)	(7)	(8)	(9)	(10)
Water Content	3	2.41	2.66	2.77	2.97	2.56	2.5	2.82	2.68
Total Ash	2	1.77	2	1.44	1.96	1.69	1.76	1.58	1.4
Acid Insoluble Ash	2	1.98	1.92	1.97	1.76	2	1.96	1.4	1.94
Microbiological Tests (Total Plate Count, Yeast &Mould Count & athogens)	6	6	6	6	6	6	6	6	6
Sensory Tests (Colour, Appearance, Odour/Flavour, Taste & After taste feel)	13	10.87	9.35	11.05	8.16	9.96	9.02	8.99	6.98
General Parameters									
Packing	2	2	2	2	2	2	2	2	2
Marking	3	2.7	3	3	2.7	2.7	2.4	3	2.7
Overall Score	100	90.63	90.56	89.92	89.78	88.81	88.05	84.91	84.21

Rating: >90 – Excellent*****, 71-90- Very Good****, 51-70- Good***, 31-50- Average**, upto 30 – Poor*

REFERENCES

1. Parle M, Bansal N. Traditional Medicinal Formulation, Chyawanprash – A Review. Ind J Trad Knowledge 2006; 5: 484-8.
2. Trivedi RP, Bhaishajya Kalpana, Aligarh: Dhanvantari Karyalaya, 1951, 260.
3. Sharma RK. Charak Samhita, Chikitsasathanam, Vol. II, Varanasi: Motilal Banarasidas, 1954, 4.
4. Srikanta Murthy KR, Sarngadhar Samhita- A Treatise on Ayurveda, Varanasi: Chaukhambha Orientalia, 1995, 111.
5. Ram G, Amrit Sagar, Khem Raj Sri Krishan Das. Bombay: Sri Vanketshwar Steam Press, 1948, 3.
6. Mehta PM, History of Indian Medicine, in: Realms of Ayurveda by Pandit Shiv Sharma, NewDelhi: Arnold-Heinemann Publishers (India) Pvt. Ltd., 1979, 66.
7. Rao RSK, Encyclopaedia of Indian Medicine-Historical Perspective, Vol. I, Bombay: Popular Prakashan, 1985, 25.
8. Panda H. Handbook on Ayurvedic medicines with formulae, processes and their uses, 2004, p. 10. ISBN 978-81-86623-63-3.
9. Bates D. Knowledge and the Scholarly Medical Traditions Cambridge University Press 1995, p. 325. ISBN 978-0-521-49975-0.
10. Anonymous. The Ayurvedic Formulary of India. Part I, 2nd ed., Ministry of Health & Family Welfare, New Delhi: Government of India; 2003. p. 37.
11. Balakrishna A, Srivastava A, Mishra RK, Patel SP, Vashishtha RK, Singh A, *et al.* Astavarga Plants – Threatened Medicinal Herbs of North-west Himalaya. Int J Med Arom Plants 2012; 2(4): 661-676.
12. Rastogi S, Bala S, Govindrajan R, Rawat AK, Mehrotra S. Quantitative Analysis of Chyawanprash: A Well known Ayurvedic Formulation. Ind J Pharm Sci 2004; 66: 753-757.
13. Kumar A, Kaur P, Rinwa P. Evaluation of Morphological, Phytochemical and Physicochemical Properties of Indian Polyherbal Formulation, Chyawanprash for Quality Evaluation. Asian J Pharma Edu Res 2012; 1(2): 121-140.
14. Wagh VD, Patil SV, Surana SJ, Wagh KV. Medicinal Plants used in Preparation of Polyherbal Ayurvedic Formulation Chyawanprash. J Med Plants Res 2013; 7(38), 2801-2814.
15. Dalai SK, Dashora MS, Dwivedi L. Numerical v/s Quantitative Variations in Ingredients of Chyawanprash- Limiting Factor for the SOP. Ind J Trad Knowl 2007; 6(3): 426-428.
16. Ayurved Sarsangarah, Calcutta: Shree Baidyanath Ayurved Bhawan Pvt. Ltd., 1965, 540.
17. Srikanta Murthy KR. Sarngadhar Samhita- A Treatise on Ayurveda,Varanasi: Chaukhambha Orientalia, 1995, 111.
18. Rastantar Sarand Sidh Prayog Sangrah, Vol. I, Ajmer: Krishan Gopal Ayurved Bhawan, Kaleda, 1961, 779.
19. Shah NC, Bharat Bhaishjya Ratnakar, Vol. II, New Delhi: B Jain Publishers Private Ltd., 1999, 164.
20. Anonymous. Handbook of Domestic Medicine and Common Ayurvedic Remedies, Central Council for Research in Indian Medicine and Homeopathy, Ministry of Health & Family Welfare, New Delhi: Government of India, 1978, 380.

21. Sharma RD, Malviya MM. Chyawanprash se kaya kalpa vatlabh kyon nahin? Ayurved Mahasammelan Patrika, 1971, 399.
22. Anonymous, Ayurvediya Aushadiyan & Samanaya Gharelu Upchar, Kendriya Ayurveda & Sidh Anusandhan Parishad, Ministry of Health & Family Welfare, New Delhi: Govt. of India, 1988, 40.
23. Ghosh A, Laloo D, Singh NK. Comparative Estimation and Chemical Standardization of New and Old Sample of Chyawanprash. Int J Pharm Pharm Sci 2013; 5(3): 801-804.
24. Ojha JK. Chyawanprash from Vedic and Genomic Era. New Delhi: Chaukhamba Sanskrit Pratishtha; 2003.
25. Anonymous: Ayurvedic Pharmacopeia of India Part–II (Formulation): Department of AYUSH, Government of India. Volume I, 1st Edition, 2007, p. 13-16.
26. Wealth of India, Raw Materials series,Vol. III, New Delhi: Publications and Information Directorate, 1989, 168.
27. Tarwadi K, Agte V. Antioxidant and Micronutrient Potential of Common Fruits Available in the Indian Subcontinent. Int J Food Sci Nutr 2007; 58(5): 341-9.
28. Anand N. Comprehensive Medicinal Chemistry, Vol. 1, New York: PD Pergamon Press, 1990, 113.
29. Anonymous. Pharmacopoeial Standards for Ayurvedic Formulation, CCRIMH, 15, 1976, 87.
30. Katiyar CK. Eastern Pharmacist, XXXVIII, 1995, 454, 4.
31. Narayanan MN. Eastern Pharmacist, XXXVIII, 1995, 451, 4.
32. Shishoo CJ, Shah SA, Rathod IS, Patel SG. Determination of Vitamin C Content of Phyllanthus Emblica and Chyawanprash. Ind J Pharm Sci 1997; 59(5): 268-271.
33. Bhandari CR. Vanoshadhi-Chandrodaya, Vol. 1, Bhanpura: Gyan Mandir, 1938, 112.
34. Manjunatha S, Jaryal AK, Bijlani RL, Sachdeva U, Gupta SK. Effect of Chyawanprash and vitamin C on Glucose Tolerance and Lipoprotein Profile. Ind J Physiol Pharmacol 2001; 45:71-9.
35. Agte VV, Mengale SS, Akkalkotkar M, Paknikar KM, Chiplonkar SA. Antioxidant and Trace Element Potential of Chyavanpraash and some Ayurvedic Preparations. Ind J Trad Knowl 2003; 2(3): 215-223.
36. Kumar A, Rinwa P Kaur P. Chyawanprash: A Wonder Indian Rasayana from Ayurveda to Modern Age. Critical Review in Pharmaceutical Sciences 2012, 1(2): 1-8.
37. Datta Goutam K, Debnath PK. Stress Adaptation in Ayurveda by Immuno Modulatory Rasayana in National Seminar on Rasayana Proceedings Published by CCRAS, New Delhi: 2001. p. 60-75.
38. Ernst, Waltraud. Plural Medicine, Tradition and Modernity, 1800-2000. London, New York: Routledge. 2002, p. 187. ISBN 0-415-23122-1.
39. Jeena KJ, Kuttan R. Hepato protective activity of Emblica officinalis and Chyavavanprash, JE thnophannacol 2000; 72: 135.
40. Handa SS, Sharma A, Chakraborti KK. Natural Products and Plants as Liver Protecting Drugs. Fitoterap 1986; 57: 307-21.
41. Jose JK, Kuttan R. Hepatoprotective Activity of Emblica officinalis and Chyawanprash. J Ethnopharmacol 2000. 72: 135-140.
42. Roy AK, Dhir H, Sharma A, Talukder G. Phylanthus Emblica Fruit Extract and Ascorbic Acid Modify Hepatotoxic and Renotoxic Effects of Metals in Mice. Int J Pharmacognosy 1991; 44: 55-60.
43. Gulati RK, Agarwal S, Agarwal SS. Hepatoprotective Studies on Phyllanthus Emblica. Ind J Experi Biol 1995; 33: 261-268.

44. Sharma PV. Dravayagun Vigyan,Vol. II, Varanasi: Chaukhamba Bharati Academy, 2003, 535.
45. Trikam Y, Dravayagun vigyanam, Datiya: Shree Sharma Ayurved Mandir, 1979, 465.
46. Chunekar KC. Bhav Prakash Nighantu, Chaukhambha Bharati Academy, Varanasi: 2002, p. 788.
47. Tripathi RD. Ashthangsangrah. Chaukhambha Sanskrit Pristhan, Delhi, 2003, p. 106.
48. Ojha JK, Khanna NN, Bajpay HS, Sharma N.A Clinical Study on Chyawanprash as an Adjuvant in the Treatment of Pulmonary Tuberculosis. J Res Ind Med 1975; 10: 11-4.
49. Ojha JK, Bajpai HS, Sharma PV, Khanna NN, Shukla PK, Sharma TN. Chyawanprash as an Anabolic Agent; An Experimental Study (Preliminary Work). J Res Ind Med 1973; 8(2): 11-14.
50. Debnath PK, Chattopadhyay J, Mitra A, Adhikari A, Alam MS, Bandopadhyay SK, *et al.* Adjunct Therapy of Ayurvedic Medicine with Anti Tubercular Drugs on the Therapeutic Management of Pulmonary Tuberculosis. J Ayurveda Integr Med 2012; 3: 141-9.
51. Sharma PV, Clinical uses of Medicinal Plants, Chaukhambha Visvabharati, Varanasi, 1996, 33.
52. Govindarajan R, Vijayakumar M and Pushpangadan P: Antioxidant Approach to Disease Management and the Role of 'Rasayana' Herbs of Ayurveda, J Ethnopharmacology 2005; 99: 165-178.
53. Jeena KJ, Kuttan R. Antioxidant Activity of Emblica officinalis. JCl in Biochem Nut 1995; 19: 63.
54. Kumar A, Kaur P, Rinwa P. Comparative Study of Various marketed Brands of Indian Chyawanprash for their Anti-anxiety and Anti-oxidant Potential. Int J Pharmaceut Res and Bio-Sci 2012; 1(4): 296-310.
55. Khopde SM, *et al.* Characterizing the Antioxidant Activity of Amla (Phyllanthus emblica) extract. Current Science 2001; 81: 185-190.
56. Kumar GS, Nayakaa H, Dharmesha SM, Salimatha PV. Free and Bound Phenolic Antioxidants in Amla (Emblica officinalis) and Turmeric (Curcuma longa). Journal of Food Composition and Analysis 2006; 19: 446-452.
57. Mehrotra S, Rawat AK, Singh S. Standardization of Popular Ayurvedic Adaptogenic Preparation "Chyawanprash" and Ethnokotary of its Ingredients. Ethnobotany 1995; 7: 1-15.
58. Yadav JS, Thakur S, Chadha P. Chyawanprash Awaleha: A Genoprotective Agent for Bidi Smokers. Int J Hum Genet 2003; 3: 33-8.
59. Middha A, Purohit S. Determination of Free Radical Scavenging Activity in Herbal Supplement: Chyawanprash. Int J Drug Dev and Res 2011; 3(1): 328-333.
60. Sur TK, Pandit S, Mukherjee R, Debnath PK, Bandopadhyay SK, Bhattacharya D. Effect of Sonachandi Chyawanprash and Chyawanprash Plus, Two Herbal Formulations on Immunomodulation. Nepal Med Coll J 2004; 6: 126-8.
61. Bhattacharya S K, Bhattacharya A., Sairam K, Ghosal S. Effect of Bioactive Tannoid Principles of Emblica officinalis on Ischemia Reperfusion-induced Oxidative Stress in Rat Heart. Phytomedicine 2002; 9: 171-174.
62. Mirunalini S, Vaithiyanathan V, Krishnaveni M. Amla: A Novel Ayurvedic Herb as a Functional Food for Health Benefits - A Mini Review. Int J Pharm Pharm Sci 2013; 5(1): 1-4.
63. Singh VK, Palbag S, Singh NK. Comparative Evaluation of Furfural in Branded and Local Honey Sample by UV Spectroscopy. Int J Pharm Pharm Sci Res 2012; 2(6): 95-96.

64. Shah R, Kathad H, Sheth R, Sheth N. In vitro Antioxidant Activity of Roots of Tephrosia purpuria Linn. Int J Pharm Pharm Sci 2010; 2(3): 30-33.
65. Bansal N, Parle M. Beneficial Effect of Chyawanprash on Cognitive Function in Aged Mice. Pharm Biol. 2011 Jan; 49(1): 2-8.
66. Sailesh KS, Archana R, Mishra S, Symphoria, Mukkadan JK. Chyawanprash on Cognitive, Autonomic, and Repiratory Parameters in College Students. Int J Res Ayurveda Pharm 2014; 5(4): 435-438.
67. Parle M, Bansal N. Antiamnesic Activity of an Ayurvedic Formulation Chyawanprash in Mice: Evid Based Complement Alternat Med. 2011: 1-9.
68. Parle M, Dhingra D. Ascorbic Acid: A Promising Memory Enhancer in mice. J Pharmacol Sci 2003; 93(2): 129-135.
69. Vasudevan M, Parle M. Effect of Anwala Churna (Emblica officinalis GAERTN): An Ayurvedic Preparation on Memory Deficit Rats. Yakugaku Zasshi 2007; 127: 10: 1701-1707.
70. Thakur CP, Thakur B, Sinha PK, Sinha SK. The Ayurvedic Medicines Haritaki, Amla and Bahira Reduce Cholesterol Induced Atheroscleros Isinrabbits. IntJ Cardiol 1988; 21: 167.
71. Sharma PV, Cakradatta: ATreatise on Principles and Practices of Ayurvedic Medicine, Varanasi: Chaukhambha Orientalia,1954, 129.
72. Shastri AD, Bhaishjya Ratnavali,Varanasi: Chaukhambha Sanskrit Bhawan, 1996, 286.
73. Verma MD, Singh RH, Upadpa KN. Physiological, Endocrine and Metabolic Studies on the Effect of Rasayana Therapy in Aged Persons. J Res Ind Med 1973; 8(2): 1-10.
74. Jagetia GC, Baliga MS. The Evaluation of the Radioprotective Effect of Chyavanaprasha (An Ayurvedic Rasayana Drug) in Mice Exposed to Lethal Dose of Gamma-radiation: A Preliminary Study. Phytother Res 2004; 18(1): 14-8.
75. Ghosh A, Sharma A, Talukder G. Comparison of the Protection Afforded by Crude Extract of Phyllanthus Emblica Fruit and an Equivalent Amount of Synthetic Ascorbic Acid Against the Cytotoxic Effect of Cesium Chloride in Mice. Int J Pharmacog 1993; 31: 116-120.
76. Hoda Q, Sinha SP. Protective Role of Ascorbic Acid and Vitamin B-complex Against Pesticide-induced Clastogeny in Bone Marrow Cells of Mice. Int J Vit Nutri Res 1991,61: 155-158.
77. Alam M, Varadrarajan TV, Venkatbushna DD. Some Studies on Chyawanprash Preparation and Standardization. J Res Indian Med Yoga Homeopathy 1977; 2: 63-73.
78. Alam M, Joy S, Dasan KKS, Bhima Rao. Analytical and Antitumour Studies on Chyawanprash. J Res Ayur Siddha 1989, IX(1-4): 43 49.
79. Jeena KJ, Kuttan G, Josely G, Kuttan R. Antimutagcnic and Anticarcinogenic Activity of Emblica officinalis Gaertn, JCl in Biochem Nut 1997; 22: 171.
80. Kohlmeier L, Simonsen N, Mottus K. Dietary Modifiers of Carcinogenesis. Environ Health Persp 1995; 103 (Suppl 8): 177-178.
81. Mathur R, Sharma A, Dixit VP, Varma M. Hypolipidaemic Effect of Fruit Juice of Emblica officinalis in Cholesterol-fed rabbits. J. Ethnopharmacol 1996; 50: 61-68.
82. Dalai SK, Dwivedi L, Dadheech G, Mishra S, Sharma P. Evaluation of Health Promotion in Elderly People through Cyavanaprasa. Ancient Sci Life 2005; XXIV: 4: 183-191.
83. Waltraud Ernst (ed.) Plural Medicine, Tradition and Modernity, 1800-2000 Routledge Studies in the Social History of Medicine; Routledge, 2002; p 272.

84. Gogate VM. Emblica officinalis. In: Drvyaguna Vigyan. 1st ed. Pune: Continental Prakashan; 1962, p. 350.
85. Economic Times SRK, Dhoni, Ravi Kishan do wonders for Chyawanprash. Available at:http://articles.economictimes.indiatimes.com/2011-01-26/news/28429729_1_chyawanprash-market-sona-chandi-chyawanprash-ravi-kishan.
86. Consumer Voice Magazine. Comparative Test. Chyavanprash Repairs and Rejuvenates. November 2011, p 20-25. available at: http://consumeradvice.in/Download/Chyavanprash.pdf.
87. Available at: http://www.foodprocessing 360.com/article/5/201112132011 1213232635201c57e81ef/%E2%80%98Chyawanprash-Cookies-with-Dates%E2%80%99-to-bring-a-evolution-in-cookies-segment.html.
88. Available at:http://www.indiamart.com/baidyanath/immunomodulator.html.
89. Available at: http://www.thehindubusinessline.com/todays-paper/sugarfree-biscuits-chyawanprash-come-under-health-scanner/article1633864.ece.
90. Sharma Y, Sharma M, Singh R, Katiyar C. Identification of Mango and Orange Flavours in Flavoured Chyawanprash by Gas Chromatography-Headspace. Int J Pharm Life Sci 2012; 3(9):1953-1957.

Index

K

L

M

N

O

P

Q

R

❑ ❑ ❑ ❑ ❑